FIELD PROJECTS

FOR SOCIOLOGY STUDENTS

Jacqueline P. Wiseman
San Francisco State College

Marcia S. Aron
City College of San Francisco

SCHENKMAN PUBLISHING COMPANY, INC.
Cambridge, Massachusetts

distributed by
CANFIELD PRESS
A Department of Harper & Row, Publishers, Inc.
San Francisco

To future sociologists

Copyright © 1970
Schenkman Publishing Company, Inc.
Cambridge, Massachusetts 02138

PRINTED IN THE UNITED STATES OF AMERICA

Library of Congress Catalog Card Number: 77-118954

Contents

Preface   v
Introduction: General Instructions for the Student   1

PART ONE. BASIC RESEARCH METHODS

   I Observation:
      Socialization   15
  II The Depth Interview:
      Religion and Religious Institutions   27
 III The Descriptive Survey:
      Social Class and Stratification   37
 IV Participant Observation:
      Primary Groups   49

PART TWO. COMPLEMENTARY APPROACHES

   V Ecology:
      Occupations   63
  VI The Case Study:
      The Family   73
 VII Role Analysis:
      Law and Society   83
VIII The Community Study:
      The City and Urbanization   98

PART THREE. SPECIAL TECHNIQUES

IX   Content Analysis:
       Collective Behavior   113
 X   Projective Techniques:
       Attitudes Toward Social Categories   126
XI   Sociometry (The Sociogram):
       Social Structure   138
XII   Panel Analysis:
       Sociology of Education   150

PART FOUR. SPECIAL PROJECTS FOR ADVANCED STUDENTS

XIII   Explanatory Survey and Multivariate Analysis:
         Ethnic Groups   167
XIV   Population Analysis:
         Social Change   187
 XV   Scales and Indices:
         Health and Illness   202
XVI   Interaction Process Analysis:
         Small Groups   221

PART FIVE. THE SUMMER PROJECT AND LIBRARY ASSIGNMENT

XVII   Ethnography:
         Small Worlds   237
XVIII   Library Project:
         Examination of Sociological Concepts and
           Hypotheses   253

       Epilogue   264

Preface

These field assignments are intended to fill a need that we, as teachers of sociology, believe exists in the curriculum of the undergraduate sociology student. Too often, students will read the assigned textbook, identify and memorize facts and theories, learn statistical techniques, but still have no understanding of what sociologists actually *do*. They have not the faintest idea of how to do an interview or observe people in social interaction, record and organize their findings, and write up their reports. Furthermore, students are often unable to develop hypotheses that they consider worth pursuing because they have never been encouraged to formulate their own, based on exploratory investigations which they have initiated and conducted.

In our own experience, the research in which we engaged during our undergraduate days consisted primarily of library work. Although this is an *essential* part of any scientific investigation, particularly in the prelininary phases of locating background material and formulating hypotheses, we feel that a preoccupation with library research inordinately restricts the students' firsthand experiences of social investigation. The major purpose of this manual, therefore, is to get the beginning student into the field so that he may get a feeling of what this important part of research is like. It is through such experience that the novice sociologist begins to learn to "see" patterns in the on-going social life around him. From insight initiated in the field, he will learn to develop his own hypotheses, and thus will gradually progress from data gathering to analysis of the empirical world.

Additionally, actual experience with techniques that sociologists use should give the student a better understanding of the material he is assigned to read. He should approach future library research with greater appreciation of the work that went into what he is reading, and a keener awareness of the problems the investigator faced and how effectively he dealt with them. Many students have the idea that subject matter falls neatly into place for a researcher during the course of his study and that "social reality" is easily translated into a well-organized report. This idea is often fostered by the ways in which social scientists write up their material, and it is further compounded by accounts of "the scientific method," which often make science sound more cut-and-dried, better planned, and certainly less exciting and problematical than it actually is.

The student exploring the sociology of social life in the field will find it more complex than he realized, and not as obviously "sociological" as it sometimes appears in journal articles or texts. Decisions have to be made as to what to consider a significant act or conversation, what is and is not important to the goals of a study, and how the data should be put together so that the reader will have confidence in the findings. By trying his hand at these decisions, the student will be in a better position to discriminate between a good job of research and a bad one.

The many research projects in this manual offer opportunities for experience in methods of research applicable to various areas and problems in sociology. Most of the assignments have been geared to three hours of work for the student—an hour-and-a-half "in the field," and an additional hour-and-a-half preparing and writing a three-page report. Those field projects requiring longer reports were designed for student teams, with a suggested maximum of three pages per team member. Assignments progress from the relatively easy to the more difficult, and the time allotted for the last six assignments (which were included primarily for upper-division students) may have to be extended somewhat.

The projects were selected in order to offer a variety of interesting and challenging field experiences that would allow the student to discover for himself how to gather data about the social world. The variety of methods also shows how each approach organizes the research enterprise a bit differently. Thus the student has opportunities to do research on large groups of people (surveys, community analysis) and on small groups (case study, depth interview, small groups). Various ways of categorizing social relationships (role analysis and the sociogram), the social effect of the physical environment (social ecology), and the social-psychological environment (content analysis) are also covered.

In order to help tie the methodological approaches to subject matter, each method is aligned with a special subject area in sociology such as socialization, family, or social class and stratification. Within these broad sub-areas, however, assignments are planned to allow the student to select specific research topics that are meaningful to him, for we feel it is important for him to be his own project director.

We gave earlier drafts of these assignments to students in both introductory sociology courses and upper-division methodology courses. We found that they worked equally well in both settings, differing only by the quality of the reports expected of beginners versus more seasoned students. We are grateful both for the enthusiasm with which these exercises were received and for the criticisms offered. We invite users of this manual to write us their suggestions so that subsequent editions will benefit from *their* field tests.

The conviction that sociology students would profit from guided experience in field work, and the writing of a manual to accomplish this, are two different things. Our task was considerably lightened by generous colleagues who read assignments and offered comments for their improvement: Jack H. Aldridge, James L. Billwiller, Sherri Cavan, Kingsley Davis, William P. Gaffey, Peter Garabedian, Jane Herzog, John Irwin, Ted T. Jitodai, Carlo L. Lastrucci, Kathryn P. Meadow, David Nasatir, Thomas E. Ryther, and Eleanor Sams. We alone, however, take full responsibility for the material presented in this manual, and any errors or shortcomings it may have.

Jean Hoy typed innumerable drafts of the manuscript and showed great patience in following arrows, paragraph re-ordering, and inserts. Special thanks goes to Charles Mohler, Schenkman editor, who suggested the project in the first place, and to Stan Wiseman, whose considerable editorial talents greatly increased the readability of the assignments. Writing the manual turned out to be a great pleasure, for it combined the satisfactions of doing something we believed in, the opportunity to work with students and colleagues, and the joy of discovering that we work well together.

J.P.W.

M.S.A.

INTRODUCTION

General Instructions
for the Student

Sociology — like anthropology, psychology, economics, political science, and history — is a commitment to learning how and why man behaves as he does in the many contexts in which he lives. To learn these things, researchers have found they must check their armchair speculations with hard facts from the real world. In so doing, they have developed various techniques of obtaining data about man and his social relationships. This manual is a tourist's guide to the study of human group life and the methods used by sociologists and other social scientists to explore various forms or aspects of social life. In it we presume you know very little about sociology. These assignments — and an adventurous spirit — will permit you to go into the field, at least to a limited extent, and study live phenomena, an experience which should make your reading material more relevant.

Each assignment covers a specific area of sociological subject matter.* By examining these subject areas with some of the current methods used for studying these topics,† you should emerge with a better understanding of sociology as a discipline and with a greater awareness of its strengths and weaknesses. Certainly you should develop a greater sympathy and understanding for those who do research in the complex phenomena of human group life.

* The order of these assignments may not quite coincide with any one standard introductory text. Your instructor may want to change the order or combinations we have suggested.

† Although we have arbitrarily assigned certain subject areas for research to specific methods, we do not mean to imply that a given method is tied to any one subject area. Obviously the researcher chooses his method for its power in answering the questions he asks in the area of his interest. For this reason, new methods or techniques of analysis are continually being devised to meet changing research needs.

Each assignment is planned to show you, with a minimum of technical language, how to handle a given method of data gathering and analysis, and also to indicate how this method of research and the data resulting from it fit into the larger scheme of sociology. We have organized these assignments so that the earlier ones contain the most familiar methods used by sociologists, in order to provide a base for the more specialized — and often more demanding — assignments in the latter part of the book. We have placed the library assignment at the end of this manual, because you probably already have had some experience with library research and we want you to capture some of the excitement of field work before you return to what is already familiar. Your instructor may feel, however, that you should do this assignment before you attempt any field work because of its emphasis upon the place of theory, hypotheses, concepts, and operational definitions in sociological research.

Each assignment contains a number of short sections to orient you to the particular method and its use in your field work. Section I of each assignment contains a general description of the method, of the way the sociologist uses it to look at the social world, some of its advantages and limitations, and, finally, some of the sociological investigations in which it has been used. Section II is a short discussion of the application of the method to the subject area in which you will use it. Section III is a brief summary of what you will be expected to do in the project assignment. Section IV specifies these general instructions by outlining (A) the steps to take before you go into the field, and (B) the steps to take once you are in the field. In Section V you are given guidance in how to analyze and present your results. Each assignment also has a selected bibliography for the student who would like to know more about the method or its application.

We advise you to read an assignment at least twice before you begin the actual field work. The best way to do this would be to read the entire assignment through to gain a general idea about it, and then go back and reread those sections you do not understand. Make notes to discuss with the instructor anything that is unclear before you go into the field.

A major purpose of this manual is to get you into the field as soon as possible. To that end we have virtually eliminated formal concern with the traditional safeguards that professional sociologists use to prevent biased, contaminated, or idiosyncratic data from affecting the results. Yet sampling, validity, and reliability are important to the professional sociologist because they assure him that his research results will be defensible. We shall discuss each of these safeguard techniques briefly here and then indicate how the consistent failure to heed them as you do your assignments will affect your findings.

SAMPLING

The goal of science is to find uniformities or "patterns" in nature, for it is a basic scientific assumption that such uniformities exist in the physical, biological, and social worlds. The scientist obviously cannot examine all instances of the data he is studying—the botanist does not look at all plants, or even all roses; the sociologist does not study all cases of juvenile delinquency, or even all cases of juvenile car theft; etc.

But even though he is unable to observe all cases in his area of study, the scientist wants to be able to *generalize to all similar cases* from the data he has collected. The problem is how to be certain that he has studied specimens that will be *representative* or typical of all similar cases of the phenomena he has chosen to investigate. To assure data representativeness, various sampling techniques have been developed. Students who decide to major in sociology will want to be familiar with them and their specific applications.

VALIDITY

Validity refers to whether you are *really* measuring or classifying what you *say* you are measuring or classifying. For example, a yardstick measures inches or feet but *not* grams or pounds. You do not measure your height by standing on a scale! There is no ambiguity or doubt about this. But the social scientist faces the problem of creating measuring instruments and classification schemes to measure phenomena that do not have physical attributes. Therefore he must try to devise other kinds of tools, such as questionnaires, attitude tests, projective techniques, and so on, which presumably *do* measure or "get at" the social phenomena in which he is interested. How does he know he has succeeded? This is where various tests of validity are helpful and should be studied by the more advanced student.

RELIABILITY

While validity refers to whether the measuring instrument *really* "gets at" the desired social phenomena, reliability refers to the consistency, dependability, or "repeatability" of the measuring instrument. Does the investigator get the same results with his instrument if he uses it more than once? If not, it is not a reliable measuring device. If you weigh the same book on the same scale day after day, you will get the same result each time. The reliability of the social scientist's instruments—for example, a questionnaire—also depends on whether he (or other investigators) could use it with the same sample or similar samples of respondents more than once and get the same results. It is clear that the reliability of the social scientist's tools of investigation is considerably more problematic than that of an instrument such as a thermometer or a scale. Methods of testing instruments for reliability are important for the more advanced sociology student.

No one claims that sampling, validity, and reliability are unimportant; in fact, they are so important that they apply to *every* method in this manual. We have omitted these concerns from your projects only because they take a great deal of time to explain and to execute, and they do not add measurably to your initial experience in handling a specific method in the field.*

As your time is limited, you will have no way of testing the *validity* of the findings—though you *can* compare your findings with the results of other investigators who have used similar measuring and classifying instruments. Nor will you be able to check on *reliability*—whether you would find the same thing if you repeated the study.†

IMPLICATIONS FOR FIELD PROJECTS

Where does the omission of these procedures leave your findings? Since we are going to allow you to "sample by the seat of your pants"— that is, to find respondents that *might* have been in the sample had you selected it scientifically—you cannot and should not generalize your findings beyond your subjects.

This restriction on the general applicability of your results does not mean that you cannot learn something about human group life from the data you collected, or that the results are totally useless. What you have completed is an *exploratory* or *pilot study,* with emphases on subject matter, methods of data gathering, and analysis of results. This is not only worthwhile in its own right, but it can also lead to a larger-scale, more carefully planned study from which generalizations about human behavior *can* be drawn. Exploratory studies that ignore sampling, validity, and reliability and concentrate rather on subject matter and data collection

---

*Your instructor may not agree with this omission, of course, and may reinstate these details into your assignments.

†You *can,* and should, see whether your findings and the analysis you make from them are *internally consistent.* This simply means that the findings and analysis seem to hang together in a logical and reasonable manner. Assignment directions will aid you with this.

are routinely used by the professional sociologist in the initial phases of a project because they aid in refining his research design for the larger-scale study. Thus, when we ask you in the assignments to suggest hypotheses growing out of your pilot research projects that could be tested by a full-scale study, we are inviting you to contribute new ideas or information that you have discovered about the nature of human group life for future testing. Furthermore, when you discuss problems you encountered and how you think these obstacles might be tackled in a future, more formal research effort, you are suggesting ways of improving the validity and reliability of future research.

By minimizing the problems of sampling, reliability, and validity you will have more time to do a careful job of using the specific method of data gathering, analysis, and report presentation suggested for your own project. This latter point deserves some amplification.

THE PRESENTATION OF EVIDENCE

A major concern of your short reports will be to present *evidence* to support your discussion points and conclusions. This evidence will come from one primary source — your field data — and will be in the form of the notes made during observations, answers received to questions, and tallies made of frequencies of behavior.* The purpose of your report is to arrange these data so as to make clear to the reader that your conclusions follow logically and legitimately from it.

How you as a researcher present your material in a written report depends to a large extent on which of two major types of data you have — quantitative or qualitative. Each of these kinds of evidence is valid within the framework of the method used to gather it.

The Presentation of Quantitative Data

If your data consist of answers to questions you have asked of a large number of persons (such as in survey research or panel analysis) or if you have made *counts* or *tallies* of a particular behavior or subject matter (such as in some small group research, content analysis, and some types of observations) the presentation of data will necessarily be in numerical

---

* We also suggest that you keep a diary of field experiences as part of each assignment. A diary can be important not only because it may contain evidence but also because it can provide insight into what was "really" going on in any field work situation — for example, how you as observer may have influenced the subject's behavior.

or tabular form. That is, you will present tables showing your results, and these tables are the *evidence* for the discussions and conclusions in the report. You should therefore know how to make tables of your findings when the research design calls for them, and you should construct tables to show the data to best advantage—for easiest comprehension by a reader. You should present explanation and interpretation of what you consider to be the most significant findings in your tables in the text of your report (usually alternately with the tables).

An example follows:

TABLE I-1

ATTITUDES TOWARD ETHNIC DEPARTMENTS OR PROGRAMS
SHOWN BY SEX OF COLLEGE STUDENT
(HYPOTHETICAL DATA)

	Students	
	Male (N = 42)	*Female* (N = 51)*
Approve program	36%	43%
Approve with some qualification	24	31
Disapprove	14	22
No response	26	4
	100%	100%

*Refers to number in sample.

The discussion accompanying such a table might go like this:

> *As noted, more women students than men students approve of an ethnic studies program. Seventy-four per cent of all females interviewed approve or approve with some qualifications, while only 60 per cent of all males express approval. A glance at the nonresponse category shows that women also seem to be more willing to give their opinions on this issue.*

You will note that the table includes the following items to make the presentation of quantitative data easily understandable to a reader:

1. Table number, *for easy reference in the text should there be several tables presented.*
2. A title *that tells the reader what the table is about.*

3. *Usually,* groups compared *on certain factors important to the study are placed side by side under the title, so that the reader can compare them by reading across.*
4. *On the left, going down, are the* answer categories *(e.g., approve, disapprove) on which each group has been compared.*
5. *The* total number of respondents *is shown at the top of each group (e.g.,* N = 41*). Answers are percentaged from these totals.*
6. Percentages *should total 100 per cent (it may be necessary to round a percentage up or down to achieve this) unless more than one answer to a question is allowed.*

Nine assignments in the manual require the collection of quantitative data and thus the presentation of evidence in numerical and tabular or graphic form:

1. Observation
3. The Descriptive Survey
9. Content Analysis
11. Sociometry: The Sociogram
12. Panel Analysis
13. The Explanatory Survey and Multivariate Analysis
14. Population Analysis
15. Scales and Indices
16. Interation Process Analysis

The Presentation of Qualitative Data

Not all evidence is amenable to tabular form, however. If a student is observing, his evidence may be *descriptions* of his observations. These are usually presented in the body of the report, indented and single-spaced. For example, suppose the researcher makes the statement, "Women at the party seemed more conscious of their appearance than men." Some of his evidence would be presented as follows:

Several women took out mirrors and lipsticks during the cocktail hour, rearranged their hair, and touched up their lips.

Women made many remarks about each other's garments and stole glances at the mirror in the dining room. I did not observe men doing this.

Conversations can also be reported as evidence:

> *How do you like my hair? My hairdresser wanted to try out a new style. Do you think it is becoming?*

Evidence can also be gathered through depth interviewing. Here the researcher would report excerpts from the respondent's discussion relating to the subject of his inquiry. Suppose he is making the point in his report that the subject felt unfairly treated as a child. He might cite as evidence the following statement:

> *My sister was older than I, and she always got all the new clothes. I had to wear them after she grew out of them. Even her toys were handed down to me. It seemed like I had nothing that was ever bought with just me in mind.*

Eight assignments rely primarily on qualitative data and thus require the presentation of evidence in descriptive form:

2. The Depth Interview
4. Participant Observation
5. Ecology
6. The Case Study
7. Role Analysis
8. The Community Study
10. Projective Techniques
17. The Ethnography

THE SOCIOLOGICAL IMPORTANCE OF YOUR FINDINGS

A primary task in the presentation of results is for the researcher to point out the way in which his findings illustrate sociological concepts (this is, in fact, what differentiates sociology from journalism). As you do your studies, be alert for the sociological importance of your findings.

For example, in the discussion of Table I-1 (concerned with student attitudes toward ethnic studies by sex), you might add the sentence: "It would seem that female students have been more socialized to the idea of an ethnic studies department in the college than have male students." A sociological interpretation of the material on consciousness of appearance might be: "Women seem to consider personal appearance and its presentation to others more important to their identity than do men."

Naturally, the more exposure a student has to sociology, the more he will be aware of the concepts his findings illustrate. Beginning students will notice that they become more adept at this as they progress through the course.

PRESENTATION OF THE REPORT

Many students (and seasoned sociologists as well) do a bang-up job formulating their research problem and collecting their data, but they literally freeze when it comes to writing a report (analysis) of their findings. This need not happen to you if you keep in mind two basic things: (1) the problem or question you were investigating in the first place (you'd be surprised how many investigators forget this!), and (2) the fact that a report is essentially a story of your findings. Try this trick. When you have just finished your field work and have all your data, imagine you are at a party explaining to someone what you have been doing. In such a relaxed setting you usually find that in a short paragraph or two you can summarize the findings so they are *understandable to someone who has never heard of your project before.* You say such things as, "Well, most people think so and so . . . , but I found that it isn't quite true. Instead, the real situation is this and that, and I have the following data as proof. . . ." And there is the outline of your analysis! (Incidentally, outlining isn't a bad idea before beginning writing. It gives you a way of knowing what you are going to say next. As you will note if you glance through the manual, we have given you a general outline in Sections IV and V of each assignment that should help you to formulate the specific outline for your own mini-project.) All your reports will be short by usual research standards, but brevity forces organization. It's amazing what can be covered in three typewritten pages if it is written in a clear, concise style.

Keep in mind that although these reports are limited in length, they should emulate the style of articles found in the professional journals. This means that a mere recounting of field experiences, followed by random or chronological listing of findings, does not constitute a research report. Rather, the student must introduce his topic and organize his findings in such a way as to make both their major point and sociological importance perfectly clear to the reader. Refer to some journal articles (see list of journals on p. 259) to see how professionals introduce their topics and present their findings.

THE INDIVIDUAL INVESTIGATOR AND THE TEAM EFFORT

A final note on conducting research should be made. Most of the projects are set up for the individual investigator, but a few are arranged for teams. This is entirely appropriate, because sociological research is conducted through both individual and team efforts. When you work as an individual you are responsible to yourself for everything from ideas to field work to analysis; but when you work as part of a team you share work and decisions equally. Each method has its strong points and its problems. By learning about each type in these exploratory exercises, you will be able to find out which research approaches you prefer, and the way you seem to work best—alone or as part of a group.

We hope that these assignments will prove to be valuable and rewarding experiences for you. We like to think that you will gain not only a broader understanding of the social world around you, but that you will also feel something of the joy and excitement that the professional sociologist experiences when he works on projects that he has conceived, directed, and carried to completion.

Two lists—books on methodology and collected abstracts of sociological studies—follow. They cover in greater detail the methods that are briefly sketched in these field assignments. As in the selected bibliographies following each assignment, we have made the bibliographic entries conform to the style set by the American Sociological Association so that you will be able to become familiar with this form of notation.

SELECTED BIBLIOGRAPHY

General Methodology

Adams, Richard N., and Jack J. Preiss (eds.)
    1960   Human Organization Research: Field Relations and Techniques. Homewood, Ill.: Dorsey.
Duverger, Maurice
    1966   An Introduction to the Social Sciences, Malcolm Anderson (trans.). New York: Praeger. (First published as Methodes de Sciences Sociales, Paris, 1961.)
Festinger, Leon, and Daniel Katz
    1953   Research Methods in the Behavioral Sciences. New York: Holt, Rinehart & Winston.
Goode, William J., and Paul K. Hatt
    1952   Methods in Social Research. New York: McGraw-Hill.
Kerlinger, Fred S.
    1964   Foundations of Behavioral Research. New York: Holt, Rinehart & Winston.
Lazarsfeld, Paul F., and Morris Rosenberg (eds.)
    1955   The Language of Social Research. Glencoe, Ill.: Free Press.

Lindzey, Gardner (ed.)
    1954   Handbook of Social Psychology. Reading, Mass.: Addison-Wesley.
——, and Elliot Aronson (eds.)
    1968   The Handbook of Social Psychology (2nd ed.). Reading, Mass.: Addison-Wesley.
Madge, John
    1965   The Tools of Social Science. Garden City, N.Y.: Doubleday.
Phillips, Barnard S.
    1966   Social Research: Strategy and Tactics. New York: Macmillan.
Selltiz, Claire, Marie Jahoda, Morton Deutsch, and Stuart W. Cook (eds.)
    1964   Research Methods in Social Relations. New York: Holt, Rinehart & Winston.
Simon, Julian L.
    1969   Basic Research Methods in Social Science. New York: Random House.
Young, Pauline V.
    1966   Scientific Social Surveys and Research. Englewood Cliffs, N.J.: Prentice-Hall.
Zeisel, Hans
    1957   Say It with Figures. New York: Harper & Row.

Abstracted Sociological Studies

Hammond, Phillip E. (ed.)
    1964   Sociologists at Work: The Craft of Social Research. New York: Basic Books. (Discussions of field problems.)
Peterson, William (ed.)
    1956   American Social Patterns. Garden City, N.Y.: Doubleday.
Phillips, Derek L.
    1965   Studies in American Society. New York: Crowell.
    1967   Studies in American Society, II. New York: Crowell.
Rosenberg, Bernard (ed.)
    1966   Analyses of Contemporary Society. New York: Crowell.
    1967   Analyses of Contemporary Society, II. New York: Crowell.

Part One

Basic Research Methods

ASSIGNMENT ONE

METHOD:

Observation

RESEARCH TOPIC:

Socialization

I INTRODUCTION

Observation as a Research Tool

Observation as a means of increasing one's knowledge is basic to the investigation of almost any phenomenon. Some types of social action can only be truly understood and appreciated when they are actually witnessed—seen "in the flesh." The pomp and ceremony of rituals, the life conditions of men in prison, and the subtle nuances of flirting are but a few aspects of social life best grasped through firsthand observation. Many of the most memorable sociological studies have been conducted by investigators who used observation techniques. That such studies are often of interest far beyond the immediate application of their findings bears witness to the vitality of observation as a research tool.

Observation of social phenomena is obviously not restricted to the sociologist. All people observe social situations to which they are privy or about which they would like greater understanding. Moreover, they offer amateur reports of such scenes by describing and interpreting them to friends or relatives who were not present, in order to increase these persons' understanding of what happened. There is an important difference between the observations of the sociologist and those of the lay observer, however. Because the sociologist must organize and analyze his data in terms of sociological theories and concepts, he is sensitized to attending to human group life in a far more systematic fashion than the average person is. The layman relies primarily on his memory, but the researcher attempts to keep written descriptions of what he sees, for he is interested in more detail than his memory can retain. For this reason the sociologist is forced to think of systematic ways to conduct his observations and record what happens *as* it happens, or soon after, without upsetting his subjects or missing significant actions. Such planning is a part of the observation technique for which laymen seldom have patience or need.

How to Do Observation Research

Observation research is part craft and part art. Anyone can observe, but it takes practice and careful planning to observe and record a scene accurately and then to analyze perceptively what happened of sociological significance. Such skills improve with experience.

An early decision the observer must make is the setting. He must choose this with the goals of the study in mind. For instance, if the observer is studying strategies of flirting, he must select a setting in which this interaction is likely to occur both openly and frequently. Furthermore, he must think of an unobtrusive way to record his observations in an organized manner. Sometimes it is helpful to set up tally sheets before going into the field.

Professional observers try to blend with others in the settings they are observing. They may dress and act as if they belong to the groups so as not to influence the interactions by their presence. Sometimes an observer also participates in the activities to get a feel for the meaning they have to the persons he is studying. (We shall discuss this technique and its problems in Assignment Four.) Blending into the scene can make the recording of data a problem. Of course, if the subjects of the research are very young, or if writing is expected in a particular setting, the problem is eliminated. But if writing might seem out of place, the observer must find a private area where he can record events and descriptions of them from time to time, because he cannot rely on memory alone.

Once on the scene the observer must remain alert and flexible. Keeping track of the interactions of even a few persons can be very demanding. An observer must be able to adjust his tally sheets and focus of attention as the situation dictates, because the true gold mined through observation is the unexpected.

At frequent intervals the sociologist observing human group life in action should stop and ponder (usually in private) what he has seen and recorded. What is its sociological significance? What sorts of interactions seem to bring on what kinds of counter moves? What sociological concepts seem to be in play? (The investigator may also discuss his findings with other sociologists to get their insights.) Once he has made some preliminary decisions about these and other questions, the investigator will try to think of ways to confirm his hunches about what is going on in the scene he is watching. Thus sensitized by his introspection, he returns to continue his observations.

Not least among the talents of an observer of human group life is the ability to organize the findings and relay them to a reader via well-written description. Deciding on the central theme of the data often aids its organization. Descriptive passages should aim at reproducing, as closely as subtleties of language will permit, the situations observed. The sociological import of descriptions should be included in order to relate the particular findings to the broader spectrum of theory about human group life.

Advantages and Disadvantages

Observation is particularly useful for gaining insight into a respondent's habitual round of activities. The average person seldom sees these activities as sociologically significant and rarely reports them to the researcher during an interview. The routines and rituals that families develop in the course of living together, for example, can so recede into the background of daily events that they do not seem sufficiently important to the people involved to mention to an investigator. Interactions that are difficult to describe or that people are reluctant to talk about are often amenable to observation, provided they are accessible to an outsider. Techniques of parental discipline, times of personal embarrassment, riots, strikes, and other collective behavior are but a few such situations.

Of course, observation research can have drawbacks. It is time-consuming and, somewhat like police stake-outs, it is not always rewarding in the type of data desired. Observations cannot be scheduled solely at the convenience of the investigator; instead he must be on the scene when the scene is on! Perhaps the most troublesome problem in observation is researcher bias that can contaminate findings. If the investigator is aware of the following sources of bias, he should be able to neutralize their effects — to some extent, at least.

1. *Unintentional selectivity in perception, recording, or reporting.*
2. *Imputation of meaning that the actors themselves do not intend or experience.*
3. *Mistaking an idiosyncratic event for a recurrent one.*
4. *Affecting the action by his presence.*

It is obvious, of course, that the lay observer also runs afoul of these biasing factors. We are often aware of flaws in the descriptions that other people offer us concerning an event at which we were not present. We know, for instance, that in reporting, some of our friends tend to select only certain features of a situation, or to emphasize certain aspects in a way that distorts it. Then, too, people frequently misinterpret the actions they witness. And we have all experienced the occasion when a person tells us that so and so is *always* engaged in a certain activity, when we know the speaker has viewed such action by the person in question only once or twice.

Some Applications of This Method

Observation techniques have been used to gather data on the means people employ to ease embarrassing moments — for example, a male doctor's examinations of female patients (Emerson, 1963). Observation has also been used to watch intake procedures at a drug and alcoholism clinic in order to detect unwritten screening principles (Wiseman, 1970); to look at the police in action (Sudnow, 1965); to see how children act and interact in a small town in various natural habitats such as the library and drugstore (Barker and Wright, 1955); and to observe men living on Skid Row to discover what their typical day is like (Wiseman, 1970). These are but a few studies based on observation.

Although many investigators use natural settings and look at whatever develops in the normal course of events, psychologists and social psychologists often use observation techniques to watch people in experimental laboratory situations. In such cases the observers often remain behind mirror-windows, unseen by the subjects — who are often aware, however, that they are taking part in a controlled experiment of some kind (Asch, 1956; Garfinkel, 1963; Lippitt, 1940; Milgram, 1965, and Bales, 1950, 1970).

II USING THE OBSERVATION TECHNIQUE TO STUDY SOCIALIZATION

Socialization, an essential process in our everyday existence, refers to the dynamics of social interaction through which people learn socially desirable actions and attitudes. As such, it is a stimulating sociological realm to study. Socializing agents develop various strategies to accomplish the socialization of a new recruit, such as rewards, honors, and punishments. These strategies may consist of the actual bestowal of an award or the infliction of a blow. More often than not, however, peer-group pressure in such forms as teasing or scolding, ostracism or temporary exclusion will be used. Rituals such as initiations are also socializing, for they give the newcomer a feeling of belonging. These techniques, ranging from the overt to the covert, may be so subtle that the subject himself is not aware he is being socialized — nor is the *socializer* always cognizant of his actual effect on others.

Usually neither participant is in a position to describe pertinent processes to an investigator in the kind of detail an investigator needs. For instance, just how does a group exert meaningful pressure on an individual to get him to conform? How much socialization is done by direct teaching, how much by illustration? What are the various techniques of exclusion and support used to bring the person "into line"? Under what conditions and in what situations are there apt to be emphases on reward rather than punishment or vice versa? How much socialization is done as a result of some of the socializers' activities, lacking conscious effort on their part? How intense can socializing pressures become without losing their effectiveness? Can too much pressure drive the subject to deviance? Such detailed information on the process of socialization is perhaps better detected through sophisticated, systematic observation than through reports based on the recollections of either the socializer or the socialized.

III PROJECT ASSIGNMENT

Where should the observer look for instances of socialization? Since socialization refers to the process of absorbing or internalizing new patterns of behavior (including thought and emotion as well as physical action), it seems logical that the best way to catch and analyze the contents of various socialization strategies is to locate persons who are new members of a group. Fortunately, society is full of them. Because the most obvious — and readily available — novitiates are young children, they will be the focus of your assignment; but sociologists also study newlyweds, rookie baseball players, newly appointed policemen, and buck privates to find out how an adult receiving group attempts to mold incoming persons to its image.

You are to observe, codify (organize into categories), and describe (report) some aspect of socialization techniques used on children of either nursery school age or early grade school, i.e., between the ages of three and ten. You will include (1) a *systematic* account of the socialization process and (2) a general description of the interactions you observed. (Note: Children of nursery school age engage in a great deal of solitary play, so their socialization is received from supervisors. Older children interact more often and peer group pressure is more important to them.)

IV STEPS FOR THE OBSERVATION ASSIGNMENT

A. Before Going into the Field

1.   Gain access to the setting. Some settings, like bus depots, are open
     to everyone. Others are closed and present problems of access. If
     you do observation research in an educational institution (for ex-
     ample, a classroom), you are likely to need permission. Often you
     need the recommendation of someone whose name carries some
     weight. If such is the case, perhaps your instructor can make ar-
     rangements for you. Where negotiations fail and the researcher
     still wishes to pursue the subject, he must locate alternative areas.
     In the case of this assignment, public playgrounds catering to small
     children would be a possibility, as would schoolyards, parks, or
     even the home of a friend with several young children.

2.   Narrow your topic of inquiry. When you stop to consider how com-
     plex a phenomenon socialization is, you become aware of the need
     to focus your efforts on one aspect of it. (All researchers have this
     problem, but it is intensified in the case of limited projects such as
     this.) Your focus might be on some aspect of reaction to aggressive
     behavior, cheating, or bad sportsmanship. Or you might wish to
     investigate how children learn table manners, appropriate behavior
     toward adults, the norms of taking turns, those of not breaking
     another's toys, etc. The list is endless. Remember to limit yourself
     to one aspect of socialization. Do not be afraid to do something
     that seems "too simple." Better a simple project elegantly handled
     than a complex one that is botched.

3.   Decide what you want to know about the topic you select. This is
     actually an additional narrowing of your inquiry. Do you want to
     compare the handling of some aspect of socialization for boys and
     girls or do you want to study the recipients' reactions to it? Are you
     interested in the socializing strategies of adults versus children
     (peer group)? Are you interested in the formal versus the informal
     approach? Overt versus covert? Would you prefer to collect and
     describe in detail the various approaches used and their apparent
     success? Would you like to take two age groups and note the simi-
     larities and differences in socialization approaches?

4.   Select a subsetting that offers an opportunity for the type of social-
     ization activity you wish to study. For example:

     A slide is a good place to observe the norm of "taking turns" being
     taught.
     A game with rules like hide-and-seek might be a good game to

watch for the norm of cheating. (An interesting problem is how children learn when cheating is part of the game and when it is not. In baseball, for instance, stealing bases is part of the game; and in "red-light, green-light," stealing space is also part of the game. But this is not true of other games.)

Building blocks or a sandpile are good situations to study aggression and its control through socialization.

5. Organize your observation and note-taking in advance. Do some preliminary planning on how you will keep track of your data. Set up some sort of tally sheet for the *structured* portion of the observations that will allow you to keep track of the acts you are interested in, the specific persons acting, and the responses to them. You will undoubtedly have to revise this after being in the field a short time, but this planning will force you to think of the types of activity to watch for and how you can organize their collection.

A sample tally sheet is shown in Fig. 1-1. An investigator used it to keep track of how children (five boys, three girls) react to the aggressiveness of their peers in a play situation. Naturally each tally sheet must be tailored to the goals of the project and may either be much simpler or more complex than the one shown (which, for the purposes of this illustration, allows three aggressive acts per child).

Figure 1-1:

A Sample Tally Sheet
(reduced in size)

INITIATION OF AGGRESSIVE ACT,
SHOWN BY CHILD AND SEX

Aggressive act *against* whom (shown by child's assigned number)*	#1 M			#2 M			#3 M			#4 M			#5 M			#6 F			#7 F			#8 F		
assigned number	5	6	8				6	7	2	1	3	5	1	6	8	2	2	4				6	3	5
Response: Anger												X	X	X										
Surprise													X		X									X
Hurt, tears		X	X				X	X							X	X						X	X	X
Little or no emotion shown	X								X	X	X													
Help from other children		X					X	X					X									X		
Help from adult supervisor		X					X									X	X							X
Resolution favors:	1	1	8				8	7	3	?	?	5	5	5	8	6	2					8	3	5

*The observer assigned numbers to the children, keyed to clothing; that is, the child in the red sweater was #1, the one in the blue shirt was #2, and so on.

(In Fig. 1-1 child #1, a male, initiated acts of aggression against one male and two females, #5, #6, and #8. Number 5 showed little or no emotion, #6 responded by tears, and #8 also cried, and got the attention of other children and the supervisor. In the act of aggression where help was not forthcoming, the aggressor—#1— won; where help came, the victim won.)

Not all tally sheets need be complicated. Figure 1-1 is an effort to keep track of reactions to specific acts by specific people, because the goals of the study were (1) to see what kinds of reactions to aggression elicited help from others, and (2) the identity of the type of helper who intervened. Students studying how children are socialized to treat animals, for instance, merely kept track of the number of adult commendations for proper handling and the number of criticisms for improper handling. The purpose of the investigation was to see whether positive or negative sanctions were used more often and which were more effective. In another study, tally was kept of the number of times young members of basketball teams threw the ball or kept it. The pass-throw differential was then reviewed in terms of the age of the children and whether the team won or lost. The results showed that the older the child the more likely he is to pass rather than hold the ball unless he is in a good position to try for the basket, and that the team whose members passed the ball more won the game, regardless of age. Thus learning team cooperation and winning in sports were seen as associated!

6. For the unstructured portions of the observation project, plan to write the details of pertinent socializing interactions and your interpretation of them at the time. This should include verbatim records of conversations (or as close to verbatim as possible) and descriptions of specific situations in which socializing appears to be taking place. Make notes of these interaction details periodically as you are observing, before you forget. Decide whether you can take notes in full view of your subjects, or whether an automobile, a bathroom, or other nearby private area will be available for this purpose.

B. In the Field

1. Find a location where you can watch without disturbing the interaction.

2. Test your tally sheet *and revise as necessary* to accommodate what is occurring.

3. If at all convenient, jot down descriptions and sociological interpretations *as they occur to you.* You may be unpleasantly surprised at the good ideas you will be unable to recall later when you are writing the report unless you note important items while in the field. This diary of ongoing events should give you some insight into recurrent patterns of socialization.

4. If you get some special, unexpected insight into your sociological problem, be flexible enough to follow it up in your systematic and descriptive observations even though you did not originally plan for it.

V PRESENTING YOUR RESULTS

Good field work is only half of any successful project. The remainder lies in an organized and easily understandable presentation of results drawn from raw field notes. Field notes are never offered as the final report; rather they are used in the composition of one. The following, presented in narrative style, are included in any good report:

1. *A brief statement of the specific problem of socialization you are investigating.*
2. *A specific description of the setting you selected and why you chose it. Include in this some of the problems you encountered in the field, what you did to overcome them, and how the findings might be affected.*
3. *A presentation and discussion of your findings. Draw on your unstructured notes to give the reader a "feel" for the setting and action. Illustrate points in your analysis with descriptions of situations or conversations or both. See "General Instructions for the Student" for suggestions on how to present descriptive evidence.*
4. *Tables developed from your tally sheet (one tally sheet can yield several tables), accompanied by narrative explanation. For instance, here are two tables and a discussion that might have been drawn from the tally sheet presented earlier. Note that this tally sheet can be added in many different ways to yield various types of information. For instance, Table 1-1 indicates that the most frequent response to aggression is acting hurt or crying. However, more youngsters showed no emotion than showed anger or surprise.*

TABLE 1-1: DISTRIBUTION OF RESPONSES TO
AGGRESSION AMONG NURSERY SCHOOL CHILDREN

Response	Total Responses to an Aggressive Act* ($N = 17$)
Hurt, tears	9
Little or no emotion	4
Anger	3
Surprise	3
Help from . . .	
Other children	5
Adult supervisor	5

Not percentaged because of small base. More observations would yield a larger base.

TABLE 1-2: RESPONSE MOST LIKELY TO GET HELP

	Response* Hurt, Tears ($N = 9$)	Little or No Emotion ($N = 4$)	Anger ($N = 3$)	Surprise ($N = 3$)
Help from . . .				
Other children	4	–	–	1
Adult supervisor	4	–	1	2
No help	3	4	2	–

Not percentaged because of small bases. More observations would yield a larger base.

The results shown in Table 1-2 indicate that a child is most likely to get help from others if he cries and makes a fuss when he is attacked aggressively. Certainly he would learn the usefulness of this response in a short time!

5. *A short summary of your major findings about socialization in terms of sociological theory and concepts, plus any hypotheses you have developed that you feel are worth testing further. You should also assess the strengths and weaknesses of observation as a research tool. These discussions should conclude your report.*

Keep your report to three double-spaced, typewritten pages (excluding tables). As we have previously stated, raw field notes per se are not part of a report but you should turn them in with this first report to give the instructor an opportunity to see your approach to the problem of data collection and its analysis.

VI SELECTED BIBLIOGRAPHY

A. Methodology

Abel, Theodore
    1948   "The operation called verstehen." American Journal of Sociology 54 (November):211–217.
Glass, John F., and Harry H. Frankiel
    1968   "The influence of subjects on the researcher: A problem in observing social interaction." Pacific Sociological Review 2 (Fall):75–80.
Heynes, Roger W., and Ronald Lippitt
    1954   "Systematic observational techniques." Pp. 370–404 in Gardner Lindzey (ed.), Handbook of Social Psychology. Reading, Mass.: Addison-Wesley.
Junker, Buford
    1960   Field Work: An Introduction to the Social Sciences. Chicago: University of Chicago Press.
Weick, Karl E.
    1968   "Systematic observational methods." Pp. 357–451 in Gardner Lindzey and Elliot Aronson (eds.), The Handbook of Social Psychology. Reading, Mass.: Addison-Wesley.
Zelditch, M.
    1962   "Some methodological problems of field studies." American Journal of Sociology 67 (March):566–676.

B. References and Studies

Asch, S. E.
    1956   "Studies of independence and conformity." Psychological Monographs 70:9.

Bales, Robert F.
   1950   Interaction Process Analysis: A Method for the Study of
           Small Groups. Reading, Mass.: Addison-Wesley.
   1970   Personality and Interpersonal Behavior. New York: Holt,
           Rinehart & Winston.
Barker, Roger, and H. F. Wright
   1955   The Midwest and Its Children. Evanston, Ill.: Row, Peter-
           son.
Blau, Peter M.
   1955   The Dynamics of Bureaucracy. Chicago: University of
           Chicago Press.
Emerson, Joan
   1963   Social Functions of Humor in a Hospital Setting. Unpub-
           lished Ph.D. dissertation, University of California, Berkeley.
Garfinkel, H.
   1963   "A conception of, and experiments with, 'trust' as a condi-
           tion of stable, concerted actions." Pp. 187–238 in O. J.
           Harvey (ed.), Motivation and Social Interaction. New York:
           Ronald.
Glaser, Barney G., and Anselm L. Strauss
   1965   Awareness of Dying. Chicago: Aldine.
Lippitt, Ronald
   1940   "An experimental study of the effect of democratic and au-
           thoritarian group atmospheres." University of Iowa Studies
           in Child Welfare 16 (February):43–195.
Milgram, Stanley
   1965   "Some conditions of obedience and disobedience to author-
           ity." Pp. 243–262 in Ivan D. Steiner and Martin Fishbein
           (eds.), Current Studies in Social Psychology. New York:
           Holt, Rinehart & Winston.
Scheff, Thomas
   1963   "Societal reaction to deviance." Social Problems 11 (Fall):
           223–232.
Sudnow, David
   1965a   "Normal crimes: Sociological features of the penal code in
           a public defender's office." Social Problems 12 (Winter):
           255–276.
   1967b   Passing On. Englewood Cliffs, N.J.: Prentice-Hall.
Wiseman, Jacqueline P.
   1970   Stations of the Lost. Englewood Cliffs, N.J.: Prentice-Hall.

ASSIGNMENT TWO

METHOD:

The Depth Interview

RESEARCH TOPIC:

Religion and Religious Institutions

I INTRODUCTION

The Depth Interview, a Definition

One of the major tools of the social scientist — the depth interview — is also a favorite of the average citizen. Everyone at one time or another has used this technique to learn more about a subject of interest. A person will start by asking someone general questions. As he receives answers, he follows up on certain points with increasingly specific questions until he has acquired "an understanding" of the topic.

Depth interviewing, as generally conducted by sociologists, has the same pattern as that used by curious nonprofessionals. The major difference is that the answers social researchers receive are usually carefully recorded and reviewed in terms of concepts and theories of concern to the discipline. As an *exploratory* tool, depth interviewing is a way to locate important information for further study. It can also become an end in itself — that is, a way to get detailed descriptions or even explanations of certain types of social behavior.

The depth interview enables the investigator to probe the intensity of an individual's feelings about a given social phenomenon, the intricacies of his definition of it, and how he relates it to other areas of his social life.

Respondents will often give their judgments of what the attitudes of others are and how these affect their own attitudes and behavior. Memories of past events (technically called retrospective longitudinal data) can be obtained through depth interviews, especially when respondents are allowed adequate time to recall past events and place them in proper order or perspective.

Depth interviewing can be viewed as a fishing expedition, because the sociologist does it to get information when he has so little knowledge on a subject that he cannot ask structured questions. He also uses it to obtain more detail than a formal questionnaire normally makes available. The depth interview is a major tool in the social sciences, one that every competent researcher should be able to handle.

How to Do Depth Interviewing

The researcher attempting a depth interview is initially faced with the problem of creating and maintaining personal rapport with the respondent. This is essential if the interviewee is to be able to express in detail his deepest thoughts and feelings. To obtain the rapport he needs, the depth interviewer must assure the respondent that his identity will be kept confidential, and that he is collecting the information as part of a legitimate research project. Throughout the interview, the social investigator must take pains to be as neutral as possible. He must resist the temptation to moralize, to give advice, or to otherwise indicate how he feels about the information given. Above all, he must encourage his respondent to keep talking. A nod of the head once in a while, to indicate understanding, is sufficient after a relationship has been established and answers are forthcoming. More reaction might interrupt the respondent's train of thought and elaboration of various points.

Because a depth interview will often last for over an hour, recording detailed answers can present problems. The tape recorder is often used, but it is by no means necessary. In fact many researchers avoid using it because of the time involved in typing tapes — approximately two to three times the length of the interview. There is also the fear that respondents may feel inhibited if they know they are being recorded, though most people forget the machine is there. Seasoned depth interviewers learn to write rapidly (using abbreviations and bits of shorthand) during an interview. They also find that respondents, far from being annoyed at the time it takes to write down their comments, are flattered that the investigator is taking pains to get what they say correctly.

Because depth interviewing is used to develop categories and hypotheses, the interviewer usually asks very general questions. "What's going on?" or some variation of this question was a favorite query of Howard Becker and his associates when they interviewed respondents for their study of the medical student world (Becker and Geer, 1960). Other examples of general questions (depending on the subject) are:

> *Would you describe a typical day here to me?*
> *Tell me about the thoughts and reasons you had before doing* _____.
> *In general, how do you feel about* _____?

The investigator may gradually *focus* a depth interview on those portions of the material about which he would like further information. To do this, he must be alert at all times for clues that could be pertinent to his problem. He may then ask more nondirective questions about these specific areas; for example:

> *You say that a typical day here always includes* _____ *activity? Why is that? Do you participate? Why or why not?*

A spot analysis of previous interviews will often reveal clues about the subject matter under investigation that can be followed up in greater detail in subsequent interviews. The more rechecking the interviewer does of past responses, the more he is able to determine areas that he has not covered or where he has only scratched the surface. Thus as the research progresses, the questions tend to become increasingly focused (Merton and Kendall, 1946).

Eventually the investigator returns to the field with a short list of topics to cover. For instance, a typical list of focused topics for a depth interview concerning the respondent's job might include:

> *Describe a typical day here. (This is always a good opening question.)*
> *What is your job here? What do you do? How do you feel about your job? Why?*
> *Describe various supervisors (or top ranking employees) you see during the day. What are they like?*
> *What are the other employees like? What do you think of them? Why?*

Note that even when the questions are concentrated on a special topic, the *tone* of the questions is as neutral and open as possible so as not to suggest answers. A question like, "What do you think of it here?" is preferable to "Do you like it here?" The same principle applies to "probing" —that is, pursuing the answer to a question to be certain you have a complete understanding of it. The best probes do not suggest answers:

> *Can you think of anything else to tell me about that?*
> *What are your reasons for feeling this way?*
> *Why do you think others do that?*

The interviewer usually inserts a hash-mark "/" where he probed for more detail. A short excerpt from his verbatim notes of the respondent's answers might look like this:

> *Well, this job pays well, but that's about all I can say for it. It's just a job, that's all./ Well, I can support my family, keep up on my bills. We aren't wanting for anything./ Well, what I mean about that's all that's good about the job is that it is boring. It's the same thing day after day and there is no real hope for advancement to something more challenging./ Oh, you know, challenging to the mind, something that really interests me and makes me think about it and makes me feel proud of what I do. It just doesn't offer that.*

Advantages and Disadvantages

A researcher uses depth interviews rather than observation techniques when he decides that the only way to know what is on the subject's mind is to ask him. As we mentioned earlier, the researcher uses depth interviewing rather than the standard structured survey interview (especially those with fixed-choice answers) when he wants detail on social interactions and interrelated attitudes that he does not have and therefore cannot "build into" his questionnaire.

A major advantage of depth interviewing is its flexibility. Instead of going into the field with a narrow and specific hypothesis that he *assumes* to be the best approach to the study area, the researcher goes in with the idea of developing hypotheses and categories *in the course of the investigation.* He can, of course, narrow the topical scope of his inquiry to the subject of his interest; but the interview framework must not be so rigid as to prohibit consideration of all material a respondent offers on this subject. The goal, then, of this unstructured approach is to obtain information that cannot be anticipated.

Obviously depth interviewing, like observation, is time consuming. Often, in order to establish or maintain rapport, the investigator must allow the respondent to tell him many things he already knows about a given phenomenon before he can work his way to new material.

As with observation, the major disadvantage of depth interviewing is the difficulty of quantifying—or even organizing—data that was collected in semihaphazard ways. There comes a time, however, when the mass of material must be put into some kind of logical order so that the investigator can present what he has learned in an understandable fashion. Usually this is accomplished by analyzing the respondents' remarks for content that will become the focus of the report. The goal of the study offers some guidance here, but many of these decisions depend on the insight of the researcher.

Among the other arguments used against depth interviewing is the presumed inability of the average person to verbalize the "true" reasons for his decisions and actions. Researchers who believe people act for reasons they are not consciously aware of will use depth interviews—if they approve use of them at all—only to get at what they call "rationalizations." On the other hand, researchers who advocate depth interviews as a tool to study motivation are convinced that people *do* know why they act in certain ways. Therefore, they say, it would be less than professional to ignore a viable, worthwhile avenue to a respondent's thought processes.

Some Applications

A person in a social grouping will ordinarily have complex feelings of satisfaction and dissatisfaction about his role there. He is also usually concerned about the judgment of his "performance" by others, and about the possibilities of gaining friends and making enemies. Depth interviewing is applicable to topics where the actor's point of view and inner feelings are important to the research goals.

The depth approach has been used as a means of interviewing deviants such as prostitutes (Bryan, 1965), alcoholics (Wiseman, 1970), homosexuals (Hoffman, 1968), and felons (Irwin, 1970; Sykes, 1965). In the area of family interaction, where attitudes and emotions are crucial, the depth interview has also proved valuable (Hess and Handel, 1959). On an institutional level, students' feelings about their curricula, their instructors, and their classmates (Werthman, 1963) have been probed through the depth interview, as have the attitudes of employees toward their jobs and bosses (Roethlisberger and Dickson, 1939).

Depth interviews are also used in combination with observation techniques as an approach to data collection. Often the information obtained through these two methods will stimulate the researcher to conduct a broader survey on a larger sample of respondents using a structured questionnaire (see Assignments Three and Seven).

II   RELIGION AS A SUBJECT FOR THE DEPTH INTERVIEW

Religious beliefs and feelings are usually very strong, as are antireligious views. In a depth interview one might try to discover if religious principles play a major role in the lives of people today. Do individuals refer to religious precepts in making decisions? How does religion relate to their day-to-day activities?

On another level, religion as a social institution presents many aspects that should respond to this method of gathering data. What are some of the relationships among members of a congregation? What are the attitudes of the congregation toward the minister, and of him toward them? What sorts of jealousies and infighting occur among members of a parish? What sorts of friendships exist? What are the social satisfactions? Depth interviewing might provide some insight into these complex questions.

III   PROJECT ASSIGNMENT

Ordinarily a depth interview lasts approximately one to one-and-one-half hours (sometimes longer), and there must be at least ten to fifteen such interviews to give the investigator some notion of the kinds of information that may be pertinent to the research problem. However, because your time is limited, your assignment is to conduct three thirty-minute depth interviews on the topic of your choice within the area of religion or religious institutions.

IV   STEPS FOR THE DEPTH INTERVIEW ASSIGNMENT

A.   Before You Go into the Field

1.   Select your specific topic of inquiry in the area of religion and religious institutions.

2. Think out a small number of neutral questions — six at most — that will lead your subject to talk about your topic. Jot these down in your interviewing notebook.

3. Decide whom you will need as respondents. In the area of religion, there are several types of respondents worth considering for depth interviews, depending on the goal of your research:

    A. *"Rank-and-file" participants in the social action — congregation members, nonchurchgoers, deep believers, nonbelievers, the "don't cares."*

    B. *Participants in position of* authority — *ministers, choir directors, Sunday school directors, aldermen.*

    C. *So-called "well-informed informants" (Back, 1960) — busybodies, gossips, coordinators, high officials, politicians — anyone who makes it his business to know everyone else's. These persons can give you a wonderful start on an overview of your subject; they can be gold mines of information (though it may be necessary later to sift this information carefully, to remove the fool's gold).*

    D. *Malcontents (persons dissatisfied with the social group under study and thus more aware of its faults than the average member) and "marginal" persons (persons trying to gain entrance to the group or not quite accepted by it and thus often more aware of its virtues — and faults — than others).*

4. Depending on whom you are interviewing, talk to respondents about (1) themselves and their interactions with others, and (2) other persons with whom they are familiar.

B. In the Field

1. As usual, you must gain access to subjects who have had experience with the topic of your interest. Tell a prospective respondent you are doing research on a given subject (make your description very general) and that you would appreciate interviewing him.

2. Once you have gained permission to interview a subject, it is im-

portant to gain *rapport* so that he will talk freely and comfortably with you. The best way to do this is to be courteous, interested in what he says, and nonjudgmental regardless of your own feelings or beliefs.

3. Get respondent's answers as nearly verbatim as possible. This means in *his own words,* not in a summary composed by you. If you try to summarize his thoughts, there is a danger that you will give them meaning they did not actually possess.

4. If you feel you are holding up the interview by writing the answers, it often helps to say, "I hope you don't mind the delay. I want to be certain to get all of your answer." An alternative is to write up the interview as soon as you are alone, counting on your memory for details, but this has definite liabilities.

    Where you probe for more detail, insert a hash-mark to indicate that you interjected a "Why?" or "What are your reasons for feeling this way?" at that point in the interview.

5. Read over each interview before embarking on the next. Watch for points that you will want to follow up in this and subsequent interviews. By the third interview, plan to focus on some of these more specific points.

V PRESENTING YOUR RESULTS

By the time you have finished three interviews, you should have some interesting information concerning the topic you have chosen to investigate. Read your interviews and make notes concerning the points you want to make and the quotations you wish to use in the report. These quotations are the *evidence* you must present to buttress your analysis. Then write your report. Include in it the following:

1. *A brief statement explaining what aspect of religion or religious institutions you are studying.*
2. *A brief list of questions you asked in the order in which they developed, from the introductory ones to those that are more focused.*
3. *A discussion of your findings and the evidence — taken from the interviews — to back them up. (See "Special Instructions for the Student" for the form of presentation.)*

4. *A discussion of the pertinent areas or hypotheses for further investigation.*

5. *A discussion of the problems you encountered in depth interviewing and any suggestions you have for surmounting them in the future.*

Restrict your report to three double-spaced, typewritten pages and include your field notes, in their original form, when you hand your project in to the instructor.

VI SELECTED BIBLIOGRAPHY

A. Methodology

Back, Kurt W.
  1960   "The well-informed informant." Pp. 179–187 in Richard H. Adams and Jack J. Preiss (eds.), Human Organization Research. Homewood, Ill.: Dorsey.
Becker, Howard S., and Blanche Geer
  1960   "Participant observation: the analysis of qualitative field data." Pp. 267–289 in Richard H. Adams and Jack J. Preiss (eds.), Human Organization Research. Homewood, Ill.: Dorsey.
Cicourel, Aron V.
  1964   Method and Measurement in Sociology. New York: Free Press. Pp. 73–104, "Interviewing."
Kahn, Robert L., and Charles F. Cannell
  1958   The Dynamics of Interviewing. New York: Wiley.
Merton, Robert K., and Patricia L. Kendall
  1946   "The focused interview." American Journal of Scoiology 51 (May):541–557.

B. References and Studies

Bryan, James H.
  1965   "Apprenticeship in prostitution." Social Problems 12 (Winter):287–297.
Hess, Robert D., and Gerald Handel
  1959   Family Worlds. Chicago: University of Chicago Press.

Hoffman, Martin
    1968   The Gay World: Male Homosexuality and Social Creation
            of Evil. New York: Basic Books.
Irwin, John
    1970   The Felon. Englewood Cliffs, N.J.: Prentice-Hall.
Komarovsky, Mirra
    1962   Blue Collar Marriage. New York: Random House.
Lewis, Oscar
    1961   The Children of Sanchez. New York: Random House.
Roethlisberger, F. J., and W. J. Dickson
    1939   Management and the Worker. Cambridge, Mass.: Harvard
            University Press.
Sykes, Gresham M.
    1965   The Society of Captives. New York: Atheneum.
Werthman, Carl
    1963   "Delinquents in schools: a test for the legitimacy of author-
            ity." Berkeley Journal of Sociology 8:39–60.
Wiseman, Jacqueline P.
    1970   Stations of the Lost. Englewood Cliffs, N.J.: Prentice-Hall.

ASSIGNMENT THREE

RESEARCH METHOD:

The Descriptive Survey

RESEARCH TOPIC:

Social Class and Stratification

I INTRODUCTION

The Descriptive Survey, a Definition

Survey research is a method for collecting and analyzing social data via highly structured and often very detailed interviews or questionnaires in order to obtain information from large numbers of respondents presumed to be representative of a specific population. The best-known example of this type of research is the so-called Gallup Poll of the American Institute of Public Opinion, a full-time survey organization that probes public attitudes about matters of general interest. Several universities also have permanent survey research centers located on or near their campuses—e.g., the National Opinion Research Center at the University of Chicago; the Survey Research Center at the University of California, Berkeley; and the Survey Research Center at the University of Michigan, Ann Arbor.

Survey research is not a new method. It began to be important as a research tool in sociology shortly before World War II, but its use only became truly widespread with the development of electronic computers. These machines perform rapid, accurate compilation and analysis of enormous quantities of "social facts" that before their development would have taken months or even years to complete.

The major aim of a descriptive survey is to establish the range and distribution of such social characteristics as age, sex, occupation, and marital status, and to determine how these characteristics are related to a particular behavior pattern or attitude. For example, an investigator might want to learn how many high school graduates in Berkeley, California, attend movies weekly as compared to the number who watch television nightly or read at least one book a year. Another investigator might want to conduct a descriptive study to discover the attitudes of students in a college toward the development of a new Ethnic Studies Department. In such a case, he undoubtedly would want to find out which particular campus groups (ethnic, religious, departmental) favor the plan and which do not.

In a *descriptive* survey the sociologist is interested in *describing* the population he is studying. Therefore he will usually include questions that ask for information about *ascribed* characteristics (age, sex, race, nationality, etc.) as well as for information about characteristics that arise from membership in social groups or categories (occupation, income, religious affiliation, etc.). Usually he will also want to know about past and present behaviors, beliefs, values, attitudes, or opinions.

Laymen constantly indulge in descriptive surveys. They collect such social statistics as: How many persons are home from the office with the flu? How many people got drunk at the party last night? Were there more friends of the bride or of the groom at the wedding? How many of that "old gang" are now married or engaged to be married? The professional survey researcher is often interested in the same types of information as the layman, but he wants to be able to generalize his findings to large populations.

In an *explanatory* survey (Assignment Thirteen) the sociologist concerns himself with *explaining* the relationships that he has shown in the descriptive survey. Often he has a hunch about the cause or causes of a particular act or belief, and he will use the data gathered in the large descriptive survey to see if his hypothesis can be verified.*

How to Do a Descriptive Survey

Survey research is usually a time-consuming and expensive proposition. When it is done by a professional sociologist, it requires the full-time efforts of a project director and a number of assistants, plus part-

---

* It should be mentioned that the distinction between descriptive and explanatory studies is often an arbitrary one, and that in practice they often merge into each other. A good description of a population often contains elements of explanation, and a good explanatory study frequently offers enlightening description.

time work by other specialists — statisticians, interviewers, coders, and computer operators. Electronic data processing equipment (EDP) is essential to large-scale survey work.

In this assignment you will be getting only a taste of this area of social research. We want you to start small, but to approach the task carefully. There are definite, standardized work patterns followed by survey researchers of which you should be aware, even though you may be unable to adhere to them completely in your own study.

First, the researcher must define the problem or area of social life he wishes to investigate as carefully and completely as possible. Second, and of crucial importance, he must select a sample in such a way as to enable him to draw conclusions that will apply to the entire "survey universe" or population pertinent to the investigation, and not just those individuals selected at random for an interview. Third, he must devise an instrument in the form of (1) a questionnaire (a form that is filled out by the respondent) or (2) an interview schedule (a form that is filled out by the interviewer while he asks the respondent questions).

The questionnaire or interview schedule can be highly structured, semistructured, or open-ended. In the highly structured, or "closed," type of questionnaire, a choice of answers is provided on the form, and no deviation in either question delivery or answer selection is allowed. The respondent must make a "forced choice." In semistructured and open-end interview schedules, the interviewer can probe by asking nondirective questions, and the informant can respond as he feels appropriate.

To avoid questions that will later prove to be ineffectual in one or more ways, a survey researcher analyzes each item on a questionnaire or interview schedule before he goes into the field. Here are some of the checks a survey researcher makes:

1. *Is a question useful? Does it get at the desired information?*
2. *Is it probable that respondents will have the information necessary to answer the question?*
3. *Are several questions needed on a specific topic in order to cover it adequately?*
4. *Is the question free from bias, or is it loaded such that the respondent might react with prejudice he would not otherwise experience?*
5. *Is the question so personal or private that the respondent will be reluctant to give an honest answer? (People are amazingly willing to talk to a stranger about their private lives. If you have trouble with a question in this area, rephrase it so that it is less intimidating or upsetting.)*
6. *Is the wording of the question clear? Does it contain difficult words that the average respondent may not understand?*

7. *Is the order of the questions both logical and helpful in keeping
    the respondent answering; that is, do the questions flow from
    easy to difficult, from impersonal to personal?*

As part of his research design the experienced investigator does a small-sample pretest before he does the main survey to determine whether there are any problems which slipped by his inspection that would be difficult and costly to correct once the project is underway. Some indications that an item in the interview schedule may not be right are (1) a large number of respondents who answer "don't know" or "don't understand," (2) a large number who answer with qualifications or irrelevant comments, (3) a high proportion of people who refuse to answer, (4) all of the respondents answer in the same way and are in complete agreement, or (5) no discernible patterning shows up on the responses. (It is a basic assumption of the sociologist that social data are not scattered or random but are "patterned," usually in a regular distribution. If the pretest results are (4) or (5) or both, it is possible that the questions are too broad to pick up nuances of opinion.)

The results are collected and coded (responses are placed in logical, mutually exclusive answer categories), the answers are assigned numbers and machine-tabulated, and descriptive percentages are made. The last step is writing the report, which includes tables composed from the tabulated categories and a discussion of the results.

Advantages and Disadvantages

When the research concern is primarily with social characteristics and with information that lends itself to numerical presentation, survey research is the best way to operate. Its adherents believe that the survey method produces results that are far more valid than those obtained by even the most intensive observations or depth interviews. Survey researchers point out that even if an entire population is observed or interviewed intensively, the sociologist cannot be as systematic in these techniques as is possible with a structured questionnaire. Different behavior is likely to be forthcoming in succeeding instances of observation situations. The course of depth interviewing can be changed by the probes of the interviewer and the associational thought patterns of the respondent. In survey research, for example, a structured questionnaire administered to a random sample of 600 to 700 individuals can give a picture of the attitudes, beliefs, and values of a much larger population (for instance, all students at the University of California, Berkeley) within a small sampling error range. Furthermore, a survey can tap both past behavior and possible future behavior. ("How did you vote?" "How will you vote?") Attitudes, beliefs, and values that might never be revealed through observation can be brought to light and their distribution in the general population assessed. Finally, survey research is relatively economical, despite its use of large numbers of respondents. Its preplanned, orderly approach to data gathering and tabulation, as opposed to the reliance of observation and depth interviewing of spontaneous situations, avoids the collection of a great deal of unorganized or extraneous information.

One of the major disadvantages of the survey is that it emphasizes scope rather than depth. This is why it is important to do depth interviewing for information on the research subject before going into the field with a structured survey interview schedule. There is less chance of formulating superficial or irrelevant questions if the information obtained in preliminary depth interviews is used as a guide to questionnaire construction. Another disadvantage is that the improperly trained interviewers may reveal their biases and influence a respondent's answers.

The very high degree of organization that gives survey research its reputation for efficiency also can result in inflexibility. Going into the field with a fixed questionnaire means that what is investigated is *predetermined* and that there is little or no allowance for adjustments in the goals of the study. This rigidity may result in overlooking pertinent data, although the survey researcher tries to reduce this loss to a minimum by extensive pretesting and preliminary depth interviewing.

Some Applications

Survey research often has been regarded as the primary method of sociologists. This is partly because sociologists have traditionally been concerned with urban societies—large, differentiated populations that are highly suited to the survey method.

Descriptive survey research is eminently suitable to study any area of social life if one's interest is in the quantity and distribution of social variables. Perhaps the best-known descriptive survey is the United States Census, which every ten years gathers social facts such as age, race, occupation, type of dwelling unit, number of children, and so on about the country's citizens. Actually, descriptive surveys are used extensively by government agencies (federal, state, and local) to help determine policy and distribution of resources. Many states—and TV networks as well—have their own private survey companies that specialize in predicting voter behavior. Businesses use market research to gather descriptive statistics to help them decide whether to initiate or keep a product, and to ascertain the needs and desires of their prospective customers.

Behavioral scientists have also made wide use of the survey research method to gather information about almost every conceivable topic, from Kinsey's inquiry into the sexual behavior of the human male and female (1948, 1953) to studies of how people in the United States view Communism (Stouffer, 1955).

Many descriptive studies also try to determine the causes of the human behavior they are investigating (see Assignment Thirteen, "The Explanatory Survey"). Surveys have been made of dropouts (Allen, 1956), mental illness (Hollingshead and Redlich, 1958), religion (Glock and Stark, 1965), education (Rogoff, 1961), and many others.

II SOCIAL CLASS AND STRATIFICATION AS A SUBJECT FOR A DESCRIPTIVE SURVEY

The classification and ranking of individuals by their fellow men and women is a fact of social life. Such stratification results in different treatment by others, different life chances, and different life styles. Of course you have observed this, perhaps without realizing its significance. Parents often interfere with their children's choice of companions (or selection of mates) on the grounds that the families are of a lower social class. Stores, by their merchandise, pricing policies, and the conduct of their clerks, attempt to cater to a certain kind of customer. Residents of a city often characterize neighborhoods and their occupants as upper, middle, or lower class. The average citizen may think of a person from the middle class as an individual who works hard to achieve success and accumulate possessions. A lower-class person, on the other hand, is seen as unambitious and careless with money or hard-pressed and exploited.

Descriptions of life in the various social classes in America give us a better understanding of the different motivations and problems of a given category of people. A number of surveys deal with the impact of *class* on attitudes and behavior patterns. Parents have been studied to see what values they use in socializing their children (Kohn, 1959). Within Protestantism, the upper class tends to be Episcopalian or Congregationalist, while the lower class tends to be Baptist (Pope, 1948). Several studies have found that the aspiration for and attainment of higher education is related to social class (Rogoff, 1961; Allen, 1956). Mental health services for each social class have been compared and found to be quite different (Hollingshead and Redlich, 1964).

III   PROJECT ASSIGNMENT

You are to work in research teams consisting of four to six persons for this assignment. Your project will consist of obtaining some descriptive information on how persons in various social classes live, or on attitudes of people in one social class toward persons in other social classes. A comparison of attitudes toward poverty programs, new proposals for social welfare reform, or tax loopholes for high-income persons might be the focus of your research. Another possibility would be to describe and compare recreation patterns, courtship patterns, or child-rearing patterns of lower- and middle-class families.

IV   STEPS FOR THE DESCRIPTIVE SURVEY ASSIGNMENT

A.   Before You Go into the Field

1.   Agree upon what aspect of social class you want to study.

2.   Decide on the population you are interested in and how you will (1) define it, and (2) sample it for this exploratory project. How will you find *instances* of the various classes — such as upper class, middle class, and lower class? For example, what will you use as *criteria* for placing a person in the middle class? Will it be income? Occupation? Education? Style of life? There are many studies that have already done this, and you might look at one or two to see how this is handled (see Hollingshead, 1949, or Warner, 1941). For an exploratory study, you need not be quite so careful in the definition and selection of people to represent the various classes as you would for the final large-scale study. You might use persons of your acquaintance whom you know to be relatively poor, middle class, or quite well off, depending on the needs of your study.

Select your sample. Though your sample will not be "scientifically" selected, you should try to obtain interviews from different social categories within your designated population. For example, you would probably try to obtain interviews from both males and females if your area of interest were tax reform legislation. You might further specify a certain number of interviews from persons representing different social categories of race, nationality, religious affiliation, etc.

3. Construct an interview schedule consisting of ten questions. We suggest that these be "closed," or "forced-choice," questions. Examples follow:

Some people have said that in a country as rich as ours everyone is entitled to a minimum annual income. Do you . . .

Strongly agree	( )
Agree	( )
Don't know	( )
Disagree	( )
Strongly disagree	( )

My favorite recreation is

Bowling	( )
Reading	( )
Watching TV	( )
Going to movies	( )
Gardening	( )
Boating	( )
Golf	( )
Other _____	

The first question is designed to get at degree or intensity of feeling; the second is a "cafeteria-style" question that allows the respondent to pick that answer pertaining to him.

Another kind of question is the "open-end" question that allows the respondent to answer in his own words: "What do you think are some of the things this country should do to help the poor?"

All these questions are useful. The first two are best when you know the possible answers but not their distribution in the population; the last is best when the possible range of answers is not known.

Check your questions against the criteria listed earlier in this assignment. You may also wish to consult one of the questionnaire-writing texts listed at the end of this chapter. The "General Instructions for the Student" section in this book also contains a bibliography with references that would be useful for this task.

You should conduct one depth interview apiece (see Assignment Two) to get some idea of the questions that ought to go into your questionnaire. This is the way most researchers go about preparing for their large-scale surveys.

4. Arrange the questions in a logical order, but be sure that you do not begin with one that could embarrass the respondent, and thus abruptly terminate the interview.

5. Do one pretest each; that is, try out your questionnaire on someone and then get together to amend your questions or change their order if it seems to be necessary.

   Be sure your interview form includes any background data you think might be pertinent, such as age, sex, income, type of neighborhood in which respondent lives, and so on.

B. In the Field

1. Locate the persons you wish to interview and arrange to interview them.

2. Have each person on the team collect at least five interviews from the population you are studying.

C. Analysis of Your Data*

1. Make a tally sheet for each set of categories you are comparing — sex, race, class, education, etc. Tabulate the number of responses in each choice offered for each question. If you use any open-end questions (such as the third one shown in the example), you must set up categories to cover the answers and then tabulate these. This is known as "coding." See Fig. 3-1 for an example. (Beginning students should not attempt to handle more than one such open-ended question.)

Figure 3-1

THINGS THIS COUNTRY CAN DO TO HELP THE POOR

	Male	*Female*
Guaranteed annual income	ℍℍ IIII	IIII
More job training	ℍℍ II	II
Higher welfare payments	I	ℍℍ I
Nothing	II	II
Etc.		

*This can be done by the entire team, or it can be divided into workable segments to be handled by individual members of the team.

2. Percentage the responses in each category. Ordinarily researchers do not percentage anything with a sample smaller than 25. However, since this is a practice exercise, percentages based on fifteen interviews—five by each member of a three-man team—are acceptable unless the instructor decides otherwise.

V PRESENTING YOUR RESULTS

1. *Identify the subject area about which you were trying to get descriptive data.*
2. *Identify the types of persons interviewed and why.*
3. *Present the results of your survey in the form of tables. For guidance in setting up readable tables, look at some of the tables in sociology texts, or refer to the "General Instructions for the Student" in this manual. A table should have clearly marked headings, a title, show the sample size, and contain other data pertinent to the information it presents. Percentage items for each question, and indicate whether the total adds to 100 per cent—or more, if more than one answer to a question was allowed.*
4. *Briefly discuss the results each table shows.*
5. *Make suggestions for further research in this area. What hypotheses about social classes are suggested by your data?*
6. *Mention some of the problems you encountered in doing the assignment. What did you do to overcome these problems, and how might the findings be affected? If you were to do this work again, would you revise the present questions in any way, or add or delete any questions?*

Please keep your presentation of results to three double-spaced, typewritten pages (excluding tables) per team member. All of your interview schedules should also be turned in with your written report.

VI SELECTED BIBLIOGRAPHY

A. Methodology

Backstrom, Charles H., and Gerald D. Hursh
    1963   Survey Research. Evanston, Ill.: Northwestern University Press.

Cannell, Charles F., and Robert L. Kahn
    1968   "Interviewing." Pp. 526–595 in Gardner Lindzey and Elliot
            Aronson (eds.), The Handbook of Social Psychology, II.
            Reading, Mass.: Addison-Wesley.

Hyman, Herbert
    1955   Survey Design and Analysis: Principles, Cases, and Pro-
            cedures. Glencoe, Ill.: Free Press.

Kornhauser, Arthur
    1951   "Constructing questionnaires and interview schedules"
            (condensed from Training Guide on Constructing Question-
            naires and Interview Schedules, prepared by the Bureau of
            Applied Social Research, Columbia University). Pp. 423–
            462 in Marie Jahoda, Morton Deutsch, and Stuart W. Cook
            (eds.), Research Methods in Social Relations, Part Two:
            Selected Techniques. New York: Dryden.

Selltiz, Claire, Marie Jahoda, Morton Deutsch, and Stuart W. Cook (eds.)
    1964   Research Methods in Social Relations. New York: Holt,
            Rinehart & Winston.

Young, Pauline V.
    1966   Scientific Social Surveys and Research. Englewood Cliffs,
            N.J.: Prentice-Hall.

B. References and Studies

Allen, Charles M.
    1956   Combating the Dropout Problem. Chicago: Science Re-
            search Associates.

Glock, Charles Y., and Rodney Stark
    1965   Religion and Society in Tension. Chicago: Rand McNally.

Hollingshead, August B.
    1949   Elmtown's Youth: The Impact of Social Classes on Adoles-
            cents. New York: Wiley.

——, and Frederick C. Redlich
    1958   Social Class and Mental Illness. New York: Wiley.

Kinsey, Alfred C., Wardell B. Pomeroy, and Clyde E. Martin
    1948   Sexual Behavior in the Human Male. Philadelphia: W. B.
            Saunders.

——, and Paul Gebhard
    1953   Sexual Behavior in the Human Female. Philadelphia: Saunders.
Kohn, Melvin L.
    1959   "Social class and parental values." American Journal of Sociology 64 (January):337–351.
Medsker, Leland L.
    1960   The Junior College: Progress and Prospect. New York: McGraw-Hill.
Pope, Liston
    1948   "Religion and the class structure." Annals of the American Academy of Political and Social Science 256 (March): 84–91.
Rogoff, Natalie
    1961   "Local social structure and educational selection." Pp. 241–251 in Amos H. Halsey, Jean Floud, and C. Arnold Anderson (eds.), Education, Economy and Society: A Reader in the Sociology of Education. New York: Free Press.
Stouffer, Samuel A.
    1955   Communism, Conformity, and Civil Liberties: A Cross-Section of the Nation Speaks Its Mind. Garden City, N.Y.: Doubleday.
Warner, William Lloyd, and Paul S. Lunt
    1941   The Social Life of a Modern Community. New Haven, Conn.: Yale University Press.

ASSIGNMENT FOUR

METHOD:

Participant Observation

RESEARCH TOPIC:

Primary Groups

I INTRODUCTION

Participant Observation, a Definition

Now that you are acquainted with the field technique of observation (Assignment One), you should be ready to take a turn with its research cousin, participant observation. Both of these techniques are important sociological tools. It is only by observing what people *do* when they interact with one another, as well as by recording what they *say* they do, that we can begin to get an understanding of the dynamics of social processes.

The method of research known as participant observation differs from the structured and unstructured observations of Assignment One in several important ways. As the name implies, the participant observer is a researcher who becomes a member of the group he is observing, while the nonparticipant observer tries to remain aloof from it. This distinction is not clear cut since there is a wide range in the level of participation— from the sociologist who stays out of the group and just watches the action to the researcher who is actually a member. Usually a researcher participates to a degree somewhere between these two extremes by either *posing* as a member or announcing himself as a scientific investigator and hoping to be accepted by the group in that role. Inevitably, a time continuum parallels the degree of participation. The longer an observer stays on the scene, the more likely he is to be drawn into participating in the group's way of life. As a general rule, the *participant* observer commits himself to a group for a considerable period of time, ranging from several weeks or months to many years.

A second characteristic of the participant observer is that he tries to understand the frame of reference of the group he is investigating. He does this primarily by joining the members in their daily activities in order to experience things as they do. The autobiographies of those who have lived for many years in institutions such as prisons (Black, 1927) or convents (Baldwin, 1959) are particularly insightful studies of these "closed" societies. Though these individuals were not trained sociologists, they were participant observers *par excellence.*

There is a certain similarity between this approach and espionage. The observer must exist mentally on two levels. Instead of being socialized to the new way of life almost unknowingly, as are most individuals after they join a group, the scientific investigator must learn to be simultaneously "inside" and "outside" the group life he is studying. He must learn the meanings that behavior has for the members of the group, and he has to become sufficiently involved with the group to be able to understand what makes it tick. At the same time, he cannot be so involved that he is unable to report accurately what is happening and why. He cannot be so far "inside" that everything seems so "normal" as to be not worth reporting. And to top it all off, he must be able to report patterns of behavior and interrelationships objectively, without moral judgment or bias. The reason for this double frame of reference is that the participant observer wants to understand the group and its actions not only in its own terms — that is, how the members themselves live and feel the culture — but also in terms of a larger and more general set of sociological hypotheses or theories about the nature of human interaction.

Do these sound like impossible tasks? They are difficult, but with practice they can be handled fairly well. Anthropologists occasionally find some of the attitudes, beliefs, and behaviors of the societies they study repugnant or immoral. However, they are trained not to judge, but rather to try to faithfully record and to determine what meaning these behavior patterns have for the people who practice them.* Perhaps an even more common outcome of close contact with a new group over a prolonged period of time is the observer's identification with the group. He starts to accept their behavior patterns as his own and may find it hard to re-enter his old way of life when he has finished his study. Many Peace Corps vol-

* The diary of Bronislaw Malinowski, the famous English anthropologist, was published recently and a great many people, including social scientists, were shocked at the disclosures he made of his personal feelings about the Trobriand Islanders (Malinowski, 1967).

unteers have had this problem after living for a year or two in a foreign culture with a way of life dissimilar from their own. These twin dangers — aversion and over-identification — can be partially neutralized if the researcher is aware that he is not *merely* a recording machine — and that he is going to have personal reactions to any new group he enters.

How to Do Participant Observation

Traditionally, participant observation requires access to a group or community over a long time period since it is essentially a research technique to learn about and describe a group's total culture or way of life. How long should an investigator stay with a group or community to obtain the information he seeks? Certainly he must remain long enough to observe recurring behavioral patterns. This may mean attendance at all the weekly activities of a small club for two or three months, or living in a community (small town or primitive society) for several years. In the first case, he may be interested in learning how the leadership of the club maintains its power; in the second, whether there is a relationship between child-rearing techniques and achievement motivation.

What should the participant observer notice and record? This depends on the purpose of the study. If it is exploratory, presumably the researcher does not know the culture of the group. Thus he must be careful to keep comprehensive and detailed notes on all that occurs around him. Even behavior that seems trivial or unimportant should be recorded in his researcher's "diary." The good investigator will record observations as often as possible and not rely on his memory, which more often than not is untrustworthy when it comes to detail. Sometimes it is necessary to record as often as five or six times a day if the observer is living with the group. No matter how difficult the circumstances, he should keep his diary current.

If the researcher is only interested in one particular aspect of a group — for example, the leadership pattern — then it would seem permissible for him to limit his observations and note-taking to those actions of the participants that exhibit "leadership" qualities. Even here, however, seemingly unimportant behavior patterns (speech, facial expressions, gestures) may offer clues that aid in giving insight into the research problem.

Because the participant observer attempts to understand how the people he is studying feel about their situation, he is trying to do more than simply *describe* the distinctive behavior patterns of the individuals interacting in a particular group — as was the task in Assignment One. He is also trying to explain *why* they, as individuals, are behaving as they are.

Whether the researcher is aware of it or not, whenever he enters a group as a newcomer he is assigned a role by the old members (see Assignment Seven regarding role analysis). He may be accepted as an "observer" or as a "member," but in whatever role he is cast, he has altered the previous structure of role-relationships. Thus he is a potential, if not an actual, disturbance in existing cultural patterns. It is only when the observer has been "placed" by the other members and is interacting with them in a "normal" way that he is able to start collecting information without arousing fear and hostility (Blau, 1967). After this normalizing has occurred will members of the group feel comfortable and act naturally.*

The degree to which a participant observer can bias his results by his mere presence can probably never be fully known. The effect of his presence varies with the size of the group (the smaller the group, the greater the effect), how deeply entrenched previous patterns of interaction were, and whether the group knows it is being studied. In this assignment you will be a participant observer in a group to which you already belong. Because you already have a place in the group and a role to play, your research efforts will probably not change previously established patterns of behavior and the biasing effect of your presence presumably will not be a problem.

Advantages and Disadvantages

A major advantage of participant observation is that the investigator need not rely totally on "empathetic insight" or intuition to understand the perspective of his research subject, as he might from observation alone. He sees the world, at least part of the time, in the same way other members of the group see it because he is living their kind of life with them. Therefore, personal introspection will provide him with clues for understanding his data. Also, as with non-participant observation, he watches human group life as it is lived, not as it is reported to an interviewer. All the contradictions between what people say they believe in doing and what they actually do, their consistencies and inconsistencies, are played out before the observer. Also, as a participant he can often casually ask for the types of explanations that an interviewer arriving "cold" on the scene cannot. He can ask, "Hey, what's so funny?" or

---

* Anything that is out of the ordinary can affect the status quo of a group, and there may be less danger that a single observer will contaminate (or bias) the group's identity and integrity than would the artificiality of a laboratory experiment. See Assignments Thirteen and Sixteen for discussions of laboratory experiments where members of a group are aware they are being "tested."

"Why did everyone look so glum just then?" and it will not sound inappropriate. The method offers great flexibility in the field. If the observer notes some activity that seems significant to the problem he is investigating and that he knew nothing about before he began his study, he can arrange his observation efforts to encompass this behavior.

Participation has one other major advantage — a built-in validity test. If the participant who is trying to "pass" as a member in the group he is studying misinterprets some bit of interaction and then *acts* on the basis of his misinterpretation, the group will soon show him the error of his ways!

Participant observation has its disadvantages too. It is time-consuming. Also, the investigator is not usually able to control the action (although this depends to a large extent on his role in the group), so that he must wait for events that are of interest to him to occur. Sometimes he will have to spend hours watching interaction he has already seen while waiting for some new data. Because of the "ongoing" nature of the happenings in the group, a participant observation project cannot be planned so completely in advance as can a survey research project (see Assignment Three).

Being a participant in some groups can be very demanding. Sociologists have performed in dance bands (Becker, 1963), successfully faked the symptoms and problems of mental illness (Caudill, 1958), and worked with the police on stake-outs (Skolnick, 1966). Often those who participated with some deviant groups found themselves faced with the choice of either joining what they considered to be immoral or illegal actions or severing their ties with the group (Whyte, 1943).

Finally, one of participant observation's greatest virtues can also be one of its most troublesome areas (we mentioned this before, but it deserves repeating). The deeper the participant investigator immerses himself in the group's culture, the more difficult he finds it to study it "objectively," and the more likely he is to miss the sociological significance of action that becomes increasingly "normal" to him.

Some Applications

Participation in the normal life of a community or group to understand its social processes better has a long and interesting history in social investigation. One of the first important studies using this technique was conducted by Frédéric LePlay (1808-1882), who studied the family life of European workers by actually living in their homes. His major interest was the interrelationships between geographical location, type of work, and a family's way of life.

Anthropologists have found this method of investigation particularly useful in studying primitive communities, and it is often associated with this branch of the social sciences. Most of what we know today of non-literate societies has been because of excellent anthropological field studies. Sociologists have found participant observation particularly valuable for the study of groups that the average American — including the investigator himself, usually — does not understand. It has been used to study mental hospitals (Goffman, 1961), delinquent gangs (Miller, 1958), and gamblers (Scott, 1968), to name but a few. Sociologists have also used the technique to study small towns (Withers, 1945; Lowry, 1965), industrial plants (Warner, 1947), and other more conventional settings.

II PRIMARY GROUPS AS A SUBJECT FOR PARTICIPANT OBSERVATION

All of us belong to social groups. The most significant of these have been identified by sociologists as *primary* groups — primary because they are the most important and meaningful groups in the life of the individual, and because they are also a potent force in socializing him to conform to the normative patterns of the society. Primary groups are small (usually not more than fifteen members) and most often engaged in face-to-face interaction. This interaction is frequently of a highly affective (emotional) nature and provides the individual with much of his sense of identity. A major primary group is the family; others include the gang, co-workers, cliques, and clubs.

There are both advantages and problems in using participant observation in primary groups. Because primary groups are small, one person can usually observe interactions without too much difficulty. On the other hand, because primary groups are almost always exclusive in membership, a researcher cannot just join one and begin to participate. He must work himself into membership. Once he is in, however, he is beset with the problems of normality and bias — and this is greatly intensified because of the nature of primary groups. Too much intimate knowledge of a group often makes it impossible to really "see" and report what is happening. Behavior that a stranger might see as important, odd, or "to be explained" is part of the normal scene for one who belongs. Furthermore, in a primary group feelings and emotions are crucial to the continued existence of the group. There is a sense of togetherness, of "we-ness," and often each member has a distinct role to play in maintaining

3. *A short paragraph giving pertinent details concerning (1) how many times you were with the group, and (2) how long you spent with the group each time.*

4. *Evidence for each finding, such as a brief objective description of the interactions or conversations you observed or overheard. (See General Instructions to the Student.)*

5. *Interpretation of your findings, using sociological concepts. What further observations, if any, do your findings prompt you to want to make? Try to formulate a hypothesis you would like to test on a primary group other than the one you have just observed.*

6. *Some of the problems you encountered in doing this assignment. What did you do to overcome them, and how might the findings be affected?*

As in all assignments, please keep your presentation of results to three double-spaced, typewritten pages. Your field diary should also be turned in so that the instructor can assess to what extent your skills in observing social interaction are improving.

VI   SELECTED BIBLIOGRAPHY

A.   Methodology

Becker, Howard S., and Blanche Geer
   1960   "Participant observation: the analysis of qualitative field data." Pp. 267–289 in Richard N. Adams and Jack J. Preiss (eds.), Human Organization Research; Field Relations and Techniques. Homewood, Ill.: Dorsey.
Blau, Peter
   1967   "The research process in the study of The Dynamics of Bureaucracy." Pp. 18–57 in Philip E. Hammond (ed.), Sociologists at Work: The Craft of Social Research. Garden City, N.Y.: Doubleday.
Bruyn, Severyn T.
   1966   Human Perspective in Sociology: The Method of Participant Observation. Englewood Cliffs, N.J.: Prentice-Hall.
Riley, Matilda White
   1963   Sociological Research: A Case Approach. New York: Harcourt, Brace & World.

B.   References and Studies

Baldwin, Monica
    1959   The Called and the Chosen. New York: New American
            Library.
Becker, Howard S.
    1963   The Outsiders: Studies in the Sociology of Deviance. New
            York: The Free Press.
Black, Jack
    1927   You Can't Win. New York: Macmillan.
Caudill, William
    1958   A Psychiatric Hospital as a Small Society. Cambridge,
            Mass.: Harvard University Press.
Dr. X
    1965   Intern. New York: Harper & Row.
Goffman, Erving
    1961   Asylums: Essays on the Social Situation of Mental Patients
            and Other Inmates. Garden City, N.Y.: Doubleday.
LePlay, Frédéric
    1879   Les Ouvriers Européens. Paris: Alfred Mame et Fils.
Lowry, Ritchie P.
    1965   Who's Running This Town? New York: Harper & Row.
Malinowski, Bronislaw
    1967   A Diary in the Strict Sense of the Word. New York: Har-
            court, Brace & World.
Olesen, Virginia L., and Elvi W. Whittaker
    1968   The Silent Dialogue. San Francisco: Jossey-Bass.
Roth, Julius A.
    1963   Timetables. Indianapolis, Ind.: Bobbs-Merrill.
Roy, Donald F.
    1960   "Banana time, job satisfaction, and informal interaction."
            Human Organization 18 (Winter):158–168.
Scott, Marvin B.
    1968   The Racing Game. Chicago: Aldine.
Skolnick, Jerome H.
    1966   Justice Without Trial. New York: Wiley.
Wallace, Samuel E.
    1965   Skid Row as a Way of Life. Totowa, N.J.: Bedminster.

Warner, William Lloyd, and J. O. Lew
    1947   The Social System of the Modern Factory. New Haven,
           Conn.: Yale University Press.
Withers, Carl [James West, pseud.]
    1945   Plainville, U.S.A. New York: Columbia University Press.

Part Two

Complementary
Approaches

ASSIGNMENT FIVE

METHOD:

Ecology

RESEARCH TOPIC:

Occupations

I INTRODUCTION

Ecological Research in Sociology

Botanists and zoologists recognize that all living creatures must have a territory where they can carry on their lives, and library shelves are filled with treatises on how various creatures and plants struggle for and use territory. Robert Ardrey's *The Territorial Imperative* (1966) is a recent popularized account of this phenomenon.

Social interaction does not take place in a vacuum, either. It is played out on some piece of territory. This area is more than just an empty staging ground. It has physical properties that affect the social occurrences that take place there. Ecological research in sociology is thus focused on the physical arrangements of an environment as they affect and are affected by social behavior.

The ecological approach in sociology began at the University of Chicago in the 1920's with the development of the famous "Chicago School" of sociology. Ernest W. Burgess and Robert E. Park were seeking ways of analyzing the development of large metropolitan areas, especially specific sub-areas of neighborhoods. They felt that the concepts of culture and socialization—traditional tools of the anthropologist studying

primitive areas—did not offer a means of analyzing the city and the processes of its differentiation into specialized social regions. Furthermore,
they saw waves of immigrants intermingling and struggling for space and
survival in Chicago, and they felt they needed a special approach to study
this state of social flux.

Borrowing from animal and plant ecology, Burgess and Park began to
look at Chicago in terms of "zones" and "groups of people competing
with each other for space." They saw geographic mobility, and barriers
to prevent it, as important to the development of "natural social areas."
Within these natural areas, Chicago School sociologists looked for "composition proportions"—that is, types of persons composing the population groupings. They sought instances of "symbiosis"—one group serving the needs of another in much the same way that plants provide oxygen
for animals, while animals give off carbon dioxide used by plants—and
"succession"—analogous to the natural succession of environmental
changes occurring in wild areas, as when a pond slowly becomes a marsh.
They conceptualized and categorized the major types of activities that
occur when different groups share an area, such as: conflict, competition,
cooperation, accommodation (symbiosis), and assimilation. Each of
these activities, they felt, represents a stage in the ultimate resolution of
the battle for territorial survival. The social ecologist thus blended the
tools of the traditional sociologist with a knowledge of the geography,
demography (population dynamics), and economics of the area being
studied.

As with most other approaches to the study of man, the ecological
approach is not without its lay counterparts. People who are house- or
apartment-hunting often ask such ecological questions as "What kind of
neighborhood is this?" The type of answer they expect requires some extensive social and physical knowledge of the area. What they want to
know is the average rental, the kinds of people living there, the access to
schools and transportation, and even the amount of business or industry
nearby. Investment men hire appraisers before they buy property, construct a shopping center, or attempt to open a new market to get the same
kinds of information. A sales map on a wall, studded with colored pins, is
a commercial version of an ecological map. It shows the geographic distribution of sales rather than of people and suggests areas where selling
will be relatively easy, where it will be so difficult that a sales campaign
would be needed, etc. Burglars must be good ecologists too, since there
is no point breaking into a home that is not likely to be worth robbing!
Restaurant owners who can create moods for their indoor space that give
them virtual control over the behavior of their customers are master
ecologists.

In those early Chicago School studies, however, social ecologists were primarily interested in social problems. They mapped the distributions of delinquency and crime, mental illness, divorce, and other deviant behavior in the city. They studied immigrants and how new waves of such persons tended to "take over" the poorest sections of a city and force others out—just as in nature where some plants crowd out others in a natural succession. The famous concentric zones theory of succession and deterioration of the city's inner core were developed by these sociologists, who noted that in almost every city there is a business section, a rooming-house section (composed of old mansions), a slum, and a middle-class section at certain distances from the center of the city.

More recently the ecological approach has been adapted to units smaller than entire cities, and culture as a conceptual tool has been reinstated as a part of the analysis. Sociologists began to take note of indoor social territory and how it affects and is affected by social life. William F. Whyte, (1949), for instance, noted that a restaurant's order counter serves as a barrier between waitresses and short-order cooks and aids in their mutual struggles for status. Howard S. Becker (1951) revealed how dance bands arrange their music stands and large instruments (drums, etc.) or even chairs so as to form a barrier between themselves and the dancing public, whom they consider to be, for the most part, "squares." Erving Goffman (1961, 173-320) noted that people in institutions tend to "stake out" and attempt to personalize pieces of territory. Anything giving an area the aspect of a "nest," from a certain chair in the patient lounge to a small corner where favorite magazines, snacks, or other personal items are kept, can become a special ecological area.

Laymen are also aware of indoor ecology. Arrangement of furniture at a party is crucial to its social success. Acceptance of a job offer or happiness in it depends in part on the work area's physical layout and the ability of employees to adapt it to their personal needs. Any employee whose department has moved to new quarters knows the effect such a change in physical arrangements can have on employees' social relationships.

How to Do Ecological Research

The first step in doing ecological research is to plot interrelationships or spatial separations between persons and groups. A minimum beginning would be to map the area under study by charting various items of interest. This might include pathways, barriers, entrances, counters, stations, desks, open or closed regions, and avenues of movement within this area.

The next step would be to observe social interaction in some detail, armed with the map as a base from which to operate. In ecological investigation, the sociologist often employs or combines some of the techniques discussed in earlier assignments; for example:

> *Observation* of social interaction within the area and the apparent boundaries of home territories (the territory considered one's own). Both descriptions and systematic tallies are useful here. For instance, how many and what kinds of people live in a certain area (which involves a count), and what types of interaction do they have (which involves descriptions)?
>
> The use of *official statistics* of the area on birth rates, death rates, and sex composition.
>
> A *descriptive survey* to get special data on phenomena not available from official sources, such as median income of the area, rentals charged, types of activities, occupations represented, or number of school-age children.

The researcher should always watch for cases of symbiosis while using these techniques, by attempting to answer such questions as: How do different elements of society cooperate and render aid to each other? What is the division of labor?

From these data, the investigator delineates activity zones or "natural areas" within the more general territory of his interest and attempts to describe what life is like in these areas, the types of social activities dominant in each area, and the kinds of problems these areas present to inhabitants. If conflict seems to be present, how is it likely to be resolved? Are there any zones where societies seem about to "break down" under pressures from other groups? To answer some of these questions, the researcher may have to gather longitudinal data—data collected over a period of time that show how the area has developed historically. Then he can compare past and current trends and attempt to make predictions concerning future social life of the area—an enterprise not without its hazards.

Advantages and Disadvantages

The most obvious benefit of the ecological approach in sociology is that it forces the researcher to interrelate many factors of human group life, both social and physical. Socio-ecological maps can contain clues to possible dominant environmental "forces" or "pressures" in an area. A heavily traveled arterial may divide a locale into two small societies. The way desks are situated in an office may contribute to clique formation, as may the placement of homes in a suburban tract (Whyte, 1963). High delinquency rates might mean that a young boy is under great pressure to participate in illegal acts and that if he refuses he will become a social isolate. Population-density maps can give clues about the availability of open areas and areas of privacy, while the sex and age composition of an area reveals opportunity for successful spouse-hunting. Obviously population analysis (Assignment Fourteen) can contribute to studies of social ecology. The search for symbiosis can also help one to understand why some social phenomena that might at first glance seem incompatible are, in fact, interconnected.

On the deficit side, much of the early theory on which social ecology is predicated is being questioned. Many of today's sociologists think that social ecology and its theories of succession (conflict, competition, co-operation, and assimilation) are too simplistic to aid in the analysis of complex human interaction processes. Furthermore, ecological theory, coupled with the concept of "natural areas," has a highly deterministic and somewhat conservative bias. Also, as we have already mentioned, the purposeful omission of *cultural* pressures from this method has been challenged (Hollingshead, 1961) on the grounds that cultural differences are, in fact, the prime movers in the conflict, competition, and ultimate co-operation and assimilation of groups. Demographic projections of future population composition in a given area are being challenged on the grounds that these computations often fail to consider cultural events that might dramatically change current trends. Certainly, there is more to human beings' competing for space than that which occurs when weeds choke out flowers!

Furthermore, there is the danger of committing what W. S. Robinson calls "the ecological fallacy." Robinson (1961) suggests that all too often ecological analysts tend to ascribe to *persons* the characteristics found by cumulative descriptive surveys of *groups*. For example, if an area has a large proportion of Italians and a high rate of alcoholism, analysts tend to describe the people in the area as alcoholic Italians, when in fact these characteristics may be quite differently distributed in the population. For instance, a substantial proportion of the Italians living in the area may not necessarily be inebriates.

The ecological fallacy can also work in another way. Researchers can interpret the high rate of a phenomenon in an area as *caused* by the area itself. Faris and Dunham, for instance, attributed the high rate of mental illness in the rooming-house section and other deteriorated parts of cities to the physical and social characteristics of those areas (1939). An alternative explanation to theirs is that persons who have become mentally ill move to the boarding-house area *after* they lose their jobs, spouses, and friends. At this point, their aberrant behavior comes to the attention of authorities, and official statistics eventually show them as residents of the area (Clausen and Kohn, 1954). This explanation is also ecological in that it suggests there are natural areas to which social misfits migrate, but it does not imply so strongly that the area *itself* is the cause of mental illness.

Some Applications

With all their shortcomings, ecological studies are extremely useful and are employed daily — perhaps more by nonsociologists than by sociologists. Urban renewal and land-use specialists rely on ecological insight for important decisions, as do architects, interior designers, and human engineers. These latter three professionals are, of course, attempting to make space within cities and buildings more liveable and serviceable. Psychologists and social psychologists use the ecological approach to study effects of crowding, isolation, and problems of communication.

II OCCUPATIONS AS A SUBJECT FOR ECOLOGICAL RESEARCH

Almost all occupations take place in areas that have unique physical attributes and lend themselves to creative, sensitive ecological study. Restaurants have tables, counters, front and back regions; doctors' offices have reception rooms, private rooms, the doctor's own office; stores have counters, checkout stands, racks; small offices vary considerably in layout from large ones; the ecological space of a school teacher varies from that of a factory worker on an assembly line. Employees in these settings must live their lives, do their work, and satisfy other social urges eight hours a day.

Employers have come to realize that many people, possibly unconsciously, quit or accept a job on the basis of the physical and social ecology of the work situation. Certainly, most of us look at pictures of large rooms with rows and rows of desks and shudder at the thought of working under the regimentation and absolute lack of privacy implicit in these conditions. People also sometimes quit small, two-man offices to get social interaction of the type to be found in large corporations. How many people have made "nests," erected barriers, torn them down, and so on in order to make their eight hours a day tolerable?

III PROJECT ASSIGNMENT

You are to pick some area of work to which you have access and study its social ecology. If you do not have a job area of your own, select one open to the public (that is, the emergency room of a hospital, a bus or train depot, a store, a restaurant). Because ecological analysis gains much of its insight from comparison, you are to join forces with another student who is studying some other type of occupational setting. For a portion of your report, *compare and contrast your two settings in terms of the social consequences of their ecological characteristics.*

IV STEPS FOR THE ECOLOGICAL ASSIGNMENT

A. Before You Go into the Field

1. Decide on the occupational setting you wish to study.
2. Find a partner who is studying a different one.
3. Discuss with your partner the activities you each might look for in your settings that will aid in understanding the overall social atmosphere in each. Look for more than just official, overt behavior. Remember people *live* in this territory for eight hours a day. Where do they socialize, congregate, exchange confidences? What kinds of activities are impossible in this set-up? What kinds are encouraged? (For instance, observe workers behind a dimestore lunch counter where it is crowded and notice that they must turn sideways to pass one another. A great deal of sexual byplay occurs here between waitresses and men delivering foodstuffs or taking away dishes, partially because of the opportunities afforded by the crowded conditions.)
4. Plan the descriptive material you might gather: sex composition, approximate age composition, ethnic and racial composition, status composition; all give insight into social activities of the region. You might anticipate some of the social action you will be viewing and

set up a tally sheet as described in Assignment One to keep track of your observations. (This planning does not mean that you can't investigate phenomena that emerge during your field work.)

B. In the Field

1. Map your area. Map paths of movement in the area and location of various people in the area. Note boundaries, physical and otherwise. Note areas of socializing and private areas.
2. Observe interaction to get some of the data above.
3. Ask questions pertinent to your study. Where do employees hide food? Cosmetics? Personal magazines? How do they keep customers out of private areas? Other workers? Is there anywhere they can go to be alone? Ask to see "back regions" if you are not privy to them (that is, behind counters, inside work-booths). Often you can gain access by explaining you are a student studying that occupation.
4. Look for instances of symbiosis. Who depends on whom for what? Does "exploitation" occur?
5. Try to determine just what is the division of labor in this setting. Is there an informal division of labor (not necessarily planned by management) of which you are aware?

V PRESENTING YOUR RESULTS

Your report should include the following:

1. *A discussion of the general interaction and atmosphere of the occupational setting you studied as compared to that of your partner's. General insights concerning the social effect of various ecological features should emerge.*
2. *Evidence for the conclusions you draw. For instance, if you say that there is not much flirting in the area, you ought to cite the fact that with the exception of an occasional office boy, it is an all-female office. Or, you could cite a count of male-female contacts that seemed to be of a friendly, social nature. If you say that the water-cooler is a socializing area, you should have some count of the number and frequency of people who meet there as compared with other areas of the office.*

about regardless of whether it is "incorrect" from an objective point of view. The problem of forgotten details can be overcome, partially at least, by interviewing more than one person in the development of a case.

Where letters and other personal documents can be used, the researcher must also be aware of the possibility of distortion. Letters are often written to impress someone or give an unduly optimistic or pessimistic view of personal matters. Diaries may be partly fabricated by romantic teenagers, as may life histories by adults. Often the only defense the researcher has against distortion is his own feeling of how the story presented by the respondent or others involved in the case "hangs together."

Finally, it may be difficult for the researcher to know when to stop collecting data for a case study. As we mentioned earlier, so many things might be or seem pertinent that there is often a temptation to use a shotgun approach. This is why a carefully thought-out theoretical perspective or framework to guide the collection and organization of data can be of great value to the field worker.

Some Applications

In addition to the pragmatic uses of case studies by physicians, social workers, and others, the technique has been successfully used again and again by sociologists and anthropologists. Case histories of deviants have been collected and analyzed in an attempt to locate the social pressures that may have led them to stray from the normative path (Keniston, 1965; McCaghy, Skipper, and Lefton, 1968; Shaw, 1930 and 1931). Case histories of families and their problems—both internal and societal—have also been traced and compared (Lewis, 1959 and 1961; Hess and Handel, 1959). They have also been used to supplement other research methods. For instance, in a study of the interplay of attitudes and personality traits, Smith et al. (1964) used case histories as part of the data to trace significant events leading to changes in their subjects. Entire gangs of delinquents have been studied by the case method (Yablonsky, 1966), as have organizations (Yablonsky, 1967). Even the social pressures affecting research projects themselves have been the focus of a study (Colarelli and Siegal, 1966).

II THE FAMILY AS A SUBJECT FOR THE CASE HISTORY

The interaction process within the family affects each member. The habits an individual forms, his outlook on life, and his attitudes and behavior toward work, the opposite sex, and himself can largely be attributed to the dynamic relationships established within this primary group. This is because the family is an enduring and emotionally charged group where many of the most important events of an individual's life take place.

The continuity of the family exists in a never-ending cycle of marriage, births, deaths, and departures. Persons of all ages, from infants to the elderly, are affected by their family—as are in-laws and even more distant relatives. Individuals have unconsciously learned many attitudinal and behavioral patterns during day-to-day activities with their families that will be passed on to succeeding generations. To some extent each family has its own culture and structure, and a few of these patterns for living are highly idiosyncratic. Family membership is so much a part of most people's lives that it is often in their conscious thoughts. They may be able to recall vividly, years after it happened, a family situation in which they considered themselves to be unfairly treated, and voice an opinion about the effect this had on their subsequent behavior. People also write about such problems in letters to others and in their diaries. There is no shortage of material on the family, and the case-study approach should yield many valuable insights concerning the effect of membership in such a primary group on an individual's subsequent behavior and attitudes.

III PROJECT ASSIGNMENT

Your assignment is to do a case history on *some aspect* of the sociology of the family. You may work singly or in teams of two or three persons. An investigator working alone may do a case history of one family member. A team effort may be devoted to the comparative study of two similar family members, such as daughters in different families or case histories on all the members of one family. Each team member should study a different person. Afterward the team members should combine their findings for the analysis.

IV STEPS FOR THE CASE HISTORY ASSIGNMENT

A. Before You Go into the Field

1. Decide on the sociological question you wish to pursue and the type of family member or family group most likely to furnish ample data on this topic. For instance:

A. How do parental attitudes and interactions of large families differ over time from those of small families?

B. What is it like to attempt to raise children when there is a serious shortage of money or when jobs are difficult to get? If you have access to a mother who is struggling against such odds, you might interview her in depth.

C. Sibling rivalry has received a great deal of attention from psychologists. How do brothers and sisters themselves describe their developing relationships? How do they "handle" each other? Do they gradually grow together or apart over the years?

D. What different kinds of feelings of love and sexual interest do spouses have for each other through time?

E. What sorts of changes are brought about in family interactions when one family member is absent as a result of death or divorce?

2. Because of the limited time for this assignment, it is highly unlikely you will have access to letters, diaries, and other human documents. Furthermore, the technique of content analysis is not covered until Assignment Nine. Therefore, you had best plan to do *depth interviewing*. Prepare in advance a list of topics you wish to cover. Keep in mind that you are interested in the process of development of your subject area over a period of time.

B. In the Field

1. Again you must face the problem of gaining access to the subject or family of your choice. Inasmuch as you don't want to influence their answers, it would be best not to be too specific about the topic of your investigation, but rather to explain that you are interested in family living patterns.

2. As usual, make provisions to get the respondent's remarks as nearly verbatim as possible. Include any observations you might make as well. It is most important to plan for some way of keeping track of change over time, and for identifying significant incidents or turning points in the subject's life. If you are studying a family relationship and its development or change over time, you might want to keep special track of such statements as, "After that I never again asked for . . ." or "That made a great impression on me and I decided that . . ."

V PRESENTING YOUR RESULTS

Read over the material you have gathered and try to find in the data some logical story or history of the family or family member of your interest. Then write your report, rearranging the order of presentation of the data so as to offer an analysis that the reader will find easy to understand. Include the following in your report:

1. *A brief statement of the problem you investigated by means of the case-study approach.*
2. *A statement of the* type *of individual or family situation you chose for your subject.*
3. *A list of the questions you asked.*
4. *Your results and the evidence for them (descriptions of significant people or events), plus any insights on the sociology of the family you think your study has generated. What hypotheses do your findings suggest for future investigations?*
5. *A discussion of the problems you encountered in producing the case study and any suggestions you have for overcoming similar obstacles in the future.*

The report, limited to three pages per person, should be typewritten and double-spaced. All field notes should also be handed in.

VI SELECTED BIBLIOGRAPHY

A. Methodology

Allport, Gordon W.
  1942   The Use of Personal Documents in Psychological Science. New York: Social Science Research Council 49.
Blumer, Herbert
  1939   An Appraisal of Thomas and Znaniecki, "The Polish Peasant in Europe and America." Social Science Research Council 44.
Dollard, John
  1935   Criteria for a Life History. New Haven, Conn.: Yale University Press.

Fuller, Richard C., and Richard R. Myers
   1941   "Natural history of a social problem." American Sociological Review 6 (June):320–329.
Goode, William J., and Paul K. Hatt
   1952   Methods in Social Research. New York: McGraw-Hill.
Gottschalk, Louis, Clyde Kluckhohn, and Robert C. Angell
   1945   The Use of Personal Documents in History, Anthropology, and Sociology. New York: Social Science Research Council 53.

B.   References and Studies

Berger, Peter L.
   1963   Invitation to Sociology. Garden City, N. Y.: Doubleday.
——, and Thomas Luckmann
   1966   The Social Construction of Reality. Garden City, N.Y.: Doubleday.
Colarelli, Nick J., and Saul M. Siegel
   1966   Ward H. Princeton, N.J.: Van Nostrand.
Freud, Sigmund
   1909   "Analysis of a phobia in a five-year-old boy." Pp. 5–149 in James Strachey et al. (eds.), The Complete Psychological Works of Sigmund Freud VII. London: Hogarth. (First edition 1909.)
   1963   "Introductory lectures on psychoanalysis: Parts I and II." Pp. 303–339 in James Strachey et al. (eds.), The Complete Psychological Works of Sigmund Freud XV. London: Hogarth. (First edition 1915–1916.)
Hess, Robert D., and Gerald Handel
   1959   Family Worlds. Chicago: University of Chicago Press.
Kardiner, Abram, and Lionel Ovesey
   1962   The Mark of Oppression. Cleveland, Ohio: World. (First published 1951.)
Keniston, Kenneth
   1965   The Uncommitted: Alienated Youth in American Society. New York: Harcourt, Brace & World.
Lewis, Oscar
   1959   Five Families. New York: New American Library.
   1961   The Children of Sanchez. New York: New American Library.
McCaghy, Charles H., James K. Skipper, Jr., and Mark Lefton (eds.)
   1968   In Their Own Behalf: Voices from the Margin. New York: Appleton-Century-Crofts.

Rubington, Earl
    1964   "Grady 'breaks out': a case study of an alcoholic's relapse."
             Social Problems 12 (Spring):372–380.

Shaw, Clifford H.
    1930   The Jack Roller: A Delinquent Boy's Own Story. Chicago:
             University of Chicago Press.
    1931   The Natural History of a Delinquent Career. Chicago:
             University of Chicago Press.

Simons, J. L.
    1964   "On maintaining deviant belief systems: a case study."
             Social Problems 11 (Winter):250–256.

Smith, M. Brewster, Jerome S. Bruner, and Robert W. White
    1964   Opinions and Personality. New York: Wiley.

White, Robert W.
    1966   Lives in Progress. New York: Holt, Rinehart & Winston.
             (First published 1952.)

Yablonsky, Lewis
    1966   The Violent Gang. Baltimore: Penguin.
    1967   Synanon: The Tunnel Back. Baltimore: Penguin.

METHOD:

Role Analysis

RESEARCH TOPIC:

Law and Society

I INTRODUCTION

Role Analysis, a Definition

Social ecology can be described as concern with the effects of fairly static geographic or physical arrangements on human behavior (see Assignment Five). Role analysis, its social-psychological counterpart, is concerned with the effects of fairly well-established social structures and their concomitant role relationships on the behavior of participants. Just as social life is not carried out in a vacuum but reflects the characteristics of its physical settings, so it is also affected by the expectations that people have developed concerning the proper role behavior for themselves and others. Thus, if a researcher can draw a map of socially important ecological elements such as barriers, pathways, hiding places, and conversation areas in a setting, he can also chart the role and counter-role relationships in society.

Sociologists have borrowed the term "role" from the theater. It refers to a cluster of behavior norms (rules) that apply to a given position in the social structure. These norms consist of a set of expectations by others that include not only how one should perform the role itself, but also how one should act toward others while performing it, and even how one should feel at the time. The term also includes the role occupant's expectations about how others should act toward him. These reciprocal norms usually remain consistent over time. Such interrelationship of role activities and the expectations it creates mean that a noticeable deviation in behavior is upsetting. Such complaints as "He doesn't act at all as a minister (or teacher, father, etc.) should act toward a parishioner (student, son)" reflect this disappointment in role enactment. The speaker is essentially arguing that the cluster of behaviors toward others by a minister and from others to a minister form a coherent whole that has social-psychological boundaries, so far as the expectations of others are concerned. This includes a minister's mode of dress, his behavior and demeanor toward others, and his status *vis-à-vis* them.

Society is possible, in part, because people go about quietly fulfilling the role expectations of the different positions they occupy. Often we become consciously aware of what those role expectations are only when someone transgresses them. When a child "smarts off" to an adult, for instance, or a professor arrives at class "inappropriately" dressed, or a low-ranking employee gets "too friendly" with the boss at a company picnic, the discomfiture signals a digression from role expectations.

Role analysts believe the concept of "internalization" of role obligations can explain much of people's behavior, and the motivations for this behavior. We have all witnessed the socializing effect of roles on their occupants: the flighty young girl who marries and slowly takes on the role of "matron" because she believes it is expected of her; the vice president who is suddenly catapulted to power by the death of the president and begins to show qualities of statesmanship no one knew he possessed; the contestant who bravely acts the role of the gracious loser, because this is part of playing the game. Some of the most dramatic illustrations of the socializing effect of acquiring a social position with accompanying role expectations are to be found in literature and the theater. In *Pygmalion,* and its musical counterpart, *My Fair Lady,* a lower-class woman is socialized to the role of "lady" and surprises everyone by feeling like one as well as acting the part. *Becket* is the story of a medieval playboy whose appointment to the position of Archbishop of Canterbury gradually socializes him to the point where he acts as is expected of a man in this position. Thus we often act to fulfill the expectations we believe others have of us.

How to Do Role Research and Analysis

Role analysis is not a method of data-gathering per se, but a conceptual and analytic tool. In action, it is an excellent illustration of the interplay between theory and method in research, because its concepts circumscribe the data to be gathered and direct the analysis.

The concept "role" is only one in a constellation of related terms used in role analysis to study the behavior of individuals. These terms are:

Position: One's "situation" in the social structure.

Role: The dynamic or behavioral aspect of position.

Status: The evaluative aspect of position—whether others see it as "high" or "low."

Counter role: A role that is complementary to the role (that is, "completes" the dyadic interaction), allowing, by its existence, the enactment of the role. Teacher-pupil, parent-child, and clerk-customer are three pairs of counter roles that reinforce and make possible each other's performance.

Rights and obligations: Every role carries with it certain actions owed by others and to others. These are the shared expectations or ideal patterns of our own and counter role enactments that we carry in our heads.

Role perception: How one thinks of his social role, what he thinks he should be doing.

Role behavior: Actual performance in a role. (Sometimes we fall below our own role expectations, or those of others. Sometimes we are gloriously successful—we "carry it off.")

Role conflict: A situation in which a person finds that his proper enactment of one role results in falling below expectations in another. Thus, no matter what he does, he has some guilt feelings. (Women who are trying to be good mothers and good students too often experience such role conflict.)

Using these concepts as guides for data-gathering, the social scientist is able to take the information he obtains and map out a "role system" that can in turn be a useful device to alert the researcher to other areas of interaction that might be fruitfully investigated. For instance, Gross (1958) suggested that one way to understand the pressures experienced by a school superintendent was first to map out the counter roles of positions relative to his, such as principals, teachers, school-board members, and students. In an analogous discussion of role and counter role, Merton (1957) uses as his illustration the student physician and focuses on persons who share the same small world—what he refers to as a "status set." In Merton's status set of the student physician, one finds physicians, nurses, social workers, medical technologists, and so on. Each of these, though fundamentally in the same "world" as the student physician (the "medical world"), looks at him from a different perspective and thus interacts with him in somewhat different ways and has somewhat different expectations of him as well.

FIGURE 7-1

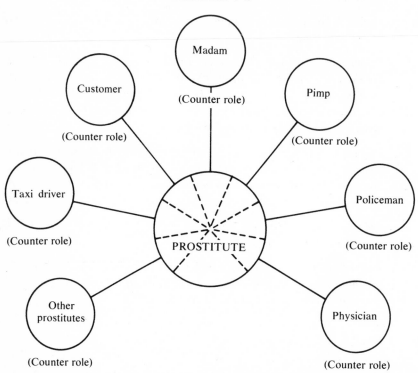

Following Gross's or Merton's lead, in Fig. 7-1 we have charted the counter roles of a prostitute. (It should be clear that the designations "central role" and "counter role" depend upon the researcher's interests. One man's counter role could be another's central role; thus the pimp could be in the focal position and the prostitute in a counter role if the pimp were the major research interest. Furthermore, counter-role occupants also interact with each other. These interactions may be included in or excluded from a research effort, depending upon the goal of the study.)

Once the researcher has mapped out (literally and figuratively) the significant counter roles that are a part of the social situation under study, he can examine the behavior of persons occupying these roles with the following questions in mind:

1. *How do individuals in a counter-role relationship interact with each other? (Specific emphasis would be placed on interaction with the designated "central role.")*

2. *What unspoken expectations do they seem to have of each other? (As mentioned, moments of obviously violated expectations — noted because of the outrage expressed by one person in a role dyad — are very revealing in this area.) For instance, what is expected of a school superintendent? What happens if he falls below expectations?*

3. *How does each person in the role apparently see himself? How does he see others? For instance, how does a pimp see himself? How do others view him?*

4. *What expectations must be fulfilled for a role to be properly played? How much leeway in performance is permitted? For instance, how must a student physician act toward others in his set?*

5. *Is there any difference in the status of the roles under study? (Here look for signs of deference shown by one role occupant for another.) For instance, does one call the other "Sir"?*

6. *What sorts of sanctions, positive or negative, do role players use on each other? What does this reveal about variations in power of the roles (and status as well)? For instance, what threats can a superintendent use to keep teachers in line? And vice versa?*

7. *Are some roles more insulated from observation than others? How can such private areas be penetrated? Where, for instance, can interns relax together?*

8. *What sorts of "props" — clothing, language, demeanor, general appearance — do persons use to maintain themselves in their roles? How does a prostitute dress, for example?*

9. *What sorts of conflicts does a person with multiple role expectations experience? What, for example, happens when a school superintendent is torn between the expectations of the teachers and those of the school board?*

How can the researcher obtain such information? Various investigators have adapted almost all of the methods discussed in previous assignments to role analysis. For instance:

1. *Observation* of persons enacting a role. This would include noting how persons in counter roles talk and act toward each other and attempting to catch their mutual expectations. *(See Assignment One.)*

2. *Participant observation* in a role set. Here the investigator notes role players' reactions to him and other persons in roles, and from these experiences (and his reactions to others in the situation) he draws some descriptions of role enactment and expectations. *(See Assignment Four.)*

3. *Depth interviews* with some persons in roles pertinent to the study. How do they see the role? What kinds of behavior would they include in a proper enactment of it? *(See Assignment Two.)* The same sort of questions can be asked of pertinent counter-role occupants. This gives the investigator a feeling for the cluster of **normative expectations and counter expectations** found in constellations of role sets.

4. *An attitude questionnaire* containing a check list of behavior and appearance traits for the respondent to use to indicate the dimensions of a role (his own or someone else's) as he sees them. Ideal versus actual role behavior can be obtained in this way. *(See Assignment Three.)* For example:

   a. A person who is a ____[role]____ should act
      Very friendly   (   )
      Cool and distant   (   )

   b. He should dress
      In a formal manner   (   )
      Informally   (   )

   c. He should
      Offer help to others   (   )
      Expect help from others   (   )

5. *Case histories* of how some people are gradually socialized to their role behavior until it becomes "second nature" to them. Here the investigator must ask respondents to recall how they felt when they were first in the role. How did they find out what to do? Did they feel awkward? Did they fail at first? And so on. *(See Assignment Six.)*

6. *The explanatory survey* (though students who have not been exposed to it yet obviously cannot use it for this assignment). How do various people assume various roles? What are the causes, as

opposed to mere associated factors? Were they drafted, self-recruited, recruited? How did this affect them? What was their education, their social background, their interests in school? Whom did they see in that role and admire? That is, did they have any role models? (See Assignment Thirteen.)

Each approach is useful in its own way in obtaining an understanding of a particular aspect of role as it affects human group life.

Advantages and Disadvantages

Perhaps the major advantage of role analysis is that a search for roles, counter roles, and the normative expectations incumbent upon each imposes an order on social life. Such organization aids the investigator to pull into a meaningful whole data about human group life that might otherwise appear to be bits and pieces of unrelated social behavior. The very act of mapping roles and counter roles helps to locate explanations for such phenomena as patterns of deference and manipulation and brings possible areas of social conflict and other problems of interaction to the investigator's attention.

Role analysis furnishes clues to motivation that may not be physically evident to the sociologist in an interactional situation; yet he knows these motives should be considered because people mentally refer to the expectations of others before acting. For instance, a person may think, "If I do something to satisfy Person A (in the counter role), what will Person B (in another counter role) think of me?" In other words, role analysis expands the boundaries of the investigation into the social-psychological histories of the actors involved.

As with all approaches to the understanding of social life, role analysis has its limitations. It can lull the investigator into perceiving a rather static social structure in which persons fulfill one role at a time for the continued successful existence of the social system. Some role theorists forget that social life is actually in a constant flux and that people may be able to play several roles simultaneously (an age role, a sex role, an occupational role, in addition to unique interpersonal roles with people). A single counter role may also have several, often contradictory, aspects rather than being the simple unity some researchers depict. For instance, the counter roles of husband and wife may be divided into several *segments:*

For the husband, there is the role of . . .

     . . . lover
     . . . provider
     . . . protector and head of house
     . . . companion

And for the wife, there is the role of . . .
>   . . . glamour girl
>   . . . good housekeeper
>   . . . interior decorator
>   . . . helper (i.e., husband's bookkeeper, etc.)

The average citizen is aware of these segments. Witness such statements as, "He's a good provider but a poor companion."

Conceptually, the term "role" has become so popularized in sociology that almost any cluster of normative expectations has been called a role. These roles are not always tied in the same way to an actual position in the social structure, nor are their behavioral expectations equally formalized. For example, there are conventional occupational roles generally associated with employment that are well demarcated in the social structure and have rather well-defined behavioral expectations. On the other hand, age and sex roles have more nebulous behavioral boundaries, and the positions associated with them are quite loosely defined. Interpersonal roles (Shibutani, 1961:323–366) established by the idiosyncratic relationships of people—such as the "fool" (Klapp, 1962) or the "tension manager" (Bales, 1950)—are so unusual that they have no formalized place in most social structures, but they still develop behavioral expectations among significant others.

The role analyst's most dangerous pitfall is to assume that all behavior is role behavior. People do act for other reasons than role expectations, and other types of theoretical approaches are often better for capturing these activities.

Some Applications

Role analysis is a useful approach to the study of how an individual is incorporated into any social structure, from the family and informal peer groups to such highly bureaucratized organizations as educational institutions and businesses. Social dilemmas can often be pinpointed through attention to problems of role conflict or role discontinuities. For instance, Komarovsky (1957) noted that college girls are expected to show an in-interest both in a career and in marriage, and that these two demands often cause problems and indecision about proper action, especially since it is considered impossible for a girl to be feminine and intelligent simultaneously. Role analyses of "middle-management" positions reveal the conflicting pressures exerted on their occupants. The foreman in a factory, for instance, deals simultaneously with executives and assembly-line workers. In attempting to cope with the problems of each, he often finds his loyalties torn, because he is in the difficult position of trying to fulfill the often conflicting demands of groups whose interests and perspectives frequently do not coincide (Roethlisberger, 1957).

Because a role can be viewed as a conceptual link between personality structure and social structure, a number of sociologists and social psychologists have been interested in the "fit" or "congruence" (or lack of it) between role demands and the personality of the individual in the role. Are bureaucratic personalities or organization men recruited, or are they created by the roles available to them? Are such roles eventually "internalized" to become the fulcrum of the person's outlook on life — the center of his self-concept? Are people pushed into roles incompatible with their self-images? Erving Goffman (1961) has suggested that in such cases the social actor will display "role distance" — that is, public disdain for the role he is forced to play.

Some sociologists (called functionalists) are interested in what each role does to help maintain the social system, and how roles in a given system support each other. The roles in small social systems such as the family or some other primary group are often analyzed — especially when there is a deviant member. Such analyses (Dentler and Erikson, 1959) may indicate that the deviant person is actually functional to the system, because his bad behavior is the one thing other members can agree upon and rally against! Occupational roles in bureaucracies can also function to reduce strain for people who must work together despite personal animosity. This is because the occupant of a position in the social system can fill a role requirement without putting his total "self" into the performance (Coser, 1963).

Social psychologists are interested in how people apprehend what their actual behavior in a role should be, and how they adjust and readjust their behavior to the expectations and counter roles of others when the standards of acceptable role behavior are nebulous. In pursuit of answers to these questions, researchers have looked at how people emulate role models (other people already in the role). Such studies often focus on mass media — movies, television, popular magazines, and newspapers — as the sources of models for individuals who wish to become something other than what they are.

Some psychologists feel that the measure of a person's successful socialization is his ability to *stay* in a role — that is, to act appropriately — regardless of inner tension (Sarbin, 1954). Children gradually develop this ability, a fact to which any parent who has given birthday parties over a period of years can testify. It has also been suggested (Brim, 1960) that the measure of a mature person is his ability to *shift* roles as the occasion demands — from boss at the office to loving husband at home, etc.

II LAW AND SOCIETY AS A SUBJECT FOR ROLE ANALYSIS

The sociology of law and society is the study of the way in which the formal norms of a society are enforced, how the enforcers act toward each other and toward deviants, and how sanctions are distributed within role interaction processes. The legal system is one of several areas in the discipline that is unusually amenable to role analysis. This is because people involved in the legal process—either as defendants or enforcers—are almost always interacting in their roles rather than as "whole persons." Other good areas for role analysis are sociology of medicine, and the sociology of occupations and institutions—wherever impersonal, regulated interaction takes place.

The sociology of law is also suitable to role analysis because it includes innumerable roles and role sets, so that the investigator has many possible choices for study. There are the police (a hierarchy of roles from chief to beat officer), judges, court aides, social workers, psychiatrists, witnesses, jailers, prison guards, lawyers, defendants, prosecutors, parole and probation officers, jury members, bail bondsmen, and so on. They form a web of interpersonal role relations that function as the legal arm of a society. Many roles are in conflict with regard to goals and guiding ideologies.

Finally, these roles in the legal system are in large proportion publicly enacted, so that an investigator has access to them and to the settings in which interaction takes place.

III PROJECT ASSIGNMENT

Your assignment is to do an analysis of some constellation of roles directly connected with law enforcement. You may work singly or in teams of two or three. A team will naturally attempt to get a more detailed view of a role set (perhaps covering more members) than would an individual.

IV STEPS FOR THE ROLE ANALYSIS ASSIGNMENT

A. Before You Go into the Field

1. Decide on the role and counter-role interaction you wish to study. For instance:

    A. Police-defendant-judge
    B. Lawyer-witness-judge
    C. Police chief-police-jailer-lawyer

2. Decide on the best setting for this study in terms of the role sets usually found there. Some suggestions follow (note that A, B, C, D, and H have some areas open to the public).

    A. A municipal or superior court
    B. A police station (the main branch) or a precinct station
    C. The office of a bail bondsman
    D. A booking area
    E. County or city jails (if you know someone in jail, go visit him and do some sociological observations at the same time)
    F. A state prison (almost all have tours in addition to having visiting days; arrange to take advantage of these public periods)
    G. A patrol car (get permission to ride around in it)
    H. A high arrest area—Skid Row, the Tenderloin, the airport, and currently, some college campuses (these are interesting places for observation for the bold and over 21)

3. Decide on your method of gathering data. Review Part B of this assignment for data-gathering suggestions. You may use more than one method if you wish. (Interviewing and observations complement each other nicely, for instance.) Remember, in asking questions the sociologist does not use technical terms, but devises laymen's substitutes. Therefore, you should not ask, "How do you see the role of mother as properly handled?" but rather, "What do you think makes for a good mother? A bad mother?" and so on.

V PRESENTING YOUR RESULTS

Data-gathering should, as usual, be limited to one hour and a half in all, with the other hour and a half utilized in writing the report. Present your findings in a coherent, organized fashion.

Include the following in your report:

    1. A brief statement of the role constellation you were investigating and the setting (if any) where role interaction took place. (It is possible to do interviews of persons about their roles when they are out of their settings, although it would be helpful if this could be supplemented with observations.)

2. *A map of roles and counter roles. Arbitrarily select one role as your focus, in the same way that the school superintendent, the prostitute, and the student physician are the foci of preceding illustrations. Then indicate the counter roles that you were able to study either directly or indirectly through the central role occupant. Do not include counter roles that you did not investigate either directly by observation or interview or by data obtained from a role set participant.*

3. *A brief description of your methodology.*

4. *A statement of your results. These should include answers to some of the following:*

   What do people consider to be the rights and obligations of their roles? (This can be inferred from observation or obtained through questioning.) What assistance do they obtain from such props as costumes and settings? Can they stay in role under tension? What differences do you notice when two different people — two different judges, for example — enact the same role? Be sure to cite the evidence you have for your conclusions — for instance, if you feel a judge expects deference from others, cite occasions or comments that indicate this.

5. *What hypotheses did this study suggest to you for further investigation?*

6. *What problems, if any, did you encounter in attempting to do your role research and analysis? What ideas do you have for overcoming them?*

If you did this assignment alone, your report should be three pages in length, but if you worked on it with others, the finished report should total three pages per person. Turn in all notes with your assignments.

VI SELECTED BIBLIOGRAPHY

A. Methodology

Bales, Robert F.
   1950   Interaction Process Analysis. Reading, Mass.: Addison-Wesley.
Balzac, Honoré de
   1963   "The genus 'clerk' and his natural habitat." Pp. 181–184 in Lewis A. Coser (ed.), Sociology Through Literature. Ellen Marriage (trans.). Englewood Cliffs, N.J.: Prentice-Hall. (First published 1837.)
Bates, Frederick L.
   1956   "Position, role, and status, a reformulation of concepts." Social Forces 34 (May):313–321.
Brim, O. G.
   1960   "Personality development as role learning." Pp. 127–159 in Ira Iscoe and Harold Stevenson (eds.), Personality Development in Children. Austin, Tex.: University of Texas Press.
Goffman, Erving
   1961   Encounters. Indianapolis, Ind.: Bobbs-Merrill.
Goode, William J.
   1960   "A theory of role strain." American Sociological Review 25 (August):483–496.
Gross, Neal, W. L. Mason, and A. W. McEachern
   1958   Explorations in Role Analysis. New York: Wiley.
Klapp, Orrin E.,
   1962   Heroes, Villains, and Fools. Englewood Cliffs, N.J.: Prentice-Hall.
Maccoby, Eleanor E.
   1961   "The taking of adult roles in middle childhood." Journal of Abnormal and Social Psychology 63 (March):493–503.
Merton, Robert K.
   1957   "Role sets." British Journal of Sociology 8 (June): 106–120.
Sarbin, Theodore R.
   1954   "Role theory." Pp. 223–258 in Gardner Lindzey (ed.), Handbook of Social Psychology. Reading, Mass.: Addison-Wesley.
Shibutani, Tamotsu
   1961   Society and Personality. Englewood Cliffs, N.J.: Prentice-Hall. (Pp. 323–366.)

Toby, Jackson
   1966   "Some variables in role conflict analysis." Pp. 348–372 in
           Carl W. Backman and Paul F. Secord (eds.), Problems in
           Social Psychology. New York: McGraw-Hill.

B. References and Studies

Cameron, William Bruce
   1957   "Social roles in a jam session." Pp. 249–253 in R. W.
           O'Brien, C. C. Schrag, and W. T. Martin (eds.), Readings in
           General Sociology. Boston: Houghton Mifflin.
Cottrell, Leonard S.
   1933   "Roles and marital adjustment." Publications of the Ameri-
           can Sociological Society:107–115.
   1942   "The adjustment of the individual to his age and sex roles."
           American Sociological Review 7 (October):617–619.
Dentler, Robert A., and Kai T. Erikson
   1959   "The functions of deviance in groups." Social Problems
           7 (Fall):98–107.
Komarovsky, Mirra
   1957   "Cultural contradictions and sex role." Pp. 230–234 in
           R. W. O'Brien, C. C. Schrag, and W. T. Martin (eds.), Read-
           ings in General Sociology. Boston: Houghton Mifflin.
Levinson, Daniel J.
   1959   "Role, personality, and social structure in the organizational
           setting." Journal of Abnormal and Social Psychology 58
           (March):170–180.
Merton, Robert K.
   1953   "Bureaucratic structure and personality." Pp. 376–385
           in Clyde Kluckhohn, Henry A. Murray, and David M.
           Schneider (eds.), Personality in Nature, Society, and Cul-
           ture. New York: Knopf.
Parsons, Talcott
   1953   "Illness and the role of the physician: a sociological per-
           spective." Pp. 609–617 in Clyde Kluckhohn, Henry A.
           Murray, and David M. Schneider (eds.), Personality in
           Nature, Society, and Culture. New York: Knopf.

Roethlisberger, F. J.
  1957   "The foreman." Pp. 243–249 in R. W. O'Brien, C. C. Schrag, and W. T. Martin (eds.), Readings in General Sociology. Boston: Houghton Mifflin.
Vogel, Ezra F., and Norman W. Bell
  1960   "The emotionally disturbed child as the family scapegoat." Pp. 382–397 in Ezra F. Bell and Norman W. Vogel (eds.), A Modern Introduction to the Family. New York: Free Press.

ASSIGNMENT EIGHT

METHOD:

The Community Study

TOPIC:

The City and Urbanization

I INTRODUCTION

A Definition of Community

When someone mentions the word "community," you probably think of a group of people with certain ties, shared interests, and concerns. You may also see in your mind's eye a place—a small town, a section of the city, a neighborhood. For the social scientist the concept of community also suggests a "togetherness," a "belongingness," and an "ongoingness" within a certain geographical locale. It also implies a certain set of relationships among the individuals who make up this rather large-scale group—relationships that are structured and that encompass the entire range of human institutions.

Despite the suggestions of some social commentators that communities have largely disappeared into the "mass society" * and therefore cannot be identified or studied, laymen and sociologists both continue to talk and

---

* The people who employ the concept "mass society" mean by it that because of increasing industrialization and urbanization the traditional ties that used to bind men together in common interests for common goals have disappeared, and that the individual now feels powerless to make any meaningful decisions regarding the focus of his life or to effect any changes in those institutions—family, church, work, politics, and so on—touching him.

act as if such entities do indeed exist. If communities are difficult to place within particular boundaries because of an affiliation with and an interpenetration by the larger society that surrounds them, they at least seem "psychologically real" to millions of people, some of whom spend a considerable amount of time trying to make "their" community (neighborhood, town, city, etc.) a "better place to live."

A community study is an attempt to understand and describe a group of people who live in a certain geographical location, share certain institutions in common, and feel that the local schools, churches, stores, theaters, parks, homes, industries, and so on somehow belong to them.* By describing one community, the sociologist hopes to reveal underlying processes and structures that are common to all such local groupings of humankind, even though he recognizes that every community is unique. The analysis of a community integrates individual, social, and institutional levels of sociological investigation.

In approaching the study of a community, the sociologist must consider the part it plays in the lives of its residents. What does the community do for them? To find out, he may look at socialization agencies such as the family, schools, churches, clubs, and voluntary associations. He investigates the processes of production, distribution, and consumption, though he realizes as he does so that on the institutional level these processes are not just the concerns of economic organizations such as the factory, the supermarket, and the local department store, but also of schools, religious groups, governmental agencies, and even of the occupations and professions. For example, the "product" that the school "processes" is the student who is to become a productive member of society. His skills are "consumed" or used by other members of the group. The individual thus contributes to and gains from his ties with the community.

The researcher may focus his attention on the family (Komarovsky, 1962), for it is through family sponsorship that an individual enters the community and thus becomes a member of the large, amorphous social grouping that sociologists identify as a class—for example, lower class, middle class, upper upper class, etc. Occupations are often used in conjunction with education and income as indicators of class membership, because the job held by the head of a family affects the life style and life chances of all family members.

The investigator can also note how community members exert social control on citizens, inducing them to conform to the community way of life. To do this the researcher looks into the formal agencies of government—police, courts, prisons, welfare agencies, etc. He may also ex-

---

* Units smaller than an entire town or city (such as neighborhoods or ghettoes) are sometimes referred to as subcommunities.

amine the family, schools, religious organizations, and peer groups for their informal controlling influence on the individual behavior.

Another aspect of community life that can be of interest is social participation. How do people in the community interact with one another in order to satisfy their needs for sociability? What web of social connections exists? Are there some connections between or among groups that are patent and overt—for instance, parents' groups concerned with the wisdom or desirability of sex education in the schools? Are there other groups that are latent and covert—for instance, the leading members of the town deciding at a cocktail party to withhold their business from a newcomer whom they consider to be socially inferior?

Laymen also do community studies—usually for practical reasons. Persons deciding where to buy a home or whether to make a job transfer may do a very extensive study in order to learn the "type of people" who will be their neighbors, the caliber of the schools, the availability of transportation, and the general outlook of the town. People often reveal—or at least lay claim to—an intimate knowledge of community norms when they make such remarks as, "This neighborhood wouldn't go for a movie like that," or "This city is very sophisticated," or "I don't think legislation like that will get much support in this town."

How to Conduct a Community Study

The way a researcher approaches a community study depends to a large extent upon his theoretical orientation. The techniques he uses are obviously not restricted to one theory or form of application, but his perspective provides a way of looking at the social world and of pointing to what data will be important, and to some degree it influences how the data will be gathered. The community study is a culmination of all the methods you have learned thus far, in that sociologists have used all these data-gathering techniques in their investigations of community groupings.

Roland Warren (1963) has identified six different ways that sociologists have employed to study a community,* all of which depend to some degree on the two major dimensions already mentioned—geographic locale and interrelationships among people.

The Concept of Space

The first and oldest approach to the study of the community was based on the concept of space. Here the ecology of the city or rural area is em-

---

*An adaptation of these approaches is presented with permission of the author and publisher. Roland L. Warren, *The Community in America,* Chicago: Rand McNally, 1963.

phasized (see Assignment Five). The investigator using this method considers such characteristics as:

1. Open space
2. Condition of buildings
3. Population density
4. Avenues of transportation and barriers to them
5. Psychological effect of the environment

Several different parts of a city (or a city and a small town) may be compared and contrasted in these terms. For instance, a slum might be contrasted with a hippie area and a middle-class section of small homes.

People Orientation

A second perspective is to look at the community as categories of people. This is essentially a description of the characteristics of the inhabitants in the area (see Assignment Three). Age, sex ratio, income, race, types of occupations, crime rates, welfare aid rates, and so on are important sociological facts to be gathered. Because census material is a primary source of data here, demographic methods can be useful (see Assignment Fourteen). The population makeup of various areas within a city can be compared with one another. The categories of people living in the city and the suburbs, of course, can be compared and contrasted. Differences between types of cities—the "white-collar" city, the "industrial" city, the "government" city, and so on—can also be revealed by this kind of analysis.

Cultural Patterns

A third view of the community—that of "shared institutions"—has been used primarily by anthropologists who concentrate on the community as a culture—norms, values, and symbols. The methodology is generally that of observer or participant observer (see Assignments One and Four). Shared meanings and values are thought to be not only basic components of the concept of community, but also important dimensions on which communities often differ from one another. These meanings and values give the community its uniqueness, its "personality."

People and Group Interaction

A fourth viewpoint is to see the community as the interaction between individuals and groups made concrete through organizations and institutions. The idea has been to look at the behavior of individuals as they go about their day-to-day business. To do this the sociologist might look at how much the local residents use institutions such as local schools, churches, and businesses.

Another study might try to determine how much change is wrought by community residents themselves as opposed to change initiated by "outside forces" such as federal or state agencies, out-of-town industry, etc. An important conceptual framework for this type of study is role analysis (see Assignment Seven), because much of the social interaction that concerns the sociologist takes place among people as they act in their official or organizational capacities.

Distribution of Power

A recently developed means of studying a community has been to analyze the distribution of power. The major focus of this approach is to attempt to determine who holds the reins of power in a given city or town. One of the most influential studies using this frame of reference was Floyd Hunter's study of "Regional City" (1953). His primary research tool was the depth interview (see Assignment Two) which he used when he conducted interviews with leading members of the town.

Social Systems

Finally, communities have also been analyzed as social systems. This approach uses the theoretical framework developed by the sociologist Talcott Parsons (1951). Its major emphasis is on the community as a system of interconnecting units (individuals *or* groups) such as the family, schools, business, the local power structure, each trying to survive and each aiding the others and the system as a whole in order to do so. It is assumed that each unit of the system has goals that mesh with the social system as a whole. To reach these goals, each unit must adapt to the physical and social environment in some way. Where goals of units conflict, there is tension in the whole system. A great deal of conflict can cause disorganization. Most of the time, however, some balance of power is maintained among the units, and the system remains in equilibrium.

The sociologist interested in studying the social system of a community tries to find out how the structure is integrated; he tries to identify the units and discover how they serve each other. He may find in the course of his investigation that some individuals in these institutions are engaged in activities that are contrary to manifest functions of the institution and the community. For example, the police may be protecting a prostitution racket or an abortion ring; or the school board may be serving as a spring-board for the politically ambitious who couldn't care less about the schools' immediate welfare.

The systems-oriented investigator also tries to identify the sources or potential sources of tension, and to investigate methods of tension management. Role analysis (see Assignment Seven) is a particularly effective means of accomplishing this, as are depth interviews with city officials, heads of organizations, and other persons "in the know" (see Assignment Two). For instance, how are the formal roles of the director, the super-visors, and the various types of social workers related within the social system of a welfare agency? How do informal or personal roles help to maintain or upset the stability of an organization's goals? How do indi-viduals in the welfare agency mesh their formal roles with counter roles in other institutions, organizations, and agencies—the police, the District Attorney's office, the school system, the public health department, the county hospital, and so on? What are some of the mechanisms within these cross-agency role relationships that lead to harmonious associa-tions among them? Are the formal roles or personal roles more important?

Depending upon the sociologist's theoretical framework, the length of time at his disposal, and the number of people collaborating on the proj-ect, he will probably rely on one or two particular techniques of collect-ing data. But if he is planning to do a long-term study, he may want to be-come a member of the community (a participant observer). He might even join some of the local voluntary associations (clubs, fraternal organiza-tions, etc.) to observe the members in interaction. He will probably con-duct depth interviews, especially with community leaders. He will also pay attention to the ecology of the community—the locations of stores, restaurants, theaters, homes, schools, and churches. He can use ques-tionnaires or interview schedules to try to get at the attitudes toward local institutions, values, and beliefs that the residents consider important. He may even examine documents (local newspapers, historical records, diaries) and some of the creative efforts of community members (plays, poems, paintings) to see if he can piece together the group's ethos or gestalt. In one participant observation study the investigator compared the data obtained from the interviewees and the local newspaper with data collected from census and historical records. His analysis showed that there was a considerable gap between the "myths" the townspeople held about the community and the "reality" of the community (Lowry, 1965 a and b).

Advantages and Disadvantages

A community study is an *exploratory* study, and also a *tool* that helps us to understand the interrelated nature of social relationships. In its exploratory function a community study can provide a fairly conclusive picture of a small society interacting over time, for it is essentially a case study or case history on a large scale (see Assignment Six). In its function as a tool, a community study, implicitly if not explicitly, sets up a comparative frame of reference for the observer and the reader. If, for example, the community under investigation appears to have certain characteristics, do other communities have the same characteristics? If not, why not? Are there common values, institutional connections, and processes of interaction found in all communities? If so, what are they? If not, what are the differences?

The major disadvantage of the community study is that the researcher must gather and organize a great deal of data, and this poses difficulties when he has only a limited amount of time and money at his disposal. Sociologists, however, are not so much interested in *describing* all the minute details of a community as they are in *understanding* its inner workings. The theoretical perspective of the researcher points him toward problem areas and thus limits what he is going to regard as relevant to his study.

Some Applications

Community studies are a good way to understand an ongoing society of individuals. Small towns and villages, large cities, neighborhoods, suburbs, and rural areas have been analyzed from a variety of perspectives. The results provide not only enlightening but lively readings. The method also has some practical applications. Not only do sociologists want to describe and understand the phenomena they study, but among some there is a growing realization that science has an obligation to make man's life a little better. Studies of a community or subcommunity can assist public and private agencies to make plans for its future. By collecting and analyzing data on categories of residents, their occupations, life styles, relationships with each other, and involvement in community life, sociologists help social engineers solve community problems. Are more elemenatry schools needed? A junior college? Where should parks and recreational facilities be located? What kinds of businesses should be encouraged and in what sections of the community? These are only a few of the questions that social scientists can help civic-minded laymen to answer in their own communities.

II THE CITY AS A SUBJECT FOR COMMUNITY STUDY

The concept of community is a relative one, and geographical boundaries are often difficult if not impossible to delineate. In our modern society even more problems confront the researcher, since federal and state agencies often alter or contaminate local institutions. Government policies can interfere with the autonomy that most people tend to feel is synonymous with community spirit. Nevertheless, the city is an ideal place for a community study, for the average citizen does identify special areas and localities as having distinct institutions and a unique flavor. Thus there are many communities within any city.

The major criterion for identifying a community is its relative exclusiveness. A community is a place that has a culture, a structured set of relationships among groups, and a delimited geographical locale. It is, however, influenced by the larger city in which it is embedded, and in turn contributes to it.

III PROJECT ASSIGNMENT

You are to pick some area of a city or small town and do a community study. For example, every large city has its ethnic clusters, and neighborhoods that seem to have their own special subcultures.

Since the community study requires a variety of methodological techniques for gathering data, you will work on teams consisting of four to ten persons. Your aim is to do a limited exploratory study of a community. What particular problem or institutions are you interested in? What social processes and institutions do you want to describe? Your team will decide on the boundaries that define your city's subarea. The techniques you choose for gathering pertinent data will depend to some extent on the focus of your project. All those mentioned in this assignment could prove useful, so if you have a large team, perhaps you will want to try each one.

Each student will spend three hours (rather than one and one-half hours) in the field collecting data for this assignment, and the project will cover a period of two weeks rather than one.

IV   STEPS FOR THE COMMUNITY STUDY ASSIGNMENT

A.   Before You Go into the Field

1.   Decide what small town or city neighborhood your team wishes to study. (The instructor can be of service here in suggesting areas or in collecting suggestions from students so that individuals might form teams around a choice.)

2.   Decide which of the six perspectives discussed in this assignment you think you want to use. With this as a guide, try to specify more precisely some of the questions you want to answer from the data you collect. For example:

Are you interested in the power structure? Who makes the decisions? Or would you like to know about the kinds of conflicts there are within the community?

Perhaps you are interested in the culture of the community. Do you want to know the major value system or what is considered important to members of this community? How do the members live from day to day? How do they dress, speak, spend their time, and so on?

Are you interested in the types of relationships between members of the community? Do neighbors know one another? Are there helping relationships? Or maybe you are interested in how adults and children interact with one another. Is there disinterest or antagonism?

Do you want to know how the major institutions of the community are related to one another? What are the causes within the community of the types of interaction that prevail? What mechanisms are used to support the bonds that tie people together, such as rituals, exchange of goods and services, and intermarriage, to name a few?

What sorts of structure does the community have? Is age, sex, wealth, and education evenly or unevenly distributed? With what effects?

These are but a few of the questions you might want to pursue. Do not, however, make the focus of your study too broad, since you will not have enough time to pursue more than one or two aspects. Choose a question or two agreeable to all members of the team so that your efforts will not be scattered.

3. Decide on the research methods most appropriate for your community study, and which member of your team is to use each technique. For example, one member might do depth interviews, two others might do an ecological study, and another two construct and administer a questionnaire or observe community groups in action. One team member might wish to consult census data or other official statistics to get some information on community structure.

B. In the Field

1. Decide on the boundaries of your community. What city blocks are you going to cover in your study? You will probably not be able to study the total geographic area, and will have to decide which locales are most important for the *data* you wish to gather. What particular behavior patterns will you examine? These decisions will impose boundaries on the investigation and cause you to look at individuals and organizations that appear to be the *focus* of your report.

2. See former assignments for a review of methodological techniques. Review your own work thus far in this course.

3. Each member of the team should concentrate on the method of research that the team has assigned him. If he runs across information that could be useful and pertinent to the total project, he should make a note of it and if possible discuss it further with his group so plans can be made to include the information or even expand on it.

C. Analysis of the Data

Data should be analyzed in accordance with instructions given in Assignments One through Seven. Review your previous work.

V PRESENTING THE TEAM REPORT

Include the following:

1. *A description of the community.*
2. *The specific questions or problems you were interested in exploring in the community.*
3. *Presentation of results using as evidence tables, quotes from depth interviews and case histories, and examples from observations. Before the final summary is written, there should be a team discussion of the various findings, their possible meanings, and how they relate to the problem you were exploring.*
4. *Suggestions for further research in this community.*
5. *Problems you encountered in doing the assignment. What did you do to overcome these problems and how might the findings be affected?*

The presentation of the results of the community study should not exceed ten to fifteen double-spaced, typewritten pages. All field notes should be attached to the report as appendices.

VI SELECTED BIBLIOGRAPHY

A. Methodology

Arensberg, Conrad M.
    1954   "The community-study method." American Journal of
            Sociology 60 (September):109–124.
Duncan, Otis Dudley, and Albert J. Reiss, Jr.
    1956   Social Characteristics of Urban and Rural Communities.
            New York: Wiley.

Hollingshead, August B.
    1939   "Behavior systems as a field for research." American Sociological Review 4 (December):816–822.
Kaufman, Harold F.
    1959   "Toward an interactional conception of community." Social Forces 38 (October):8–17.
Kimball, Solon T.
    1952   "Some methodological problems of the community self-survey." Social Forces 31 (December):160–164.
Lamb, Robert K.
    1960   "Suggestions for a study of your hometown." Pp. 422–430 in Richard N. Adams and Jack J. Preiss (eds.), Human Organization Research: Field Relations and Techniques. Homewood, Ill.: Dorsey.
Long, Norton E.
    1958   "The local community as an ecology of games." American Journal of Sociology 64 (November):251–261.
Parsons, Talcott
    1951   The Social System. Glencoe, Ill.: Free Press.
Sanders, Irwin T.
    1958   The Community: An Introduction to a Social System. New York: Ronald.
Stein, Maurice R.
    1960   The Eclipse of Community; An Interpretation of American Studies. Princeton, N.J.: Princeton University Press.
Warren, Roland I.
    1947   Studying Your Community. New York: Scribner.
    1963   The Community in America. Chicago: Rand McNally.
Wormser, Margot H., and Claire Selltiz
    1951   "Community self-surveys." Pp. 611–641 in Marie Jahoda, Morton Deutsch, and Stuart W. Cook (eds.), Research Methods in Social Relations. New York: Dryden.

B. References and Studies

Clark, Kenneth B.
    1965   Dark Ghetto: Dilemmas of Social Power. New York: Harper & Row.
DuWors, Richard E.
    1952   "Persistence and change in local values of two New England communities." Rural Sociology 17 (September):207–217.

Gans, Herbert J.
  1962   The Urban Villagers: Group and Class in the Life of Italian-
          Americans. New York: Free Press.
Hunter, Floyd
  1953   Community Power Structure. Chapel Hill, N.C.: University
          of North Carolina Press.
Komarovsky, Mirra
  1962   Blue-collar Marriage. New York: Random House.
Lowry, Ritchie P.
  1965   Who's Running This Town? New York: Harper & Row.
  1965   "The myths behind small-town conservatism." Trans-action
          3 (November-December):31–36.
Lynd, Robert F., and Helen Merrill Lynd
  1956   Middletown. New York: Harcourt, Brace & World (First
          published 1929.)
Seeley, John R.
  1959   "The slum, its nature, use, and users." Journal of American
          Institute of Planners 25 (February):7–14.
——, Alexander Sim, and Elizabeth W. Loosley
  1956   Crestwood Heights: A Study of the Culture of Suburban
          Life. New York: Basic Books.
Vidich, Arthur J., and Joseph Bensman
  1958   The Small Town in Mass Society. Princeton, N.J.: Princeton
          University Press.
Vogt, Evon Z., and Thomas F. O'Dea
  1959   "A comparative study of the role of values in social action in
          two Southwestern communities." American Sociological
          Review 18 (October):645–654.
Warner, William Lloyd, and Paul Lunt
  1941   The Social Life of a Modern Community. New Haven,
          Conn.: Yale University Press.
Wirth, Louis
  1939   "Urbanism as a way of life." American Journal of Sociology
          44 (July):1–24.
Young, Michael, and Peter Willmott
  1957   Family and Kinship in East London. New York: Free Press.

Part Three

Special Techniques

ASSIGNMENT NINE

METHOD:

Content Analysis

RESEARCH TOPIC:

Collective Behavior

I INTRODUCTION

Content Analysis, a Definition

Up to this point we have examined man's behavior more or less directly. We have observed how he attempts to control or adapt to his ecological environment and how he tries to adjust himself to the demands of group pressures. We have interviewed him about his past and questioned him about his ideas and attitudes. From these diversified data we have tried to locate and isolate important variables in an attempt to understand human group life better.

Much of man's behavior is not directly observable, however, nor is it possible to interview people who might know of such behavior from first-hand experience. Content analysis is a technique that enables the sociologist to observe men's behavior in an indirect way, through an analysis of the things they write (their verbal symbols). The social researcher who uses content analysis as a method for gathering data is usually concerned with the manifest content of the written document—with that which is openly stated. It should be noted that a group's conscious and unconscious beliefs, attitudes, values, and behavior patterns are revealed not only in newspapers, magazines, literature, drama, advertisements, and so on, but that such nonverbal symbols as architecture and art can also contain clues of society's life styles (Spengler, 1950).*

The sociologist assumes that communication both affects and is affected by the social environment. It follows, therefore, that an analysis of communication messages could reflect a great deal about human group life at any given point in time. To analyze these messages, the sociologist needs to order the vast amount of material available to him. So he develops pertinent categories that allow him to count or compare what he thinks is important. For example, what was the role of women in America in the mid-1800's? This is so far in the past that persons who could tell us about attitudes toward women in those days are no longer living. But the researcher could examine short stories in magazines of the decade 1850 to 1860 and, by using categories of the "types" of women portrayed — traditional housewife, mother, career girl, glamour girl, pal, and so on — he could tell us about the roles that women played or were supposed to play and the incidence of each.

It is apparent that by using this technique the investigator can observe, indirectly, anything from trends in child-rearing practices (comparison over time) to types of heroes preferred by people of different cultures (cross-cultural comparison). Material can be analyzed for propaganda content; differences can be revealed in the handling of the same event by mass media in different countries — or by different media in the same country. Or, through the analysis of literature and popular magazines, comic strips, cartoons, and movies, the researcher can reveal how countries differ in their emphasis on sex, crime, religion, ethnic groups, expressions of affection and love, or violence and hatred. The rise and fall of fads can be noted. From these data, a researcher can make comparisons about the attitudes and beliefs of various groups of people separated by time, geographic locale, or culture.

How to Do Content Analysis

Content analysis, like other techniques of collecting data by sociologists, is a refinement of ways used by the layman to describe and explain social phenomena and changes in the social world. For example, the parents of an unruly and aggressive boy may say the cause of his behavior is

*This assumption, that man reveals himself through his productions, is a basic tenet of those who use projective techniques to understand human behavior. See Assignment Ten.

that there is "too much violence on television these days." Parents may blame the promiscuous behavior of their teen-age daughter on "all that sex in the magazines and movies." They may emphasize that "it wasn't this way when I was your age," much to their children's anger, disdain, or amusement. What the layman is saying is that—based on his impressions of the contents of television, movies, magazines, and other mass media—there is a greater emphasis on violence and sex now than in his own formative years. He is also saying that the contents of mass media influence the behavior of his children.

The social researcher also looks at mass media (as well as other types of symbols) to try to describe their contents. He too makes some assumptions about change over time and the impact the material could be having on the audience it reaches. The major difference between a layman's intuitive impressions and the sociologist's approach is that the sociologist tries to describe the messages contained in these communications in an objective and systematic way. The sociologist tries to define as precisely as possible what aspects of the content he is going to investigate and then to formulate categories that are relevant to his investigation—categories that are so explicit that another analyst could use them to examine the same material and obtain substantially the same results—that is, find the same proportion of topics emphasized or ignored. This introduces a second characteristic of content analysis—*quantification*. Each time a unit in a pertinent category is found it is "counted."

Counting certain words, for instance, may be an important way to analyze content if he is interested in determining the prevalence of terms that convey group stereotypes or that have loaded emotional overtones, such as nigger, honky, dago, red, hippie, beatnik, right-wing agitator, or commie. Here the categories would be relatively easy to formulate, since each title would constitute a separate type. For example, the words "black" and "Negro" in a magazine (or magazines, depending on the sample) could be tallied to see if there had been a significant shift in the preference of one word over the other in a specified period of time.

It may be that the researcher wants to determine certain characteristics of a specific group. For example, he might want to compare short stories in women's magazines to see what kinds of heroes are presented to the readers. He would first select his sample—that is, which magazines he would read, over what time period, and which issues (for instance, 25 issues of each magazine between 1945 and 1965, selected by a set of random numbers). He could then formulate tentative categories representing characteristics of heroes, which might include physical, emotional, social, and personality characteristics. These in turn he would break down into even smaller coding units such as:

Physical Characteristics	*Emotional Characteristics*	*Social Characteristics*
Color of hair	Warm	Race
Color of eyes	Aloof	Religion
Height	Stable, secure	Occupation
Weight	Anxious, insecure	Income
Age	Hostile	Housing
Scars	etc.	etc.
etc.		

A third possibility for category creation might be to attempt to isolate the major ideas, values, attitudes, or behavior patterns expressed in some communication. The sociologist could want to see if there are different attitudes expressed toward intimate human relationships described in the mass media of the United States, England, France, and Sweden. Films would be an excellent and accessible source for this analysis, though obviously the categories and coding units within each category would be much more difficult to formulate (not to mention the problem of taking notes in the dark), but it could be done. For instance, three general categories could be formed using Karen Horney's typology (1945) of relationships: "going toward," "going away from," and "going against." The researcher would then look for instances of these concepts expressed in the movies. Such units of behavior as hitting or slapping someone, sarcasm, aloof behavior, and holding hands or kissing are illustrations of possible categories.

A final way to analyze the content of mass media is to use "space" or "time" units. For example, in the past few years, how many inches or newsprint have been devoted to student demonstrations on campuses? How many minutes have television news programs devoted to the riots in Watts or Chicago?

Advantages and Disadvantages

As we have indicated, much of what we know is obtained, not through direct interaction with others, but through books, newspapers, and other symbolic products of man. One of the major advantages of content analysis is that the researcher can delve into past records and documents in order to get some feeling for the social life of an earlier day. He is not limited by time and space to the study of present events.

Content analysis is also useful because it is an unobtrusive measure (Webb et al., 1966); the investigator can "observe" without being observed, since mass media are not influenced by the investigator's presence. Information that might be difficult or impossible to obtain through direct observation or interview techniques can be gained through available communication material without the producer's awareness of its being examined. Finally, since the data is always available (except for television and movies, and even these media offer reruns), the method allows replication of a study by other researchers.

There are major disadvantages to content analysis too. Foremost is its limited nature. If we are studying the past, we normally have records only of what has survived or was thought to be of sufficient importance to write down. Since each generation has a somewhat different perspective, what may be considered important today might not be available from years past. Parallel to this disadvantage is the possibility that what mass media present are often of an ideal nature, in the sense that media reflect cultural ideals rather than actual activities. To offset this kind of bias, an investigator might wish to check his analysis of mass media against a content analysis of letters and diaries of the times (if they are available), on the assumption that personal documents are more forthright about what human group life was really like in those days than materials produced for public consumption. (This assumption may not always be warranted, however.)

Finally, there is sometimes a temptation among social scientists to consider that the data gleaned from a content analysis were *causes* of social phenomena rather than reflections of them. For example, violence in the mass media may be pointed to as a cause of violence in the streets (Wertham, 1954), but a more reasonable conclusion is that mass media both reflect and change the social world around us. Certainly much work has to be done to determine the relationship between mass media and human behavior. For example, some people think that reading pornographic books and magazines causes decay in the moral fiber of all individuals who read them. It is up to the sociologist, however, to check out such assumptions by finding out who the targets of the message-makers are, whether these targets are reached, and what effect, if any, the message has.* Pornography may (and probably does) affect groups differently because of such factors as selective perception, group affiliation, and past experience.

Some Applications

Content analysis is a technique that has almost unlimited applicability in social research. It can be used as the primary method to:

---

*The identification of the message-makers and their targets and a determination of their degree of influence are also integral parts of content analysis, but these topics will not be dealt with here.

1. *Describe trends in science, leisure, politics, and human relationships (Bronfenbrenner, 1958; Lowenthal, 1950; Rosen, 1964).*
2. *Reveal propaganda themes (Evans, 1967; Stewart, 1964; Berelson, 1946).*
3. *Show how different levels of communication media handle the same material (Winick, 1963).*
4. *Infer attitudes, values, and cultural patterns of historical and foreign peoples (McClelland, 1961; Sebald, 1962).*
5. *Compare the myths people hold of their cultural past with historical records and documents (Lowry, 1965; Lantz et al., 1968).*

Content analysis can also be used to supplement other, more direct methods of research. Attitudes toward women who are working in so-called men's occupations can be investigated in a variety of ways: by questionnaire, depth interview, participant observation, and content analysis of magazines, television, newspapers, films, and autobiographies that touch on this subject. The "boss lady" stereotype may be more a creation of the media than a case of spontaneous social typing. Once established, however, it creates expectations in others about women in executive positions.

Content analysis can also be used to give the researcher insight into problems or hypotheses he can test by a more direct method. A sociologist might analyze the content of an underground newspaper to obtain information for use in devising questionnaires or formulating questions for depth interviews with members of the hippie youth.

Finally, content analysis can be used to make practical decisions. For example, a recent study by the Federal Communications Commission determined the percentage of television time the major networks throughout the United States gave to cigarette commercials, as compared to the time allowed for warnings against the use of cigarettes for health reasons. The results led to the threat of loss of license for several television stations because of unequal time allotment.

II COLLECTIVE BEHAVIOR AS A SUBJECT FOR CONTENT ANALYSIS

The phenomenon of collective behavior covers a wide range of activities, such as mob action, riots, crowd behavior, fads, fashions, and any other type of action that occurs on a collective level as a result of what some have called "social contagion." Collective behavior is different from other group behavior that sociologists study because it often occurs among people who do not form a society or social grouping. Members of collectivities often have no other historical social relationship than the casual ones of being in the same place, being exposed to identical stimuli, or having attitudes about the same thing at the same point in time. There- fore the concerted action that occurs among human collectivities cannot be explained by any long-standing social ties; rather, all the people pres- ent are caught up in the common excitement of the event. Such emotion- charged activities do not lend themselves to dispassionate reporting on the part of the mass media. Thus the sociologist may become interested in comparing treatment of the same incident as reported in the different mass media—newspapers, television, popular magazines, etc.

In the past few years there have been increasing instances of collective behavior—mobs, crowds, riots, civil-rights marches, demonstrations—in the United States. Many reasons have been suggested for this phenome- non—the Vietnam War, the social conditions of minority groups, the dis- affection of middle-class youth with the materialistic values of the Ameri- can culture, anomie, permissive child-rearing techniques, and so on. This behavior has been chronicled in magazines, books, newspapers, and, per- haps most potently, television news broadcasts. Sometimes we get the impression that there is no serene and stable life left in the United States. Therefore it would be both interesting and useful to find out if indeed more coverage of such collective behavior of other types of news is now being presented by the mass media as compared to the coverage of ten years ago.

The norms of a society are also reflected in the fads and fashions adopted by its people. A comparison of photographs in magazines and newspapers of fifty years ago with those of today would undoubtedly reveal that the permissible limits within which a woman can expose her body in public has been considerably expanded. It can be assumed that this shift in "style" may also be an indicator of other changes in the so- ciety—the role relationships between men and women, for example. Other fashions, too, both reflect and influence cultural behavior patterns. Advertisements of children's toys will reveal current thinking about what a child's nature is—or should be. Attitudes toward the morality of saving money and paying cash versus installment buying can be noted by comparing today's financial pages with those of many years ago. The list is endless.

III PROJECT ASSIGNMENT

You are to do a content analysis of some aspect of collective behavior as described by the mass media. For your data you may select one topic below and do a comparative analysis as described:

1. *The major themes in the fiction of two different kinds of popular magazines. For example:* Playboy *and* Ladies' Home Journal, McCall's *and* True Confessions, *etc. (One issue of each magazine you select is sufficient.)*
2. *The types of news emphasized in two daily newspapers — one issue each, a current issue and an issue of fifty years ago.*
3. *The general subject matter of a foreign film (Swedish, French, Italian)* and *an American film.*
4. *The cartoons in two issues of the* New Yorker *(one a current issue and the other a ten-year-old issue),* or *of an issue of* Punch *and an issue of the* New Yorker *for the same year.*
5. *Three thirty-minute television news broadcasts, two during the week and one on a weekend.*
6. *The fads or fashions being created — aside from the product advertised — on television commercials; i.e., the fashions worn by models, male and female; the way mothers speak to children, and so on.*

IV STEPS FOR THE CONTENT ANALYSIS

A. Before You Go into the Field

1. Choose one of the topics in the project assignment.
2. Formulate a problem or hypothesis that will allow a comparison between two groups or two types of activities. For example: a comparison between television time devoted to college demonstrations versus time devoted to sports.
3. Decide on the content you want to describe. What categories are you going to use? Do you want to study riots? Fashions? Fads?
4. Decide on your unit of analysis. What will you "count"? All advertisements in the magazine that pertain to clothing styles or only the color ads? All news dealing with collective behavior, or only that mentioning college demonstrations and war protests?

5. Prepare a coding sheet, as you did in Assignment One, for tallying the data you plan to collect (a sample is shown in Fig. 9-1). If you plan to analyze men's and women's fashions in two popular magazines, you might want to see if there is a difference in types of clothing considered appropriate by each type of magazine. A sample tally sheet is shown in Fig. 9-2. Repeat the tally sheet for readers of magazine #2.

Figure 9-1

INSTANCES OF COLLECTIVE BEHAVIOR
(TV NEWS BROADCASTS)

	College Demonstrations	Race Riots	War Protests
30 sec.			
60 sec.			
90 sec.			
120 sec.			
etc.			

Figure 9-2

CLOTHING CONSIDERED APPROPRIATE FOR READERS OF
(MAGAZINE #1)

	Men	Women	Both
Slacks or pants			
Tailored shirts			
Frilly blouses			
High-heeled shoes			
etc.			

B. In the Field

1. In every case, be sure you tally *all* instances of descriptive behavior (or active behavior on TV and film) that applies to your study. If you are unsure of an item, note it and decide later if a new category should be made or if the item should be omitted. In any case, but especially when you are analyzing written documents, keep a record of how each item was coded. (If you are coding magazines, newspapers, or cartoons, you can usually make a note directly on the document itself, at the side of each item you use, as well as tabulating it on your sheet. This allows you to check your accuracy.)
2. In order to code a movie with a fair degree of accuracy, it may be necessary to see it two or three times. A news broadcast, of course, allows no such rerun unless you look at early and late news. It is probably easier (and more accurate) to do a time analysis in this case, by counting the number of seconds or minutes an item takes to be shown. Ads on TV are rerun many times, and therefore it should be relatively easy to code content accurately.

V PRESENTING YOUR RESULTS

Present your findings in a clear and organized fashion. Include the following:

1. *A brief statement of your problem, the media and subject-matter you examined, and the comparisons you made.*
2. *A presentation of your results in table form. (Look at some tables in other sociology texts for guidance or in the "General Instructions for the Student" in this text.) All tables should have clearly marked headings and a title. Show percentages for each item.*
3. *The significance of the results shown in each of your tables.*
4. *Suggestions for further research in this area.*
5. *A list of some of the problems you encountered in doing the assignment, how you overcame these problems, and how your findings could be affected.*

Please limit your presentation of results to three double-spaced, typewritten pages. Hand in all of your tally sheets and notes with your written report.

VI SELECTED BIBLIOGRAPHY

A. Methodology

Berelson, Bernard
  1952   Content Analysis in Communication Research. New York:
          Free Press.
Cartwright, Dorwin P.
  1953   "Analysis of qualitative material." Pp. 421–470 in Leon
          Festinger and Daniel Katz (eds.), Research Methods in the
          Behavioral Sciences. New York: Dryden.
Holsti, Ole R., with the collaboration of Joanne K. Loomba and Robert
C. North
  1968   "Content analysis." Pp. 596–692 in Gardner Lindzey and
          Elliot Aronson (eds.), The Handbook of Social Psychology
          2. Reading, Mass.: Addison-Wesley.
Lasswell, Harold D., and Nathan Leites (eds.)
  1949   Language of Politics. New York: George W. Stewart.
McGranahan, Donald V.
  1951   "Content analysis of the mass media of communication."
          Pp. 539–560 in Marie Jahoda, Morton Deutsch and Stuart
          W. Cook (eds.), Research Methods in Social Relations. New
          York: Dryden.
Webb, Eugene, and Donald T. Campbell, Richard D. Schwartz, and Lee
Sechrest
  1966   Unobtrusive Measures; Nonreactive Research in Social
          Science. Chicago: Rand McNally.

B. References and Studies

Albrecht, Milton C.
  1956   "Does literature reflect common values?" American So-
          ciological Review 21 (December):722–729.
Berelson, Bernard, and Patricia J. Salter
  1946   "Majority and minority Americans: an analysis of magazine
          fiction." Public Opinion Quarterly 10 (Summer):108–190.
Berkman, Dave
  1963   "Advertising in Ebony and Life: Negro aspirations vs. real-
          ity." Journalism Quarterly 40 (Winter):53–64.

Bronfenbrenner, Urie
  1958   "Socialization through time and space." Pp. 400–425 in
          Eleanor E. Maccoby, Theodore M. Newcomb, and Eugene
          O. Hartz (eds.), Readings in Social Psychology. New York:
          Holt, Rinehart & Winston.
DeCharms, Richard, and Gerald H. Moeller
  1962   "Values expressed in American children's readers: 1900-
          1950." Journal of Abnormal and Social Psychology 64
          (February):136–142.
DeFleur, Melvin L.
  1964   "Occupational roles as portrayed on television." Public
          Opinion Quarterly 28 (Spring):57–74.
Evans, James F.
  1967   "What the church tells children in story and song." Journal-
          ism Quarterly 44 (Autumn):513–519.
Hoopes, Paul R.
  1966   "Content analysis of news in three Argentine dailies." Jour-
          nalism Quarterly 43 (Autumn):534–537.
Horney, Karen
  1945   Our Inner Conflicts. New York: Norton.
Lantz, Herman R., Eloise C. Snyder, Margaret Britton, and Raymond
Schmitt
  1968   "Pre-industrial patterns in the colonial family in America:
          a content analysis of colonial magazines." American Socio-
          logical Review 33 (June):413–426.
Lowenthal, Leo
  1950   "Biographies in popular magazines." Pp. 289–298 in Ber-
          nard Berelson and Morris Janowitz (eds.), Reader in Public
          Opinion and Communication. Glencoe, Ill.: Free Press.
Lowry, Ritchie P.
  1965   Who's Running This Town? New York: Harper & Row.
McClelland, David C.
  1961   The Achieving Society. Princeton, N.J.: Van Nostrand.
Rosen, Bernard
  1964   "Attitude changes within the Negro press toward segrega-
          tion and discrimination." Journal of Social Psychology 62
          (February):77–83.
Sebald, H.
  1962   "Studying national character through comparative content
          analysis." Social Forces 40 (May):318–322.
Spengler, Oswald
  1926   The Decline of the West. Authorized translation with notes
          by Charles Frances Atkinson. New York: Knopf.

Stewart, James S.
   1964   "Content and readership of teen magazines." Journalism
          Quarterly 41 (Autumn):580–583.
Wertham, Frederic
   1954   Seduction of the Innocent. New York: Holt, Rinehart &
          Winston.
Winick, Charles
   1963   "Trends in the occupations of celebrities—a study of news
          profiles and television interviews." Journal of Social Psy-
          chology 60 (August):301–310.

ASSIGNMENT TEN

METHOD:

Projective Techniques

TOPIC:

Attitudes Toward Social Categories

I INTRODUCTION

What Projective Techniques Are

In most of the previous assignments, you have used two basic methods of obtaining information about individuals and groups: direct observation and direct interrogation (interviews and questionnaires). In this assignment, as in Assignment Nine ("Content Analysis"), you use an indirect method to obtain data about your respondents. The researcher who utilizes a projective test is primarily interested in analyzing a certain kind of content—an individual's responses to such unstructured stimuli as pictures, stories, words, ink blots, and so on. By examining the content of these responses the investigator hopes to obtain information about the person's attitudes, beliefs, values, motivations, and behavior.

As you may recall, there are some major drawbacks to the techniques of observation and interviewing: when an investigator observes people, he may misinterpret the meanings of their actions; when he asks questions, he may lose rapport with a respondent by asking questions that are too personal. Furthermore, people do not always know themselves well, they may not be accustomed to introspection and therefore cannot tell the investigator what he wants to know even if they are willing to do so. They may simply be unaware of the motives for their behavior.

Projective techniques were originally devised by psychoanalysts to reveal the motives for men's actions that were hidden or disguised not only from others but, more importantly, from their own consciousness. It is a basic tenet of psychoanalytic theory, beginning with its originator Sigmund Freud, that most of man's behavior is directed by unconscious needs and modified by unconscious defense mechanisms. The demands these needs make are imperious, yet so socially unacceptable to an individual that he probably will not admit to their existence even if he is confronted with evidence. Freud, in attempting to understand and help his patients, tried to discover their unconscious motivations by asking them to talk to him. He encouraged them to say whatever came into their thoughts, regardless of whether it seemed "logical" or proper. Freud called this method *free association* and made it the primary approach to the development of his theory of human personality and behavior. It was part of his theoretical position that individuals reveal unconscious motives in their behavior—in their speech, thoughts, dreams, and actions. It was the task of the psychoanalyst to analyze the latent content of these behaviors and ferret out the "true meanings" in order to cure the patient. Most of Freud's data were collected from his patients, but he also used himself as a subject and throughout his lifetime recorded and analyzed his own thoughts and behavior.

The originator of projective methods as they are used today by psychologists was Carl Jung, a psychoanalyst who for many years was a close associate of Freud, but who later evolved his own theory of the development of the human personality. It was Jung who in 1918 introduced the word-association test, which consists of a standard list of words that is read to the subject one at a time. The subject is supposed to respond with the first word that comes into his mind, and the analyst notes how long it takes him to answer. The word association test was one way Jung used to unmask an individual's "complex"* or "complexes." He also thought that fantasies, drawings, paintings, and other objects created through the exercise of imagination could be analyzed to uncover unconscious thoughts and feelings.

The rationale of the projective method is to make the individual organize a series of "unstructured" situations or objects in some way. Since perception is selective and idiosyncratic—that is, since each person perceives the world differently because of biological, psychological, and cultural factors—it is assumed that the structure he imposes or "projects" onto the material is a reflection of his inner state.

* In Jung's terminology a *complex* is an organized or structured group of feelings, thoughts, memories, and so on in the unconscious. Thus a person with a "father complex" would be dominated by thoughts of the father and his actions will reflect unconscious feelings, memories, and perceptions of the father.

Many other projective methods besides the word-association test have been developed. Most of these are used to discover more about the personality of an individual, his motives, and his emotional makeup. Movies, television, fiction, and drama have acquainted most of us with at least a few of these tests. For example, not only are caricatures of the word-association test a familiar and even trite scene—where the subject replies to a word like "night" with "blood"—but so is the administration of the Rorschach test, in which the subject is to tell the analyst what objects he sees in a series of ink-blots.

Not so well-known to laymen, perhaps, is the *Thematic Apperception Test* (T.A.T), in which the subject is to respond to a series of situationally ambiguous pictures by writing or telling a complete story about each one. The story may be only a sentence or two, but it must have a beginning, middle, and end. A well-trained psychologist is supposed to be able to reveal the individual's attitudes, values, motives, hopes, wishes, fears, goals, how he sees himself, and how he acts in relation to others by analyzing these stories. For example, one of the pictures shows a young woman standing with her head down and her face covered by one of her hands. The other hand is stretched forward against a door. A young girl might tell the following story about this scene: "A young woman is crying because she has just learned that her boyfriend has been killed in the war. She will eventually gain control of her emotions and go on to lead a happy life. But she will always remember her first, lost love." A man might give this story: "This is a woman who has just had a fight with her husband and is trying to gain sympathy by resorting to tears. The husband will be obliging so as to restore harmony to the household. She will stop crying—until next time." As you can see, there is a vast difference in what is "seen" by these two individuals. The psychologist could interpret the results as follows (although he would *never* make a personality assessment on the basis of *one* test picture alone): "The first subject is a woman who is capable of warm and tender feelings toward another person. She also has a strong enough ego (or sense of reality) to cope with problems in her life." On the other hand, he might say about the male subject: "He is a person who feels women are manipulative. He resents them but is also a bit afraid of them. He identifies his wife with his mother."

Almost any object produced by man can be used as a projective test, and many devices have been developed to gather data for analyzing personality and motives. For instance, David C. McClelland (1961, 1964), in his investigations of the "achievement motive," has used such items as children's primers, fairy tales, and designs on pottery as raw materials for analyses of entire societies. Another researcher (Knapp, 1958) built a projective test around Scottish clan tartans, and found that achievement-motivated people tend to choose blue or dark plaids rather than red or bright plaids!

Lindzey (1959) has identified five different types of projective techniques: * (1) word-association techniques that require the individual to respond to the stimulus with the first thing that comes into his mind; (2) construction techniques that require the individual to construct something — a drawing, story, and so on; (3) completion techniques that require the individual to finish a sentence or story; (4) expressive techniques in which the individual is allowed to play, dance, paint, or play roles as in the socio-drama (where the individual acts out another person's role) or psycho-drama (where the individual "plays" himself); and (5) choice or ordering techniques, which are more recent attempts to quantify or objectify projective devices such as the Rorschach test by providing multiple-choice answers (Campbell, 1950; Hammond, 1948).

Obviously there is no one "right" set of responses for a particular projective test. What the investigator is interested in obtaining is the *pattern* that develops from the respondent's set of responses. He then interprets this pattern according to valid and reliable categories that have been developed for the test.

The layman uses projective methods in everyday life when he interprets the actions and consumption choices of friends, relatives, and even strangers. For example, we usually note house furnishings when we are first invited to someone's home because we "know" that these are reflections of the person in some way. We may casually examine his doodles to see if the absent-minded squiggles tell us anything about his mood or feelings. We make speculations about an individual's personality based on the kind of car he buys and the kinds of clothes he wears. There is the "sports-car type," the "tweedy type," the "cigar smoker," the "bead-wearer," etc.

How Projective Techniques Are Used in Sociology

Sociologists have adapted projective tests to their own needs. Their concern is not so much with the underlying personality traits of an individual as it is with the attitudes and behavior of individuals with regard to specific issues or groups in society. Projective techniques allow the sociologist to obtain such information without influencing answers in the process, and to find out things about the respondent that he could be unwilling to reveal.

In view of these differences in the ways that sociologists use projective techniques, it is not surprising that they usually devise more structured and less ambiguous tests than those that psychologists use. Psychologists assume that the less structured a test the deeper the level of personality

* You will choose one of the first three types for this assignment.

it taps, and this is what interests them. The sociologist, on the other hand, is more interested in social attitudes that presumably are more "available" — in the individual's consciousness—and that he could express if it were not for his reluctance to reveal them openly to others. Sociologists tend to avoid projective techniques that require relatively lengthy and intensive training, such as the Rorschach, to interpret.

Modifications of the T.A.T., however, have proved to be useful to sociologists. Variations of this test usually consist in selecting sets of pictures that will focus the respondent's attention on a specific topic. For example, if the investigator wants to learn about attitudes toward elderly people, he can select test pictures showing both young and old persons in a variety of social contexts and ask respondents from a particular social group—for example, members of the lower class—to tell him a story about each picture. Then he can analyze the responses to see if there is a consistent set of attitudes among lower-class persons toward old people.

Another technique the sociologist might use is the sentence completion test. If the researcher wanted to determine attitudes toward drug addicts and people who experiment with drugs, he could construct a test that might include the following items:

Joe saw some marijuana weeds growing behind the house.
He _____

Mary's friend offered her an LSD sugar cube. Mary
_____

Tom read a novel in which the hero took cocaine. Tom
_____

It should be noted that most projective tests allow the subject only a limited amount of time in which to respond. Presumably this makes it difficult for him to fake consistent answers to the test, and the patterning of his responses reveals "true" attitudes.

Advantages and Disadvantages

The major advantage of this method is that the researcher can elicit attitudes without the subject's becoming aware of the researcher's aims. If the sociologist feels that the issue he is exploring is sensitive, he can hide the purpose of the test by interspersing the key elements—words, stories, cartoon, etc. — with more neutral stimuli. Even if the subject is aware of the test, he may find it easier to respond to such unstructured stimuli than to answer direct questions.

Like the depth interview, the data obtained through the use of a projective test may be utilized to formulate questions to use in a more structured approach — an attitude survey, perhaps. However, because projective techniques are difficult to devise and interpret, they would ordinarily not be used if the data could be obtained in other ways.

The major disadvantage of the projective test is its subjectivity. There is no assurance that two sociologists will interpret the same data in the same way. For example, suppose a sociologist is testing the following hypothesis: "Young people (under twenty) will not see or notice old people (over sixty) unless it is in a negative way." This sociologist might interpret a young respondent's story about a picture showing a youth saying to an older person "Do what you like" as negative because it ignores the older person as an individual. Another sociologist might say that the same response is a positive statement indicating respect of the other's worth as a person and his right to "do his own thing." The interpretation of the data from the responses would depend on the context of the statement in relation to the total answer pattern, and also on the researcher's theoretical perspective. In other words, it is very difficult to agree about the "true meaning" of a response to a projective test in comparison with the meaning of a more structured objective test.

Psychologists have standardized most of their projective tests so that different psychologists (with intensive training) will be able to code responses uniformly. But many projective tests are subject to the individualistic interpretation of the sociological researcher, since he has adapted the test to the goals of his study. Therefore, in spite of the potentialities of projective tests to provide insight into a social issue, extreme care must be used in administration and analysis.

Some Applications

As you have probably gathered, projective techniques have been used in many ways. Some typical studies have been to determine interracial attitudes (Brown, 1947); reactions to Negro sales personnel (Saenger and Gilbert, 1950); achievement motives (McClelland, 1964); life styles (Rainwater et al., 1959); opinions on methods to prevent war (Fromme, 1941); race conflict in children (Axline, 1948); and reactions of children to physical disabilities (Goodman et al., 1963).

II SOCIAL CATEGORIES AS A SUBJECT FOR PROJECTIVE TECHNIQUES

As mentioned, projective tests are most appropriate for sociological investigations when the researcher feels that the respondent either may not want to talk about the issues because he fears his attitudes are unpopular, or that he may not be sufficiently aware of his attitudes to be able to verbalize them without aid. Some of the most sensitive topics are those concerned with different "social categories" of people as determined by their age, sex, race, religion, physical appearance, mental disease, criminal record, and so on. Social categories are important for sociologists to study because they affect social interaction. Even when the people who fall into these categories are not aware of their common characteristics and thus do not identify themselves as a distinctive group, other people may see them as such and respond to them in certain positive or negative ways solely on the grounds of one or two characteristics.

An example of a "sensitive" social category might be the physically handicapped. Our society has a youth-oriented culture that emphasizes a beautiful and normal body; therefore when respondents are asked to give their attitudes or opinions about people who fail to attain this ideal, their answers are apt to be circumspect or altogether evasive. If, however, a series of pictures is given to the respondent in which handicapped people are depicted in a variety of situations, the researcher can determine how the respondent handles situational stories about them. The same type of tests could be used to obtain attitudes toward individuals who represent other social categories—the aged, the unmarried, people of ethnic and religious groups, welfare recipients, alcoholics, drug addicts, homosexuals, ex-convicts, and so on.

The tendency to hide one's feelings will, of course, vary from individual to individual, but it is assumed that the social groups to which the respondent belongs will have an influence on his attitudes. Thus, one might hypothesize that it is likely fat people will be more sympathetic to the plight of the obese than will those who are of average weight. The slim person might be "polite" in his response to a direct question about a particular friend who is somewhat heavy, but if he had to make up a story about an overweight couple sitting on a park bench he might reveal more negative feelings, such as disgust or pity.

III PROJECT ASSIGNMENT

In this assignment you will devise a projective test and administer it to six subjects. The test should explore attitudes toward a social category that people may be unwilling to discuss openly, or about which they may have conflicting attitudes. (Some of the social categories that seem to have these properties have been listed above.)

Your test can be either any of those mentioned—word association, pictures, sentence completion, story completion, cartoons in which the subject "makes up" the conversations of the characters—or any other test you feel will elicit responses revealing an individual's attitudes.

IV STEPS FOR THE PROJECTIVE TECHNIQUE ASSIGNMENT

A. Before You Go into the Field

1. Decide what social category you are interested in. The aged? The crippled? Drug addicts?
2. Decide what kind of test you want to use. Be sure to choose one that will be most appropriate for your social category. For example: pictures might be appropriate for the aged or the physically handicapped, but less so for such deviant behavior as alcoholism or drug addiction.
3. Construct your test. Use two pictures or cartoons, five completion sentences, or ten words for a word-association test.

B. In the Field

1. Administer your test to six people. Choose two sets of individuals differing on one characteristic you think is important to the topic of your investigation so that you will be able to compare the attitudes of each group. On all other characteristics each group should be approximately the same. For example:

   Three young housewives and *three female college students.*

   Three middle-aged men and *three middle-aged women, all in the same occupation or working for the same company.*

   Three female blacks and *three female whites of approximately the same age.*

2. Find a way to obtain access to the group you wish to examine. For example, you may be able to test housewives by attending a PTA meeting, or possibly your parents belong to a club from which you can secure volunteers. Old people often go to public parks or libraries, or sit around bus depots.

C.   **Analysis of Your Data**

1.   Formulate categories for coding your data, and code and tabulate
     them with the aid of this guide. See Assignment Nine ("Content
     Analysis") for more specific details, since you are actually doing
     a content analysis of the data collected from your projective
     test.

2.   Compare the patterns of your groups' responses. Note differences
     and similarities and how these are indicated.

V   PRESENTING YOUR RESULTS

Include the following in your report:

   1. A brief statement describing the social category you investigated,
   why you chose this social category, and how you constructed the
   test.
   2. A description of the two groups you tested. Why did you feel that
   they would be pertinent to your study? How did you locate them
   for testing?
   3. A statement of how the test was administered.
   4. A presentation of your results in narrative form. (Tables may also
   be used if applicable to the data.) What kinds of attitudes did you
   feel were expressed toward the social category in question? Did
   you discover any differences in attitudes between the two groups
   to whom you administered your test? What were they? Why do
   you think there was such a difference (or no difference at
   all)?
   5. Any hypotheses for future research that your findings suggested.
   6. Problems you encountered in attempting to do this assignment.
   How might they have affected your results? What suggestions do
   you have for overcoming them in a future study?

Data gathering should, as usual, be limited to one hour and a half; your
report should be three typewritten pages. Hand in your projective test and
notes with your assignment.

VI SELECTED BIBLIOGRAPHY

A. Methodology

Brown, Roger
1965   Social Psychology. New York: Free Press.
Campbell, Donald T.
1950   "The indirect assessment of social attitudes." Psychological
        Bulletin 47 (January):15–38.
Hammond, Kenneth R.
1948   "Measuring attitudes by error-choice and indirect method."
        Journal of Abnormal and Social Psychology 43 (January):
        38–48.
Henry, William E.
1945   "The Thematic Apperception Technique in the study of
        group and cultural problems." Pp. 230–278 in Harold H.
        Anderson and Gladys L. Anderson (eds.), Introduction to
        Projective Techniques. Englewood Cliffs, N.J.: Prentice-
        Hall.
Lindzey, Gardner
1959   "On the classification of projective techniques." Psycholog-
        ical Bulletin 56 (March):158–168.
Rotter, Julian B.
1945   "Word association and sentence completion methods."
        Pp. 279–311 in Harold H. Anderson and Gladys L. Ander-
        son (eds.), Introduction to Projective Techniques. Engle-
        wood Cliffs, N.J.: Prentice-Hall.
Sayles, Leonard R.
1954   "Field use of projective methods: a case example." Sociol-
        ogy and Social Research 38 (January-February):168–173.

B. References and Studies

Aronson, Elliot
1958   "The need for achievement as measured by graphic expres-
        sion." Pp. 249–265 in John W. Atkinson (ed.), Motives in
        Fantasy, Action and Society. Princeton, N.J.: Van Nostrand.

Axline, Virginia M.
  1948   "Play therapy and race conflict in children." Journal of
         Abnormal and Social Psychology, 43 (July):300–310.
Brown, J. F.
  1947   "A modification of the Rosenzweig Picture-Frustration
         Test to study hostile interracial attitudes." Journal of Psy-
         chology 24 (October):247–272.
Fromme, Allan
  1941   "On the use of certain qualitative methods of attitude re-
         search: a study of opinions on the methods of preventing
         war." Journal of Social Psychology 13 (May):425–429.
Goodman, Norman, Sanford M. Dornbusch, Stephen A. Richardson, and
Albert H. Hastorf
  1963   "Variant reactions to physical disabilities." American Socio-
         logical Review 28 (June):429–435.
Haire, Mason
  1950   "Projective techniques in marketing research." Journal of
         Marketing 14 (April):649–656.
Jung, Carl G.
  1918   Studies in Word-Association, M. D. Eder (trans.). London:
         Heinemann.
Kerr, M.
  1943   "An experimental investigation of national stereotypes."
         Sociological Review 35 (January-April):37–43.
Knapp, Robert H.
  1958   "Achievement and aesthetic preference," pp. 367–372 in
         John W. Atkinson (ed.), Motives in Fantasy, Action and
         Society. Princeton, N.J.: Van Nostrand.
McClelland, David C.
  1964   "Achievement drive and economic growth," pp. 16–45 in
         David C. McClelland, The Roots of Consciousness. Prince-
         ton, N.J.: Van Nostrand.
  1961   The Achieving Society. Princeton, N.J.: Van Nostrand.
Proshansky, Harold M.
  1959   "Projective techniques in action research: disguised diag-
         nosis and measurement." Pp. 462–485 in Lawrence E. Abt
         and Leopold Bellak (eds.), Projective Psychology. New
         York: Grove.
  1943   "A projective method for the study of attitudes." Journal of
         Abnormal and Social Psychology 38 (July):393–395.
Rainwater, Lee, Richard P. Coleman, and Gerald Handel
  1959   Workingman's Wife. New York: McFadden-Bartell.

Saenger, Gerhart, and Emily Gilbert
    1950   "Customer reactions to the integration of Negro sales per-
            sonnel." International Journal of Opinion and Attitude
            Research 4 (Spring):57–76.
Sanford, Fillmore H., and Irwin M. Rosenstock
    1952   "Projective techniques on the doorstep." Journal of Ab-
            normal and Social Psychology 47 (January):3–16.
Seeman, Melvin
    1947   "Moral judgment: a study in racial frames of reference."
            American Sociological Review 12 (August):404–411.

METHOD:

Sociometry (The Sociogram)

RESEARCH TOPIC:

Social Structure

I INTRODUCTION

What Sociometry and the Sociogram Are

All of us must make a certain number of choices during our lives. Perhaps the most important of these is the choice of the people with whom to associate. How do we decide this? Intelligence? Beauty? The social situation? Common interests? It is not as though relations with others can be avoided; those who live in society must interact with people in some way — on jobs, with friends, or in families — and these associations involve choices which result in social relationships of many kinds.

Sociometry is the study and measurement of the social choices that people make. There are three major techniques used to study these choices — the sociogram, the sociometric index, and the sociometric matrix. The latter two methods include complex mathematical formulations and are beyond the scope of this manual. We shall focus here on the sociogram, which is simply a diagram of the social choices (and rejections) made by members of a group.

The sociometric test was originally devised by J. L. Moreno in 1934 as a technique to discover the attractions and repulsions that individual group members have toward one another. The sociogram is designed to give an objective picture of the relationships resulting from these feelings. By means of a sociogram, an investigator can study the organization within a group or clarify relationships among groups in a larger community or society. For example, he can identify social choices of individuals, and whether these are reciprocated by being able to find those who are the most popular members of a group—the "stars"—the rejectees, and the isolates. Essentially, the sociogram is a *descriptive* technique that helps the sociologist to locate group structure.

The following simple example shows how the sociogram works. Each of five members in a small group is asked to select the two members with whom he would most like to work. The results are diagramed in Fig. 11-1. (Individuals are represented by small circles, while initials identify individuals.) An arrow proceeds from each person toward his choices. An arrow with two points indicates a mutual selection.

Figure 11-1

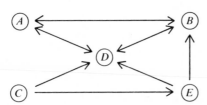

This sociogram shows that *D* is the most "attractive" work-partner, since he is chosen by all four of the other members. *B* is second, as he is chosen by *A*, *D*, and *E*. *A* is chosen twice, by *B* and *D*. *E* is chosen only by *C*, and *C*, not chosen by anybody, is thus identified as a "neglectee." Some other typical structures delineated by sociograms are shown in Fig. 11-2 (Evans, 1962).

Figure 11-2

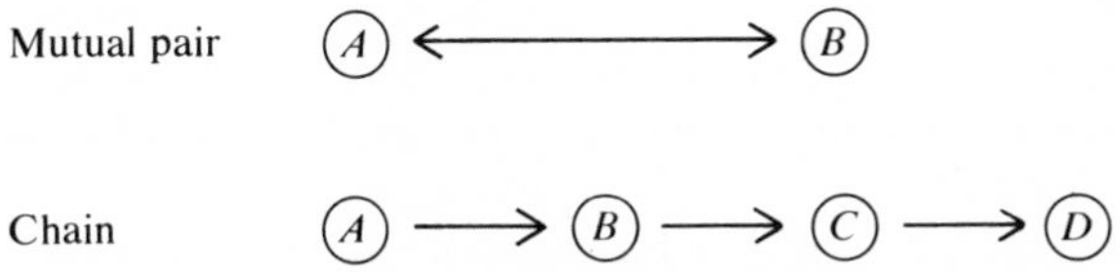

Mutual pair   (A) ⟷ (B)

Chain   (A) ⟶ (B) ⟶ (C) ⟶ (D)

(continued)

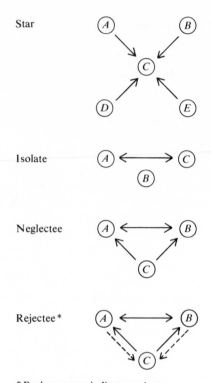

* Broken arrow indicates rejectee.

How to Make a Sociogram

The sociometric test must be administered before a sociogram can be drawn. For this test, the sociologist must decide on the specific type of situation he wants to explore, because members of a group may prefer different persons for different kinds of activities. The most desirable companion for an evening at the theater, for example, may be less desirable as a fellow hiker on a mountain climbing trip or as a bridge partner. Thus the sociologist must formulate a question that asks for a choice in a particular type of social interaction, such as:

1. *Whom would you choose as a laboratory partner in your chemistry class?*
2. *Which of your neighbors would you choose to work with in a fund-raising campaign for a block party?*
3. *Which of your friends would you choose for membership in a current-events discussion group?*

It is customary for the researcher to ask the members of the group to indicate not only their choices but also their rejections. This is important because there is no way of knowing whether those individuals who are not chosen are simply being ignored by others or whether they are actively rejected. (The question "Whom would you least like to work with?" — play with, have as a partner, and so on — should not be used, however, if it is believed that group members might feel too threatened by revealing hostility or dislike toward the other members.*)

Often the researcher also asks each member to choose more than one person and to indicate his choices in order of preference. For example: first, Jack; second, Ken; third, Bob; and so on. Ideally a respondent should be allowed to indicate as many persons as he wishes; but because of the difficulty of graphing and analyzing more than three choices without the use of mathematical techniques such as those used with sociometric indices and matrices, a respondent's choices usually are limited to three.

The group to be tested must be relatively small if the sociogram is going to be utilized — certainly not more than twenty, and half this number is better. If there are too many members, the sociogram becomes cumbersome and complicated, with many crisscrossing lines that offer more confusion than help in clarifying the group structure.

After each group member has chosen, the researcher draws his sociogram. Many kinds of lines can be used — for example, red lines for positive choices and black lines for negative choices. Choices and rejections are then numbered to indicate whether they were the member's first, second, and third choices. Another way is to mark positive choices with solid arrows (as in Fig. 11-1) and negative choices, if they are asked for, with broken arrows. First, second, and third choices can be shown by different-colored lines. The researcher will, of course, discuss the implications of his sociogram in his report.

Advantages and Disadvantages

One of the major advantages of the sociogram is the ease with which it can be understood. It is not necessary to have any technical knowledge to assimilate the information, as is true for the sociometric matrix or index. Furthermore, all the important relationships can be presented simultane-

* It goes without saying, of course, that the sociologist informs the group that their choices will be kept confidential and not revealed to the other members. The researcher must have the complete trust of the group members that he will abide by his word.

ously. Both these qualities are particularly desirable when the researcher wants to show the structure of a group to an audience of laymen. For example, a community leader may wish to show the lines of communication within a neighborhood to block workers.

The sociogram can also be useful in the beginning stages of a small-community study. For example, it can give the researcher clues concerning group interaction, friendship patterns, and so on. He can learn rather quickly who are the leaders, the participators, and the isolates. These are facts that might take longer to obtain if the investigator merely observed the members in action. Outsiders often pretend to be in, or do not recognize their "outsidedness," and they interact in much the same way as others in the group; leaders also often have challengers that cloud the scene. In either case, the identification of the most and the least attractive members would give the investigator two persons who would be ideal subjects for more intensive interviews, since presumably they would hold diametrically opposed views about the same situation. Therefore because the sociogram clarifies the pattern of group relationships, it is useful as a practical way for determining leadership and morale problems, the existence of cliques within a group, and the identities of those individuals who are high and low in social acceptability.

Not only does the sociogram allow a sociologist to locate cliques within a small group or community, but it can provide knowledge about the formation of intergroup relations. For example, in an experimental test situation the researcher could give the sociometric test to two matched groups. Then he might expose one group to a stimulus or test condition — perhaps shifting the work assignments for some reason that the members would consider legitimate or reasonable (i.e., he could shift members from a job that required group cooperation to one that required a number of different partnerships). He would then test both groups to see if there had been any modifications in friendship patterns. If there were changes in the experimental group and not in the control group, these could be attributed to the changed work conditions.

One disadvantage of the sociometric test is also shared by any approach relying on interviewing or structured questionnaire. It is not always easy for members of a group to be honest about their feelings toward others, especially those in primary relationships. It is also possible that members may be influenced by the investigator's preferences even though he is trained to conceal them.

As far as the sociogram itself is concerned, a major limitation is the difficulty of showing relationships clearly when the respondent is allowed a large number of choices. Furthermore, it is difficult to draw these relationships, since the reader may interpret closeness between circles in the diagram as "closeness" of choice. The use of a "target sociogram" has been suggested as one way to alleviate this problem (Northway, 1940a). In the target sociogram there are four concentric circles, much like a bull's-eye target for archery practice. Individuals are placed in these circles according to the number of choices they receive; those most frequently selected are placed in the innermost circle, those least frequently chosen in the outermost, and those chosen an intermediate number of times in the two circles in between.

Sociograms also tend to oversimplify human relationships. While a subject *can* select a work partner *as if* this were the only factor, in an actual situation he might be faced with a number of other pressures that would influence his choice. For instance, he might select a good worker if he wanted to get the job done, or a bad one if he wanted to impress the boss by contrast. He might even select a coworker whom he had been trying in vain to date! The specific situation always affects actual decisions.*

Finally, the sociogram does not explain why certain relationships exist or how they developed, nor does it indicate the intensity of the feelings held. The primary usefulness of this technique is the start that it gives the researcher in locating group structure. Used in conjunction with other techniques—the experimental test situation, the interview, the case history, and especially observation—it can lead to insight for further exploration into group dynamics.

Some Applications

There have been numerous applications of the sociogram. Anthropologists have used it to identify informal community groupings (Loomis, 1941); attractions and repulsions in an Indian society (Danielsson, 1949); comparison of status systems (Loomis and Powell, 1949); and social attraction patterns in a village (Lundberg and Steele, 1938). Sociologists and social psychologists have used sociograms to study neighborhood interaction (Caplow and Forman, 1950); work groups in industry (Jacobs, 1945); cleavages in schools (Becker and Loomis, 1948); summer camps for boys (Sherif et al., 1961) and numerous other settings. Psychologists and teachers have made extensive use of the sociogram, too, in analyzing play and classroom groups of children not only to understand group dy-

---

* This is one reason why Moreno felt that any choice an individual made should be a "real" one—that is, it should have actual consequences in terms of job placement, seating arrangements in a classroom, and so on. Moreno was interested in real group situations and the amelioration of human problems through the use of sociometrics. This is clearly indicated in the title of his major work: *Who Shall Survive? Foundations of Sociometry, Group Psychotherapy, and Sociodrama* (1934).

namics better but also to make changes in the social environment that would lead to more satisfying human relationships.

The sociogram has other practical applications. For example, it can be used by administrators who want to ease tense work situations. With the information obtained from the sociometric test and the resulting sociogram, employers can place people together who like each other and who work well together. By using the sociogram, it is possible to discover, without too much expenditure of time and money, why some work crews have high morale and others do not or, given equal qualifications, who would make the best foreman or team leader, at least in the opinion of other members in the group. One of the most effective potential uses of the sociogram is in the mobilization of community residents for social action (Wolman, 1938; Sanders, 1949).

II SOCIAL STRUCTURE AS A SUBJECT
FOR THE SOCIOGRAM

As we noted previously, a sociogram is helpful when the sociologist wants to present group relations and group structure in a clear, unambiguous way. Any small group of from three to twenty members, whose members can be asked to choose or reject others in the group on the basis of some criterion, can be used. Here are some suggestions.

In many occupations, such as an office, a garage, a flight crew, a branch post office, the effective work groups are small—not more than six or seven members. These groups develop sets of status positions that may be very different from those recognized by the formal organization. For example, one man may have seniority and be considered by his supervisor to be the most competent worker in the group, but the others go to a different worker for advice when they have problems with job decisions. A knowledge of this informal structure can be of use to both the pragmatically oriented administrator and the theoretically oriented social scientist.

Another possibility is a recreation group—a bowling team, a dancing club, a sewing group. In these activities members also form stable relationships. A question to pursue here might be to ascertain whether there are more mutual choices made among members of a team (bowling, baseball, football, etc.) than among members of a group engaged in a competitive sport (golf, tennis, fencing, etc.).

Classrooms provide still another setting in which the sociologist can study group relationships. In some high-school and college classes students are required to participate in group discussions with four or five other student members; in drama or dance classes students may be involved in putting on shows or recitals; or in science courses it may be necessary for students to have laboratory partners.

III PROJECT ASSIGNMENT

In this assignment you will give a sociometric test of two questions to two *different* groups of not fewer than five or more than ten members each. Each member of both groups is to choose the person he would most like for a particular activity and the person he would least like for the same activity. If you feel it is not feasible to ask for the "least liked," ask each member for his first three choices, in order of preference. After collecting your data, draw two sociograms, one for each group. Finally, write a summary of your findings in which you make comparisons between the two groups you studied.

IV STEPS FOR THE SOCIOGRAM ASSIGNMENT

A. Before You Go into the Field

1. Select two groups of not fewer than five or more than ten members whom you can ask to choose or reject other members in their groups on the basis of some criterion. Any of the suggestions made in Section III ("Social Structure as a Subject for the Sociogram") will be acceptable. For example, you can choose two recreational groups, two work groups, two clubs, and so on, or any combination of types of groups for comparison.
2. Obtain a first choice and a last choice from *each* member in *both groups, or* obtain the first three choices in order of preference from *each* member in *both* groups.
3. Ask questions of your group members that would be appropriate for the type of group you have chosen. For example:

Whom would you choose to go to among your coworkers if you had a question about the job? Whom would you be least likely to consult?

Whom would you choose to work with you on a panel discussion? Whom would you least like to have work with you on this project?

Who would make the best leader in the group? Who would make the worst leader?

B. In the Field

1. Administer your sociometric test to both groups.
2. Have the members of the groups write their choices on uniform sheets of paper which you have supplied to them. Each member should sign his own name on the sheet so that you will be able to draw the sociogram indicating the choice and rejection. You may assign each individual a pseudonym (false name) or a letter (*A, B, C*, etc.), or you may designate him by his work title. He *must*, however, be identifiable or you will be unable to do the assignment.
3. Be certain you make very clear to the members of the group that the information you have collected will be kept completely confidential, especially that information concerning who chose whom will not be released to any member of the group.

C. Analysis of Your Data

1. Draw two sociograms from the data obtained from the sociometric test.
2. Examine each sociogram to ascertain the pattern of choices, especially the pattern of mutual choice or rejection, the stars, isolates, rejectees, etc.
3. Compare the sociograms with each other to see if they differ in any respect. What do you think might explain similarities and differences?

V PRESENTING YOUR RESULTS

Include the following in your report:

1. *A brief statement identifying the groups you tested and indicate why they were chosen.*
2. *A description of your test and how it was administered.*

3. *Two sociograms. They are evidence for your conclusions. Draw the sociograms neatly and large enough so they can be easily compared by the reader. If necessary, use two separate sheets of paper. Be sure to identify the group members by pseudonyms, letters, or work titles, not by their actual names.*
4. *A discussion of the sociograms. What are the similarities and differences?*
5. *Any hypotheses for future research that your findings suggest. What practical applications, if any, do your findings have?*
6. *Problems encountered in attempting this assignment. How might they have affected your results? What suggestions do you have for overcoming them in future sociometric research?*

You should limit the time devoted to preparing your sociometric test and presenting it to your two groups to one hour and a half. Your report should consist of three typewritten pages. Hand in your rough field notes along with your assignment.

VI SELECTED BIBLIOGRAPHY

A. Methodology

Borgatta, Edgar F.
  1951   "A diagnostic note on the construction of sociograms and action diagrams." Group Psychotherapy 3 (March):300–308.
Bronfenbrenner, Urie
  1944   "The graphic presentation of sociometric data." Sociometry 7 (August):283–289.
Chapin, F. Stuart
  1940   "Trends in sociometrics and critique." Sociometry 3 (July): 245–262.
Evans, K. M.
  1962   Sociometry and Education. London: Routledge.
Moreno, Jacob L.
  1953   Who Shall Survive?: Foundations of Sociometry, Group Psychotherapy, and Sociodrama. New York: Beacon House. (First published 1934.)

Northway, Mary L.
　1940a "A method for depicting social relationships by sociometric testing." Sociometry 3 (April):144–150.
　1940b A Primer of Sociometry. Toronto: University of Toronto Press.

B. References and Studies

Altmann, Margaret
　1951 "Horse-mule group (with animal sociograms)." Sociometry 14 (December):351–354.
Becker, Myron G., and Charles P. Loomis
　1948 "Measuring rural urban and farm and nonfarm cleavages in a rural consolidated school." Sociometry 11 (August):246–261.
Caplow, Theodore, and Robert Forman
　1950 "Neighborhood interaction in a homogeneous community." American Sociological Review 15 (June):357–366.
Danielsson, Bengt
　1949 "Some attraction and repulsion patterns among Jibaro Indians: a study in sociometric anthropology." Sociometry 12 (February-August):83–105.
Hoffer, Charles R.
　1948 "The family doctor, sociometric relationships." Sociometry 11 (August):244–245.
Hunt, J. McV., and R. L. Solomon
　1942 "Stability and some correlates of group-status in a summer-camp group of young boys." American Journal of Psychology 55 (January):33–45.
Jacobs, John H.
　1945 "The application of sociometry to industry." Sociometry 8 (May):181–198.
Loomis, Charles P.
　1941 "Informal groupings in a Spanish-American Village." Sociometry 4 (February):36–51.
　1948 "The most frequently chosen sociogram: or the seduction of rural sociologists by the neighborhood theory." Sociometry 11 (August):230–234.
——, and Reed M. Powell
　1949 "Sociometric analysis of class status in rural Costa Rica: a peasant community compared with a *hacienda* community." Sociometry 12 (February-August):144–157.

Lundberg, George A., and Mary Steele
    1938   "Social attraction patterns in a village." Sociometry 1 (January-April):375–419.
Potashin, Reva
    1946   "A sociometric study of children's friendships." Sociometry 9 (February):48–70.
Sanders, Irwin T.
    1939   "Sociometric work with a Bulgarian woodcutting group." Sociometry 2 (October):58–68.
    1949   "The use of block leaders in effective community mobilization." Sociometry 12 (November):265–275.
Sherif, Muzafer, O. J. Harvey, B. J. White, W. R. Hood, and Carolyn W. Sherif.
    1961   Intergroup Conflict and Cooperation: The Robber's Cave Experiment. Norman, Okla.: Institute of Group Relations, University of Oklahoma.
Wolman, Shepard
    1938   "Planning a new community." Sociometry 1 (July-October): 220–254.

ASSIGNMENT TWELVE

METHOD:

Panel Analysis

RESEARCH TOPIC:

Sociology of Education

I INTRODUCTION

What a Panel Study Is

Earlier in the course, while you were doing the interviewing assignments, you possibly had some thoughts that the answers you received
reflected a person's opinions at only one point in time in a moving, changing world. Could not people be expected to change their minds if something happened to alter their current situation or social environment? A
statistician might answer that this really doesn't matter, since a new and
different sample could be drawn from the same population to determine
whether there had been any change in the attitudes of a similarly sampled
group. "But," you may have thought, "what about the *individuals* in the
original group? Have any of them changed from the position they once
held? Would it not be useful to have this information?" The statistician
would then acknowledge that this information could not be known from a
second, though similar, sample.

Perhaps you also realized, with some concern, that in interviewing
people about past events you had to rely on the individual respondent's
all-too-fallible memory, for there was no way to know if he really had a
certain attitude at one time merely because he said he had.

The panel study is a technique for dealing with these problems of development and change. The term itself simply means that a group (or panel) of the same individuals is interviewed at regular intervals over a specified period of time. It is the essence of the panel study that the researcher can individually identify those subjects chosen to be members (though their identity will remain anonymous in the final report). How many times the panel members are reinterviewed, over how long a time period, and the size and selection of the panel are matters the researcher should determine in terms of the purpose of the study. Panels as small as ten and as large as a thousand have been used.

The classic example of a panel using a relatively large sample of persons interviewed over a period of months was a study by Lazarsfeld, Berelson, and Gaudet (1948). Before and after the national elections, these sociologists interviewed 600 respondents every month for a period of seven months to determine the formation, change, and development of public opinion. These researchers were not just interested in describing public opinion at a single point in time, or even in comparing opinions from time to time. They wanted to discover the factors that influenced peoples' voting decisions. Did people change their minds about candidates in the months preceding an election, and, if so, what caused them to change? In analyzing the results obtained by interviewing the same people over this period, these sociologists discovered that certain individuals in the community exerted significant influence on the political opinions of others. When these persons were designated "opinion leaders," a new sociological concept was born. (See Assignment Eighteen for a discussion of concepts.)

Theodore M. Newcomb conducted a panel study (1943) utilizing an entire group with interviewing spread over a period of years (1935–1939). He measured the attitudes of Bennington College students from their freshman through their senior years on a number of social issues. One of Newcomb's interests was to test the hypothesis that the more students become assimilated into a college community, the more they will agree with prevailing student opinion. Many students did change their political views in a liberal direction over this four-year period, though some did not. Newcomb, by using the panel technique, was able to study intensively the attitudes of these respondents over an extended period of time to come to some conclusions regarding the factors and processes that led to the stability or instability of opinions.

A panel study has one major characteristic that makes it comparable to the classic "before-and-after" experimental study (Assignment Thirteen). There is a testing of the *same* subjects after a special condition or treatment has been introduced that presumably will alter the responses of the subject. In the foregoing examples, this condition or stimulus was a "natural event"—an election and an entry into an institution of higher learning. However, the researcher could contrive a situation. For example, he could arrange for panel members to experience a certain event, such as a movie, a lecture, an initiation, a product (in market-research panels), and so on. The panel differs from the classic experiment, however, in at least two ways. First, the panel researcher cannot control the stimulus to the extent that laboratory conditions permit, especially when a natural event is the focus of the study. The sociologist cannot, for example, manipulate the speeches given during a political campaign, or which particular aspects of pre-election events the panel might be interested in. Certainly he cannot alter in any pronounced way the social environment of his subjects, although he can select his sample so as to represent various factors important to his study.

Second, in the laboratory experiment all possible variables that might affect the results can be altered or manipulated one at a time while everything else is held constant. This allows the experimenter to feel that he can say with some certainty which of the stimuli are most important for inducing change in the subject's behavior. A researcher who uses the panel technique has no such control over the important events, even when they are known; but he does have an advantage over the laboratory experimenter, since he is often dealing with "real life" events that are more likely to touch and affect his panel members.

The sociologist who uses a panel study is interested in change over time. He wants to determine the *net changes*—any changes in attitudes or behavior in the total group or panel occurring after the introduction of the stimulus. If this were his *only* interest, however, he could have selected two samples from the same population at different points in time and determined the net amount of change, despite the fact that the same individuals were not necessarily involved. But the panel study has something in common with the case study. Like the case study the panel researcher's prime interest is in developing a history of *individual* shiftings of attitudes or behavior. He wants to know which members of the panel change, in which direction, and how much, so that he can identify possible causal factors. He wants to be able to explain the change, not merely describe it. He can obtain this data with more certainty by interviewing the same persons at least twice. The goal of establishing individual, as well as collective, change forces the panel researcher to devise a way of tabulating his data so that each individual is identified every time his answers are tallied (see Section IV of this assignment). Not to do this would leave the investigator without a way to compare his data on individuals from one time period to another, and the major advantage of the panel study would be lost.

Whether drawing a sample from a large population or studying an entire group, the panel researcher will probably use a questionnaire or interview schedule with open or closed questions—or both—in his first interview (see Assignment Three). After this interview, he will wait until the group has experienced a certain "change" in the environment. The panel members will then be reinterviewed to ascertain if this new experience has indeed changed them. It is possible (but not probable) that the researcher will find there have been no net changes, that the panel still holds the attitudes it had on the first interview. This in itself is a worthwhile finding, especially if opinion-changing events took place in the interim. On close examination of the data, however, the researcher may discover that there have been individual changes in opposite directions, that there appears to be no change only because the changes that individuals have made have cancelled each other out. This is a finding the researcher can study further only because he knows the individual changes.

Whether there have been net changes or not, the researcher begins to look at those individuals who did shift their opinions after experiencing the stimulus. For this phase of the research he will probably use depth interviewing (see Assignment Two) in an attempt to find the reasons for the changes in attitude in one direction or another.

Advantages and Disadvantages

There are several advantages to the panel method over those of the one-shot interview (structured or depth). First, as we have already mentioned, it allows the researcher to determine changes both in the aggregate and in individual opinions. He can then isolate and determine the relative importance of the factors that produced these individual changes. Second, the researcher does not have to depend so heavily on the respondent's memory of how he felt and acted in the past, because by asking these questions directly at different times throughout the study he learns the person's current opinions (though of course he may still use questions that rely on the individual's memory in the course of his investigation). Finally, and really implicit in all of these, is the advantage the panel gives the researcher in some measure of before-and-after behavior.

As with other research techniques, there are several disadvantages to panel studies. One of the most important is *respondent mortality*—the researcher's inability to interview panel members for the second or third time around. Respondents may be unavailable for future interviews for a variety of reasons. For example, they may have disliked the first interview, or they may be on vacation, sick, or have moved. In any event, the researcher must cope with the fact a certain proportion of respondents will be lost through attrition, by planning for it at the outset.

One way for the researcher to compensate for this expected loss is to select more panel members from the population than he will need. Thus if he desires a panel of 500 persons, he could draw a sample of 600, which would allow for a 20 per cent dropout loss. If this technique is not possible because the sociologist is interviewing an entire group—for instance, the members of a club—he can lessen the impact of the loss by gathering as much information as possible about his panel members in the first interview or questionnaire so that later he can make a close analysis of the dropouts and adjust his final interpretations of results accordingly.

A second major disadvantage is that the researcher may find it difficult to know what is a "real" change in any respondent's attitude. If there is a difference in his answers from the first interview to the second, this may have been occasioned not by the intervening event but because he misunderstood the question or was in a bad mood. (It is amazing how many "changers" there can be on such simple factual items as age, amount of education, and birthplace!) Closely connected with this problem is that of the panel's becoming sensitized to the repeated interviewing. This eventuality is most likely to happen if the study is a long-term one, extending over several interviews, or several months or years, or both. Some possible effects are that the members of the panel may try to find out more about the topic in which the researcher seems to be interested and thus become better informed than they might otherwise have been. Panel members may also begin to see themselves as a special group and therefore answer in ways that would not be typical of others in the same situation. Or, they may not want to appear "inconsistent" in their answers from the first interview to the next and thus attempt to hide genuine change in attitude.

One way to minimize the problems of identifying "real" change and sensitization is to have a control group for the final set of interviews. There should not be any difference in the reactions of the control group and the original group if they have experienced the same conditions. If there is a significant difference, it is possible that repeated interviewing has caused a bias in the original group. However, a control group is possible only if the original panel was drawn from a large population. Panels of entire groups do not have anyone left over for control. Another way to minimize the danger of sensitization might be to refrain from telling the panel members that they will be reinterviewed in the future, but this ploy obviously loses its potency each time the person is recontacted.

As we noted earlier, another problem for the investigator is that he has no way of knowing for certain whether the change in attitude was caused by the "natural event" or stimuli he thinks is pertinent to the study, or whether the change was because of factors that are extraneous to the problem being studied. A researcher can correct for this to a limited degree by including questions in his subsequent interviews on issues that have occurred in the intervening time (days, weeks, months) and that could also be causal factors in changing attitudes under investigation. This presumes a high degree of sociological sophistication on the part of the researcher, however. A more frequent solution to this problem is to do a short-term rather than a long-term study. This of course shortens the time span for events to occur that could influence the respondent.

A final disadvantage of the panel approach for the sociologist results also from its longitudinal nature. Terman began his study of 1000 gifted school children, for instance, in 1925, and reinterviews with panel members were conducted in 1947 and 1959. Such a long-term affair is, of course, very expensive, and many investigators feel that the expenditure of months or even years is not worth the time it takes to collect the data, especially if there is a good possibility that the dropout rate will be high. Thus, researchers often use panels only to study changes of specific attitudes over relatively short spans of time, so that they have to interview respondents only two or three times (Rosenberg et al., 1951). This procedure reduces field time, minimizes respondent loss, and lessens the risk of exposing the respondents to possible contaminating intervening events.

Another solution to the time and expense of panel management worth mentioning is the *cohort analysis,* a kind of "poor man's panel," based on longitudinal data without following the same group through time. In this technique, different groups that are at different points in the same course of experiences are measured at some one point along the time continuum. For example: first-year medical students, second-year medical students, and third-year medical students (or cohorts) could be compared on a subject such as conformity to the norms of the school. Differences between or among these groups can be attributed to their increasing experience with the patterns of punishment and reward as they move through each school year. The underlying assumption is that if first-year medical students are followed through time they would be very similar to current third-year students. Thus, cohort analysis saves both the time and money involved in keeping track of persons throughout the study period. It does not have the panel's major advantage, however—obtaining information from the same individual over time. Furthermore, the cohort analysis has to make the assumption that all things were the same for each group of students as they proceeded through the institution, and obviously this position may be unwarranted in a society where rapid change is itself a norm.

Some Applications

The many advantages of this method have led to numerous studies in a variety of sociological areas. Panels have been used to study the effects of social environment on an individual's attitudes and behavior (Newcomb, 1943); shifts in political attitudes (Lazarsfeld et al., 1948; Berelson, 1954); the attitudes and life styles of the aged (Lowenthal, 1964; Lowenthal and Haven, 1968); and the effect of school environment on IQ (Klineberg, 1935). The panel technique has also been employed in the identification of reference groups (Stouffer, 1949).

Recently a group of doctors have been studying their patients in an attempt to discover the correlations between certain diseases and other attributes of the individual (for example, the relationships between lung cancer and smoking). In the mass media the Nielsen television rating service and other consumer-research organizations have permanent panels to gauge the reactions of individuals to new programming or new products.

II EDUCATION AS A SUBJECT FOR A PANEL STUDY

The beginning phases of life in institutions such as military posts or camps, monasteries, nunneries, mental hospitals, and prisons engage the individual "totally" in every phase of his life, from the time he gets up in the morning to the time he goes to bed at night. The individual is, in fact, *supposed* to change his values, outlook, and skills to fit into the social environment. Schools also have some of the same qualities as these "total institutions" (Goffman, 1961), since school children, too, are in a sense captive audiences who are supposed to learn new facts and values to help them cope with their future roles in the society. This socialization process is especially important in the primary grades in schools. The student is moving through a step (year) at a time, and presumably he is being changed in some way or another by contact with socializing agents of the school community, both the teacher and his peer group. The school milieu is thus an appropriate—in fact, an almost ideal—place for the panel researcher to conduct a study. In the higher grades there are additional influences within the educational environment that can also be evaluated. In the college community, for example, there are numerous socializing agents—school activities and clubs, fraternities and sororities, ethnic groups, athletics, school politics, and so on.

Panel studies are also appropriate for other aspects of the educational process. For instance, how do people in the community—not just the vocal members, but a cross section of the citizens—feel toward integration of the schools? Do these citizens retain their original attitudes, or do they change them over time? If there is change, who changes? What are their social characteristics and the reasons they give for the shift in attitude?

III PROJECT ASSIGNMENT

Since the time for you to pursue a panel study is limited, you should choose an area of investigation that will fit your needs. In order to complete the before and after interviews within the time period available for the course, you will want to choose a topic in which there is some probability that events could occur that might change some persons' minds about the issues. On most campuses there are always issues and events that actively involve some students and interest most of the others. Typical issues include attitudes toward college politics (elections, sit-ins), educational issues (experimental courses, attitudes toward types of teaching methods), or recreational activities (sports, clubs). The college community also consists of various groups that are ideal for panel studies. For example, there are many formal subgroups for potential panels: student activity and social clubs, vocational departments in which registration is fairly stable because of the required sequence of courses (engineering, school of business, social welfare, nursing, dental assistant, hotel and restaurant management, photography, and so on). You could also use one of your classes, or a sample of it, as a panel.

For this assignment you are asked to conduct a structured ("closed") interview with a panel of individuals. Each panel member will be interviewed twice, with three to four weeks between the first interview and the last. The topic you select should be one of current interest on campus, one likely to develop or change in some way. The more advanced students will also reinterview, in depth, those individuals whose attitudes changed to determine why these shifts came about. Since this assignment has three separate steps—interview, second interview, and, for more advanced students, depth interview of changers—you will need more time than the usual one to one and one half hours in the field. We suggest that you spend the equivalent of two assignments on this assignment—approximately four hours in the field and four hours on the analysis and write-up of your findings.

IV STEPS FOR THE PANEL STUDY

A. Before You Go into the Field

1. Decide the campus issue or event on which you want to obtain opinions and attitudes. This can be either educational, political, or recreational. For example:

    A. Attitudes toward a course or a professor (educational).
    B. Development of career choices (educational).
    C. Development of friendship or dating patterns (recreational).
    D. Attitudes toward the football or basketball team at the beginning of the season and later (recreational).
    E. Attitudes toward college administrators (political).
    F. Political awareness of, and attitudes toward, changes on campus (political).

2. Decide on your panel members. Will you choose these from some club, department, or another class? What social characteristics do you want them to possess? For example, if you are going to do a panel study on attitudes toward a course taught by a particular instructor, you would choose your panel from students who are presently taking the course. On the other hand, if you are doing a panel study on the development of friendship patterns, you might choose the panel members from a club or vocational department where students stay together throughout their school careers.

3. Prepare for each panel member a background sheet of social characteristics that you think will be important in determining the attitudes toward the issue you have selected. These might be age, sex, race, social class, semester on campus, vocational goal, and so on. Because each panel member in the panel study will have to be identifiable, this sheet should also contain the name of the respondent. (You can assign numbers, but if you do this, make certain you will be able to match the respondent and the number for the second interview.) It might also be a good idea to obtain addresses and phone numbers so you can locate missing panel members for later interviews.

4. Construct a structured interview schedule consisting of five questions, all of which will give relevant information in the area you are investigating. Use questions that offer Agree-Disagree, "don't

know," or "no opinion" choices. (See Assignment Three for more detailed information on interview schedule and questionnaire construction.)

5. Prepare a coding sheet for each respondent on which you can record the responses from both interviews. (This material would be put on IBM cards if you were interviewing a large sample with a great many questions and had a computer available for the analysis of the data.)

EXAMPLE OF INDIVIDUAL CODING SHEET OR CARD

Respondent: (Name or I.D. #)	Question:	Interview #1 (Answers)	Interview #2 (Answers)
Sex: (Male or Female)	#1		
	#2		
	#3		
Semester in College: (1st, 2nd, etc.)	#4		
	#5		

Later you will compare the answers of people who differ in their social characteristics, and select *two* such characteristics from the background data sheet that you think could account for significant differences in response. (In the sample coding card above these characteristics are sex and semester in college.)

B. In the Field for the First Set of Interviews

1. Interview at least ten persons, plus perhaps two extras as substitutes in case you lose any original panel members.
2. Inform your panel members that they will be reinterviewed at a later time. Always reassure them that their answers to the questionnaire will be held in strictest confidence.

C. Organization of Data

Code the data from the questionnaires to the individual coding sheets or cards.

D. In the Field for the Second Set of Interviews

1. Wait for three to four weeks before you repeat the interview — depending upon the length of time available in the course, or until the stimulus event has occurred that could change the opinions of some of the panel members.
2. Reinterview the panel members. Use the same questions as before.

E. Analysis of Data from First and Second Interviews

1. For net changes of the entire group:

    Sort your cards into three piles for the first question: (1) those who changed their opinions in a more positive direction, (2) those who changed in a more negative direction, and (3) those who did not change at all. Record or tally this data on a card or sheet. Repeat this operation for all five questions. You will then have for each question the net amount of change, both positive and negative, for each question asked, regardless of the social characteristics of these changers.

EXAMPLE OF A TALLY SHEET

Question #	No. of changers (positive)	No. of changers (negative)	No change
1			
2			
3			
4			
5			

2. For social characteristics of types of changes:

    Take your coding sheets or the cards that you have re-sorted into "positive," "negative," and "no change" piles for the first question. Sort each of these piles on those two social characteristics which you decided to use from the background sheet. For instance, tally the number who are males and females and those who are first- and second-semester students. Do this for each *question.* See example tally sheet below.

Question #1: Responsiveness to Student Needs

Social Characteristic	No. of changers (positive)	No. of changers (negative)	No change
Male			
Female			
1st Semester			
2nd Semester			

3. For further examination of individual changers:
   A. Examine the card of each respondent to identify the "changers" — those who consistently changed their opinions in one direction or another for each question.
   B. What *combinations* of traits are they most likely to have — i.e., first-semester males? second-semester females? etc.
   C. Decide which three "changers" you would want to interview more fully concerning the reasons for their shifts in attitude. Try to select persons who changed in opposite directions.

F. For Advanced Students

Depth interview the three panel members you selected in E3c above. Try to determine what could account for these changes.

V PRESENTING YOUR RESULTS

Include in your report the following:

1. *The issue you decided to explore.*
2. *The identity of the group from which your panel members were chosen. Where and how did you obtain your members?*
3. *The results of your panel study.*
   A. *Make the following tables (although percentaging is generally not done on a base of less than 25, you are asked to percentage tables for this assignment):*
      (1) *Tables showing the net changes for the entire group, regardless of social characteristics, on each of the questions — a total of five tables.*

(2) Tables showing changes for the group that are associated with characteristics you considered important. Make tables for two different questions. For example:

COLLEGE RESPONSIVENESS TO STUDENT NEEDS
(Hypothetical Data)

	Changers (positive)	*Changers (negative)*	*No change*	*Totals*
First-Semester Males (N = *xxx*)	25%	10%	65%	100%
Second-Semester Males (N = *xxx*)	15	25	60	100
First-Semester Females (N = *xxx*)	25	5	70	100
Second-Semester Females (N = *xxx*)	30	10	60	100

* Usually the total number of cases is inserted here, so that the reader will know what the percentage is based on. However, since this is a "made-up" example, no totals are shown.

4. *A brief discussion of the results shown in your tables.*
5. *An explanation of why you would want to interview the three changers you selected.*
6. For advanced students: *The reasons for individual changes in opinions as gained from reinterviewing three changers in depth.*
7. *Suggestions for further research in the area.*
8. *Some of the problems you encountered in doing this assignment. What did you do to overcome these problems and how might the findings be affected?*

Please keep your presentation of results to five double-spaced, type-written pages. All of your interview schedules, tabulations, face-sheets, coding cards, and notes should be turned in with your written report.

VI SELECTED BIBLIOGRAPHY

A. Methodology

Eckland, B. K.
    1968   "Retrieving mobile cases in longitudinal surveys." Public Opinion Quarterly 32 (Spring):51–64.

Festinger, Leon, and Daniel Katz
  1953   Research Methods in the Behavioral Sciences. New York:
          Holt, Rinehart & Winston.
Lazarsfeld, Paul
  1953   "The use of panels in social research." Pp. 511–519 in Ber-
          nard Berelson and Morris Janowitz (eds.), Reader in Public
          Opinion and Communication Supplement. New York:
          Free Press.
Rosenberg, Morris, and Wagner Thielens with Paul F. Lazarsfeld
  1951   "The panel study." Pp. 587–609 in Marie Jahoda, Morton
          Deutsch, and Stuart W. Cook (eds.), Research in Social
          Relations. New York: Dryden.

B.   References and Studies

Berelson, Bernard, Paul F. Lazarsfeld, and William N. McPhee
  1954   Voting: A Study of Opinion Formation in a Presidential
          Campaign. Chicago: University of Chicago Press.
Deutsch, Morton, and Mary E. Collins
  1951   Interracial Housing: A Psychological Evaluation of a Social
          Experiment. Minneapolis, Minn.: University of Minnesota
          Press.
Goffman, Erving
  1961   Asylums: Essays on the Social Situation of Mental Patients
          and Other Inmates. Garden City, N.Y.: Doubleday.
Klineberg, Otto
  1935   Negro Intelligence and Selective Migration. New York:
          Columbia University Press.
Lazarsfeld, Paul F., Bernard Berelson, and Hazel Gaudet
  1948   The People's Choice: How the Voter Makes Up His Mind
          in a Presidential Election. New York: Columbia University
          Press.
Lazarsfeld, Paul F., and Morris Rosenberg (eds.)
  1955   The Language of Social Research. Glencoe, Ill.: Free
          Press.
Lowenthal, Marjorie F.
  1964   "Social isolation and mental illness in old age." American
          Sociological Review 29 (February):54–70.
——, and Clayton Haven
  1968   "Interaction and adaptation: intimacy as a critical variable."
          American Sociological Review 33 (February):20–30.

Maddox, George L.
  1968   "Persistence of life style among the elderly: a longitudinal
          study of patterns of social activity in relation to life satisfac-
          tion." Pp. 181–183 in Bernice L. Neugarten (ed.), Middle
          Age and Aging. Chicago: University of Chicago Press.
Newcomb, Theodore M.
  1943   Personality and Social Change: Attitude Formation in a
          Student Community. New York: Dryden.
Stouffer, Samuel A., Edward A. Suchman, Leland C. DeVinney, Shirley
A. Star, and Robin M. Williams, Jr.
  1949   The American Soldier. Vol. I. Adjustments During Army
          Life. Princeton, N.J.: Princeton University Press.
Stouffer, Samuel A., Arthur A. Lumsdaine, Marion Harper Lumsdaine,
Robin M. Williams, Jr., M. Brewster Smith, Irving L. Janis, Shirley A.
Star, and Leonard S. Cottrell, Jr.
  1949   The American Soldier, Vol. II. Combat and Its Aftermath.
          Princeton, N.J.: Princeton University Press.
Terman, Lewis M.
  1943   "Mental and physical traits of a thousand gifted children."
          Pp. 279–306 in Roger G. Barker, Jacob S. Kounin, and Her-
          bert F. Wright (eds.), Child Behavior and Development, A
          Course of Representative Studies. New York: McGraw-
          Hill.
  1947   The Gifted Child Grows Up. (With Melita Oden.) Stanford,
          Calif.: Stanford University Press.
  1959   The Gifted Group at Mid-Life. Stanford, Calif.: Stanford
          University Press.

Part Four

Special Projects
for Advanced Students

ASSIGNMENT THIRTEEN

METHOD:

Explanatory Survey and Multivariate Analysis

RESEARCH TOPIC:

Ethnic Groups

I INTRODUCTION

The Explanatory Survey, a Definition

In seeking a better understanding of human group life, sociologists try to do one or both of the following: describe the behavior and attitudes of people interacting in groups, and explain in some detail the cause of behavior and attitudes.

In Assignment Three, we presented survey research as a way to describe certain behavioral and social characteristics in a given population. The explanatory survey assignment builds on those skills and adds another element—that of finding causal relationships between behavioral and social characteristics. To do the kind of survey research that attempts to explain the existence of a given phenomenon, it is important that you understand the basic mechanics and assumptions of multivariate analysis. Multivariate analysis is a method the sociologist uses to locate and test causal elements.

To find the cause or causes of a social phenomenon is a more difficult task than merely to describe it. Sociologists and lay persons both seek explanations for why things are the way they are. All of us have come up with clues or hunches (technically called hypotheses) that lead us to believe we may have located the cause for a given phenomenon. Have we? To be fairly certain, we must test our hypothesis by attempting to answer the following:

1. *Is the presumed cause always present when the effect is? Are these factors (variables)—the presumed cause and the effect—associated or related in some way?*
2. *Does the presumed cause always precede the effect in time? If it doesn't, it can't very well cause it, so we know the effect is truly antecedent. (Therefore establishment of time order of the relationship between an effect and its presumed cause is important.)*
3. *Is the factor truly causal, or is it merely something associated with either the true cause or the effect? (Such an association is called spurious—i.e., noncausal—and will be explained shortly.)*
4. *Is the presumed cause solely responsible for the effect, or is it merely one of a constellation of causes that together produce the effect? That is, is the factor sufficient to be the cause, or is it merely one necessary part of the causal picture, with other variables intervening?*

If the investigator can rule out the time order problem and spurious association, and can select from the vast number of possible social factors those which are most likely to have produced the effect, he will feel he is on the right track in the search for causal factors. Once he has reached this point, he may want to know the following:

5. *Under what conditions is the cause-effect relationship stronger, weaker, or changed? (This is called* elaboration *of the causal relationship.)*

Let us look at an example. Suppose you want to test the idea that people who study hard will get good grades on an examination. You would have to examine the following:

1. **Are the factors associated?** *Are studying and good grades related? Does a larger proportion of students who study hard get good grades than students who do not study?*
2. **Does the presumed cause precede effect?** *Does studying hard result in good grades or is it the other way around? Maybe the student who gets a good grade in an earlier test is so encouraged that he begins to study hard to keep his grades up for the big examination.*

3. **Is the relationship spurious?** *Maybe studying hard is really not the true cause of good grades at all. Perhaps good grades are actually the consequence of a fairly high IQ. Studying hard and good grades could be related, but this relationship would not be causal if those persons who get good grades do not really have to study hard but do so out of habit.*

4. **Is one factor enough to account for causation?** *Maybe studying hard is just one of many things that aid a student's grade. Others might be his attitude toward the school, the parents' attitude toward school, the availability of privacy for study, the instructor's fairness, and so on.*

If investigation shows that people who get good grades also study hard, that their study preceded the grades, and that they could not get the good grades without hard study, a researcher might then claim a causal association; but then he would doubtless want an answer to the following question:

5. **Under what conditions might the causal relationship vary?** *Whatever the causal relationship between study and grades, it might vary because of the student's age, sex, the course material, the type of school, the skill of the instructor, and so on.*

Before we consider the multivariate analysis as a way to answer the five questions above, it would be helpful for you to know some of the terms used and some of the logic behind cause-effect investigation procedures. The *dependent variable* is the *effect;* in this case, good grades. It is *dependent* because the investigator assumes that its existence or form depends on the presence of other causal factors. It is *variable* because the investigator assumes that the effect will vary in intensity or quantity with the strength and mixture of the presumed causal factors. Anything that might affect the dependent variables—such as studying, in this example—is called an *independent variable,* independent because the investigator assumes that it affects the dependent variable—not the other way around.

Scientists have developed many techniques for checking out the meaning of an association between two variables so that causal relationships can be more firmly established. The most notable of these techniques is the laboratory experiment. Multivariate analysis, as used in survey research, is actually an adaptation of the laboratory experiment, and so to understand the logic of one is to understand the logic of the other.

The Laboratory Experiment and Its Relationship to Multivariate Analysis

The classic laboratory experiment is a development of the physical sciences. For instance, an agronomist will establish that a certain fertilizer (independent variable) makes corn grow taller (dependent variable) by putting two corn seeds from the same ear into identical boxes of identical dirt. Both receive identical amounts of sunshine and water. The difference is that only one seed receives fertilizer. If the fertilized seed grows taller than the unfertilized seed, the scientist can assume that the fertilizer caused the difference, since all the other factors (variables) that might have affected growth were the same in each box (matched).

What does the agronomist know from such an experiment? He knows:

1. *That fertilizer and good growth in corn are somehow related or associated (where one was present the other was also).*
2. *That the fertilizer preceded in time the growth of the corn (after all, the investigator put it in right after he planted the seed).*
3. *That it is possible that the way in which he administered the fertilizer to the corn might have affected growth. Perhaps he stirred it into the soil and thus loosened the soil in that box; this might be the true cause of the difference, and he would have to check out this possibility by subsequent experiment.*
4. *That everything else was the same in both boxes—soil, sunshine, and water—so he can feel safe in saying that the fertilizer was a sufficient condition for the added growth of the corn.*
5. *That the effect of the fertilizer on corn growth might vary with different varieties of corn, size of box, amount of fertilizer administered. He would have to perform another set of experiments to test these possibilities.*

For laboratory studies in the social sciences, the experimenter attempts to approximate this sort of close control (1) by matching two groups of subjects on all the social characteristics that he feels might influence responses to the stimulus he will administer, or (2) by matching the distribution of characteristics within groups by means of random assignments of subjects. Then if the members of one group receiving the stimulus react by changing in some way, while members of the other group do not, the stimulus can be assumed to have caused the change.

For example, subjects might be given a test designed to indicate their attitudes toward minority groups (the dependent variable). The experimenter then exposes one group (the experimental group) to some new condition (the independent variable), such as a film portraying minority groups in a sympathetic manner. The other group (the control group) is not exposed to this film. The attitudes of the two groups are then re-measured, and any change in the attitudes of the experimental group is assumed to be a result of the film's message. At the heart of this method is *comparison* of groups that differ in one experience or characteristic.

The laboratory experiment is most typically a tool of psychologists and social psychologists. Many sociologists do not like its artificiality. This reluctance to employ laboratory experiments to investigate social behavior results from the belief that conclusions based on laboratory tests about the relationships between social characteristics and behavior may not actually reflect how these are associated in the world outside the laboratory. Not only is it difficult to match groups on all variables presumed to be important—even when large masses of people are screened for the right combination of social characteristics—but it is almost impossible to know in advance every factor that it might be important to control (though theory does offer guidance here). Furthermore, there are some factors that can't be controlled, regardless of the investigator's intentions or resources. There is also a growing body of evidence that the artificial conditions of the laboratory experiment actually alter subjects' responses (Sherif and Sherif, 1969).

The panel study (Assignment Twelve) is an attempt to locate causes by sidestepping the artificiality of the laboratory environment. Panel members are usually not brought together for test-stimulus-retest procedure, but rather are selected so that in the course of their everyday lives they will be exposed to some factor of interest to the sociologist. They are then questioned (or tested) at prescribed intervals to discover if their attitudes have changed over time. If there is change, it can be attributed, at least in part, to the influence of the stimulus because the investigator knows when the stimulus is introduced—in many cases he arranges it!

The panel approach is a way of answering questions 1, 2, and 4 of a presumed causal relationship (outlined earlier in the assignment). The investigator tries to assure some kind of relationship by exposing panel members to the presumed cause; he knows the time-order of the cause and the appearance of effects; and if he selects so that the panel members match on pertinent social characteristics, he can rule out these possible causes. He might need to do more investigating for questions 3 and 5, but so does the investigator who uses the laboratory experiment.

The Explanatory Survey and Multivariate Analysis

The explanatory survey, through multivariate analysis, uses the logic of the laboratory study to establish relationships of a probable causal nature, but it dispenses with the test-retest approach and the time-consuming panel study. Checking out a possible cause through the five test-questions outlined and illustrated earlier is accomplished by *manipulating records of the data rather than manipulating actual people.* That is, the survey researcher collects data from people on a considerable number of topics he believes are related to the subject of his investigation. Then he puts these data on cards, and sorts them (usually with the aid of electronic equipment) into piles. Each pile contains data on a group of individuals with the behavioral characteristics that the sociologist wishes to compare on their relationships to the dependent variable. Several piles of cards sorted on, say, the number of years of education completed is analogous to several laboratory rooms each with persons of different educational attainment, or several boxes of growing corn seeds each with a different kind of fertilizer. By this method the sociologist can study many more people than the average laboratory experiment can accommodate. He can leave the respondents in their natural habitat, and he need contact them only once.

Let's see how the survey researcher, with the aid of multivariate analysis, tests his hypothesis that studying "causes" good grades. (For the present we shall take for granted that he has already written and administered his questionnaire.) Because he was well read in the literature relevant to his investigation and familiar with pertinent theories, this researcher had the foresight to ask many questions about such things as study habits, school, grades received on various tests, attitudes toward instructors, easy and hard subjects, and to gather necessary background data such as IQ, social class, sex, age, and so on. Thus he has an abundance of possible causal factors (independent variables) to test and to aid him in the establishment of time order, the rejection of spuriousness, and an elaboration of the relationships he should locate.

How Association Is Established

Now let us consider how the survey researcher decides which factors or variables are associated, since this is the first step in locating causality. Like the laboratory test and the panel, comparison of groups that are different on some significant feature is the crux of the method.

As previously mentioned, the association of factors refers to a situation in which one variable is present if the other is also present, and in which each variable exists to a greater degree, and more consistently, when the other is present than might be expected by chance alone.* If

---

*There are complicated statistical techniques to test such associations, but we shall not consider these in this assignment.

65 per cent of the students who studied pass an examination, while only 15 per cent of those who did not study pass, we can say that passing the test and studying seem *positively* associated. If the findings had been the other way around—that is, if more of the nonstudiers had passed—the association would have been classified negative. If an equal proportion of both groups had passed then it might be assumed there is no association at all, in which case there would have been no hope of proving causality.*
However, neither positive nor negative association is necessarily causation, though it does give us a basis on which to proceed with further tests.

Before he attempts to establish association and, ultimately, causality, the investigator has some important decisions to make: he must determine whom he is going to label a "studier" and whom a "nonstudier," and also what he is going to call a "good grade" and what a "poor grade." This procedure—making concepts usable (operable) so they can be located in the real world—is called *operationalizing concepts* (see Assignment Eighteen). Such operationalizing is often done by arbitrary criteria, dependent on the good sense of the investigator. For instance, he might label anyone who spent four hours or more preparing for an examination a studier; he might designate a good grade either an A or a B; etc.

Now that he has defined his variables, the survey researcher is in a position to see if there is any association between them. Studiers and nonstudiers will be compared by sorting their answer cards into two groups—in the same way that the laboratory test puts people into two different situations. Then he would sort each of these groups according to the examination grades they received. Next he would percentage the findings in each group he is comparing (studiers and nonstudiers), and present the results somewhat as in Table 13-1. Because a higher proportion of studiers than nonstudiers passed, the survey analyst can say that studying and passing are related and in a positive direction. Next he asks: Does the relationship appear to be a strong one—that is, is the difference between the grades received by studiers and nonstudiers a *substantial* one? (The definition of "substantial" depends to a great extent upon what is being studied and upon sampling exigencies, but as a rule of thumb 10 to 12 per cent is a minimum for the researcher to consider worth further investigation for possible causality.)

---

*There is the possibility, however, that the initial lack of relationship might result from the fact that some other related characteristic, also evenly distributed in the sample canceled the grades-study association out. For instance, the bright students might be studying while the dull ones are not. The totals would show no relationship between studying and grades because each factor canceled the other out. One would have to test for this possibility by stratifying by IQ, as is done on page 176.

TABLE 13-1

THE EFFECT OF STUDY ON EXAMINATION GRADE
(Hypothetical Data)

Grade received on examination	Students who studied for examination (N = xxx)*	Students who did not study for examination (N = xxx)*
A or B	65%	15%
C or lower	35	85
	100%	100%

* Usually the total number of cases is inserted here, so that the reader will know what the percentage is based on. However, since this is a "made-up" example, no totals are shown.

How Time-Order Is Established

How can the researcher locate the time-order of these variables so as to ascertain whether study is responsible for good grades or whether it is the other way around — whether it is success on a test that encourages study? Suppose he had the foresight to collect some data from a previous "snap" (unannounced) quiz in the same class. He might sort his cards to compare respondents who had studied for the examination and received A or B with those who had passed without study. Then he would see how each group did on the earlier snap quiz. The results might be as shown in Table 13-2. From this table the analyst can say that passing the quiz and experiencing "success" is not strongly associated with studying for the exam, and that good grades do not precede the urge to study in time order; quite the contrary, the students who failed the quiz *then* apparently decided to study for the big examination. In fact, in our example situation a larger proportion of those students who did not study for the examination passed the snap quiz than those who did study (55 per cent, as opposed to 10 per cent). (From the evidence it is apparent that there are some students who do not need to study in order to receive good grades, but that they are a very small group.) Had the findings been the reverse — had a large proportion of students who studied for the announced examination previously passed the snap quiz (90 percent, say, instead of only 10 per cent) — the investigator might suspect that early success influenced studying patterns in a positive direction. His investigation would then take a different turn — specifically, finding out how feelings of "getting the material" increased interest in it.

TABLE 13-2

DISTRIBUTION OF PASS AND FAIL GRADES ON A SNAP QUIZ
AMONG THOSE RECEIVING AN A OR A B ON THE EXAMINATION
(Hypothetical Data)

	Students who studied for examination (N = xxx)	Students who did not study for examination (N = xxx)
Passed snap quiz	10%	55%
Failed snap quiz	90	45
	100%	100%

How to Test the Spuriousness of a Presumed Causal Relationship

Making certain that a statistical relationship is actually an *explanation* for the existence of an attitude or behavior, and not just *associated* with it, is an important problem in an explanatory survey. The problem of spurious correlations is usually attacked with the aid of a third variable that might be the cause and that is also associated with the two variables central to the hypothesis.

Zeisel (1957, pp. 197–200) gives an example that shows single people regularly eat more candy than married people. But he also found that young people eat more candy than older people. Which is the cause of the change in rate, and which is spuriously associated? Do married people eat less candy because they are married or because they are older? Zeisel found the answer by breaking down the data into smaller categories. The percentages of younger married *and* older married who eat candy and the percentage of younger single *and* older single who eat candy were compared. From this new tabulation, the researcher found that it was the *younger group* in both married and single categories who eat candy regularly, and that consumption declined with age. Marriage was not the causal factor for lowered candy consumption, but was merely associated with getting older. As a result, Zeisel concluded that marriage was spuriously associated with eating less candy.

To return to the grades and studying example, the investigator next asks whether studying causes good grades or whether the high IQ students get good grades and study out of habit—which would mean that studying was spuriously associated with the true cause, high IQ. Since the investigator anticipated that IQ might be an important variable and collected IQ data, he can test the relationship between studying and good grades for possible spuriousness by comparing the grades of high IQ students who studied for the examination with those of high IQ students who did not study. The results of this comparison are presented in Table 13-3. From this table we can see that although a high IQ does help a student get good grades to some extent, studying is the major factor. Thus more than ever, studying appears to be causal. On the other hand, if the high IQ group that did not study had about the same proportion passing (75 per cent) as the studious group, then studying and good grades would be related only spuriously because they are·both related to the *real* cause — high IQ. (To complete the picture, the researcher should also see how much studying helps low IQ students.)

TABLE 13-3

COMPARISON OF GRADES RECEIVED ON EXAMINATION BY HIGH IQ
STUDENTS WHO STUDIED FOR EXAMINATION WITH THOSE WHO DID NOT
(Hypothetical Data)

	High IQ students (over 115)	
	Students who studied for examination	*Students who did not study for examination*
Grade on exam	(N = *xxx*)	(N = *xxx*)
A or B	75%	35%
C or lower	25	65
	100%	100%

Naturally the analyst may have to check out many possibilities to rule out a spurious association between hypothesized cause and effect. He is limited only by time, the quality and breadth of his data, and his own insight and knowledge of the theories and findings in the field.

How Other Possible Causal Factors Are Located and Checked Out

Can study alone account for good grades? There are many other possible causes that might be working in conjunction with study: encouragement of parents, being a member of a clique that approves of good grades, liking the subject, and so on. To see whether any or all of these factors combine with study to assure good grades, the analyst would "control" his respondents according to each variable; that is, he could sort the data cards into those with and those without encouraging parents, those in and those outside study-oriented cliques, those who liked the subject and

sample, or he may decide to dispense with the random sample of the entire population and instead get large samples of special subgroups of his interest.*

When the investigator has constructed his questionnaire and decided upon the sample, he must interview as carefully as in the descriptive survey. Following collection, he codes the open-end questions and usually puts all the answers on IBM cards. In small-sample surveys, white cards or the interview form itself are used for sorting purposes after the field work is completed. Then the multivariate analysis begins!

Finally he writes a report, including the tables resulting from the analysis. This report will contain (1) a discussion of each of the tables presented, (2) the analyst's discussion of what he thinks the findings mean, and (3) the way he thinks the variables fit together to create causation.

Advantages and Disadvantages

Like the descriptive social survey, the explanatory survey can be used to investigate larger numbers of people and a wider range of social categories than either observation or depth interviews. Furthermore, unlike the classic experiment the explanatory survey is not limited to those variables that can be manipulated by the experimenter. Machine sorting allows unlimited manipulation. Data gathering also has a greater range than the laboratory method. The survey researcher can use the retrospective memory of respondents to ascertain past attitudes. He can also use the respondent's anticipations of how he might act in future or different situations.

This latitude is a disadvantage as well, as it was in the descriptive survey, because the researcher must rely on what people say about how they felt in the past or will act in the future. Both of these data have the danger that they are removed from actual situations and behavior in them.

Another problem is that the researcher is not an omniscient superman —though he often tries to be. He cannot know all the possible factors that could affect his data before he goes into the field, even though he does many pre-tests. Once he has started the field work he usually has no provisions for adjusting his design to accommodate the unexpected, since question-asking uniformity is necessary. Nor can he make certain he has

---

*While sampling and methods of drawing samples are beyond the scope of this assignment, the student undertaking an actual explanatory study should consult a good book on sampling or an expert in the field. (This latter course is, in fact, taken by many professional sociologists who have mastered the techniques of multivariate analysis but who need assistance on the technical aspects of sample selection to fit the goals of their study.)

checked all possibilities that the presumed cause-effect relationship is spurious. All he can do is to attempt what seems to him to be a reasonable explanation of the phenomenon he is studying.

The tendency to generalize from the findings on group data back to an individual is a dangerous temptation. For example, a finding that those individuals with some college education are less prejudiced than individuals with only a high-school education does not mean that any particular individual with some college background is less prejudiced than any particular high-school graduate. To be more accurate, the researcher with the above data might suggest that a group with similar characteristics in a similar situation will have a similar proportion of its members behave or have attributes like the sample group.

Furthermore, the association of characteristics, attitudes, or behavior may *seem* to point to causation, but it is not conclusive proof of it. What the investigator has when he has completed a multivariate analysis is a cluster of associated factors and a plausible discussion of their interrelationship in the real world.

Perhaps the most serious shortcoming of the explanatory survey is that in its emphasis on finding relationships between variables the method fails to deal with social processes as they are actually experienced. That is, by implication it reduces social interaction to variables affecting each other. Certainly there is more to social life than this. This is another reason why the explanatory survey should not be viewed as the means to a complete explanation of any social phenomenon. Despite these restrictions, the explanatory survey is still extremely useful because it can provide clues that may help explain many social mysteries.

Some Applications

Explanatory surveys have been used to study every conceivable facet of human group life. The relationship between various child-rearing techniques and adult response-attitudes and response-behavior has been probed (Miller and Swanson, 1958; Kohn, 1962). Attempts to predict marital happiness by correlating the "success" of a sample of marriages with various background factors of the two spouses have also been made (Burgess and Cottrell, 1939). The factors influencing people to become politically liberal or conservative or to vote for one candidate or another have been probed (Lazarsfeld et al., 1944; Lipset, 1960).

Attitude surveys are used both to explain past actions and (hopefully) to predict future ones. The reasons the International Typographical Union developed a democratic organizational structure in contrast to the more oligarchical form of a majority of unions were probed (Lipset, Trow, and Coleman, 1956). Both whites and blacks were interviewed concerning their attitudes toward interracial housing in an attempt to see how they would react when this situation becomes a reality (Deutsch and Collins, 1951). The causes of various deviant behavior, such as juvenile delinquency (Glueck and Glueck, 1950) and alcoholism (McCord and McCord, 1960), have been sought through the aid of multivariate analysis. An explanatory survey was also used to test hypotheses that the prevalence, diagnosis, and treatment of mental illness is differentially related to social class (Hollingshead and Redlich, 1958). In public health, epidemiologists use the explanatory survey to locate social factors related to and possibly causing disease. Currently such studies are being used in attempts to find clues to both heart disease and cancer.

II   ETHNIC GROUPS AS A SUBJECT FOR ATTITUDE SURVEY RESEARCH

The attempt to determine attitudes toward various ethnic groups within American society has been a continuing topic of interest for social scientists. Today, as minority groups strive to establish an identity and a base of political power for themselves, research on attitudes of various groups toward each other is more important than ever. It is important to know how such attitudes are formed and changed. What situational and sociological factors are crucial in that change? Do racial attitudes have more or less impact on behavior than other kinds of attitudes—for instance, the basic beliefs an individual holds toward self identity, or toward authority?

Some interesting experimental work in this latter area reveals that individuals, if given a choice of working with someone of the same basic beliefs and attitudes or with someone of the same race almost always chose the person who had similar views regardless of race (Rokeach, 1968). Rokeach's findings, based on small-group research, provide a challenge for researchers who are interested in explanatory attitude surveys to design a research project that would test this hypothesis on a wider scale.

III   PROJECT ASSIGNMENT

Multivariate analysis is a demanding undertaking. The beginning student might limit himself to a "dry run" such as the following:

FOR THE BEGINNING STUDENT

Using the examples in this assignment as a guide, plan a small study and make five or six dummy tables showing its outcome.

In discussing each table, tell the reader what you were trying to accomplish by sorting the data in this fashion, what your results were, and what you think they mean from a sociological point of view. (Remember, you can "make up" the results.)

Limit your discussion to six typewritten, double-spaced pages.

If the regular assignment is to be followed, the student will formulate a hypothesis on race relations to be tested by a survey. Because of its many tasks, survey research of this type is necessarily handled on a team basis and you will work with three to five persons on this assignment. Your aim is to see if there is any relationship between social characteristics of groups and their attitudes toward members of an ethnic minority, and try to isolate possible causes for such attitudes.

IV STEPS FOR THE ATTITUDE SURVEY ASSIGNMENT

A. Before You Go into the Field

1. Formulate a testable hypothesis. Your hypothesis must state that one variable causes the other variable to be different or change. For example: "People of lower socioeconomic status are more prejudiced toward ethnic minorities than people of high socioeconomic status because the poor are competing for the same types of jobs."
2. Formulate your operational definitions, as these will influence the content of your questions. For example: What will be your definitions of "high" and "low" socioeconomic status? Will it be income, education, occupation, or all of these? How will you find instances of "prejudice"? What will you regard as job competition?
3. Try to identify other social factors that could explain greater prejudice among low socioeconomic groups. For example: Where did

the respondents grow up? In what state and city? In a rural or an urban environment?

4. Select your sample, but do not worry in this assignment about the technicalities of sampling for explanatory surveys. Concern yourself instead with what types of people you will select to be representative of the low socioeconomic status and of the high socioeconomic status (if that is a part of your study).

5. Construct a structured attitude questionnaire of not more than ten questions that will give relevant information for the hypothesis you wish to test. Decide whether you want to ask for information on attitudes toward ethnic groups directly or indirectly—that is, whether you wish to "hide" the nature of your investigation. More advanced students should have two open-end questions—questions in which a choice of answers is *not* provided so that the respondent is urged to discuss his feelings at length in his own words.

6. Prepare a background sheet of "sociological facts" that you will need to know about each respondent, that is, age, sex, religious affiliation, nationality or race, socioeconomic status, or any other variables that you feel will help explain (or is a cause of) an attitude. For example: If you are studying two groups of college students, you want to know their semester in college, among other things. Items on the background sheet should be selected with the idea that they might provide means of testing spuriousness, time order, or elaborating on the hypothesized relationship being tested.

7. Plan to have each team member do one pretest of the questionnaire. Then get together and revise it where necessary. Watch especially for questions that seem ambiguous or that offer an opportunity for two kinds of meanings.

B. In the Field

Each person on the team is to administer at least five attitude questionnaires to persons who fit their sample.

C. Analysis of Your Data

This process can be handled by the entire team or it can be divided into workable segments for processing by individual members of the team. Eventually, though, you will have to work together to follow up clues to causation that are revealed by early tabulations.

1. Coding. This step is necessary for any open-end questions in your questionnaire. Set up categories by sampling the answers, then tally. (See Assignment Three, page 45, Fig. 3-1.)
2. Tabulation. Count the number of responses given in each choice for each question, maintaining separate counts for the groups you are comparing. Keep in mind at all times that the goal of your study is to establish, as well as possible, the viability of your hypothesis, or to reject it. Don't go off on tangents of analysis not related to your central theme.
3. Percentage the responses for comparison of various subgroups. Make understandable, well-labeled tables to display this information. (See General Instructions for the Student.)
4. Determine whether your hypothesis has been confirmed on the basis of your findings and whether it is modified in some way when you subject it to some of the "tests" of causality discussed in this assignment.

V PRESENTING YOUR RESULTS

Include the following in your report:

1. *The hypothesis you tested and its relevance to the sociology of attitudes toward ethnic groups.*
2. *The types of people you decided to include in your "sample" in order to test your hypothesis.*
3. *Your tables and a discussion of their meanings. Help the reader see the logic of the comparisons you are making. Tell him when you are testing for time order or spuriousness, and why. Point out the significant findings in each table so that the reader will see how your findings "fit together" as a test of your hypothesis. (Tables and the paragraphs explaining them should alternate.)*
4. *Suggestions you have for further research in the area.*
5. *Problems encountered in doing the assignment. What did you do to overcome these problems, and how might the findings be affected by them?*

Please keep the presentation of your results to five to seven double-spaced, typewritten pages. The completed interviews should also be turned in with your written report.

VI   SELECTED BIBLIOGRAPHY

A.   Methodology

Backstrom, Charles H., and Gerald D. Hursh
    1963   Survey Research. Evanston, Ill.: Northwestern University Press.
Galtung, Johan
    1967   Theory and Methods of Social Research. London: Allen and Unwin, pp. 229–354.
Hyman, Herbert
    1955   Survey Design and Analysis, Glencoe, Ill.: Free Press.
Kerlinger, Fred N.
    1965   Foundations of Behavioral Research. New York: Holt, Rinehart & Winston, pp. 603–649.
Selltiz, Claire, Marie Jahoda, Morton Deutsch, Stuart W. Cook
    1961   Research Methods in Social Relations. New York: Holt, Rinehart & Winston, pp. 127–143, 422–432.

B.   References and Studies

Benson, Purnell
    1952   "The interests of happily married couples." Marriage and Family Living 14 (November):276–280.
Blood, Robert O., Jr., and Donald M. Wolfe
    1960   Husbands and Wives: the Dynamics of Married Living. Glencoe, Ill.: Free Press.
Burgess, Ernest W., and Leonard S. Cottrell
    1939   Predicting Success or Failure in Democracy. Englewood Cliffs, N.J.: Prentice-Hall.
Burgess, Ernest W., and Paul Wallin
    1953   Engagement and Marriage. Philadelphia: Lippincott.
Deutsch, Morton, and Mary E. Collins
    1951   Interracial Housing. Minneapolis, Minn.: University of Minnesota Press.
Glueck, Sheldon, and Eleanor Glueck
    1950   Unraveling Juvenile Delinquency. Cambridge, Mass.: Harvard University Press.

Hollingshead, August B., and Frederick C. Redlich
    1958   Social Class and Mental Illness. New York: Wiley.
Kohn, Melvin L.
    1962   "Social class and parental values." Pp. 304–321 in Robert
            F. Winch, Robert McGinnis, and Herbert R. Barringer
            (eds.), Selected Studies in Marriage and the Family. New
            York: Holt, Rinehart & Winston.
Lazarsfeld, Paul F., Bernard Berelson, and Hazel Goudet
    1944   The People's Choice. New York: Columbia University
            Press.
Lipset, Seymour M.
    1960   Political Man. Garden City, N.Y.: Doubleday.
——, Martin A. Trow, and James S. Coleman
    1956   Union Democracy. Glencoe, Ill.: Free Press.
McCord, William, and Joan McCord, with John Gudeman
    1960   Origins of Alcoholism. Stanford, Calif.: Stanford University
            Press.
Miller, Daniel, and G. E. Swanson
    1958   The Changing American Parent. New York: Wiley.
Ohlin, Lloyd E.
    1951   Selection for Parole. New York: Russell Sage Foundation.
Rokeach, Milton
    1968   Values, Attitudes, and Beliefs. San Francisco: Jossey-Bass.
Stouffer, Samuel A., Edward A. Suchman, Leland C. DeVinney, Shirley
A. Star, and Robin M. Williams, Jr.
    1949   The American Soldier, Vol. I, Adjustment During Army
            Life. Princeton, N.J.: Princeton University Press.
Zeisel, Hans
    1957   Say It with Figures. New York: Harper & Row.

METHOD:

Population Analysis

RESEARCH TOPIC:

Social Change

I INTRODUCTION

Population Analysis, a Definition

Since population refers to *people* in the mass or aggregate, the subject is bound to be of interest to sociologists. The study of population is sometimes called *demography,* and concern with this aspect of human life cuts broadly across the social sciences.

Demography is the statistical study of human populations. It includes their size, distribution, and characteristics (such as age, sex, and race) as these are affected by births, deaths, and migrations. How these *population* variables affect and are affected by such *sociological* variables as social class, social mobility, and educational level is also investigated, as is the effect of such *economic* variables as gross national product, per capita income, and cost of living index. The study of population, then, is one approach to understanding the structure of society.

The population analyst is interested in both describing and finding causal relationships. How does a drop in the number of children under fifteen affect the composition of the population? How is this effect distributed throughout the population? He might also want to know if a change such as this is related to an increase in the proportion of married women in the labor force or in the use of birth-control methods among lower-class women.

The major unit of analysis for demographers or population analysts is usually a political territory such as a nation, state, city, or rural district, or areas that exhibit social cohesiveness (such as neighborhoods), special social characteristics (such as slum areas, Skid Rows, suburbs, ghettoes, and wealthy districts), or a political entity (such as census tracts or school districts) where arbitrary boundaries are assigned.

As with almost every other approach to the gathering of social data, population analysis is not solely the province of the professionals, but is indulged in daily by laymen as a means of making more intelligent decisions. Women who move to areas where there is an abundance of single men of marriageable age (Alaska, for instance) have done a practical population analysis on the probable effect of sex composition on their social life. Stock market analysts of the 1930's who followed national economic trends and then correctly predicted lowered birth rates as a result of the Depression were analyzing the effect of social conditions on rates of reproduction and, ultimately, on the composition of the population itself. When a popular restaurant moves out of a neighborhood that is increasingly dominated by incoming drug-taking hippies and narcotics pushers, its owner is predicting the effect of the changing population on its paying customers.

Population specialists are of course much more systematic in their data-gathering and analysis than the average citizen. They follow numerous trends in population composition, increases or decreases in rates of birth, death, and migration, and other social variables, for the purpose of understanding present social conditions and making some cautious future predictions. For instance, almost all sociology textbooks make note of the current trend for the middle-class white family to move from the city to the suburbs as soon as it can afford this change of residence. As this trend continues, cities are left with a population composed of a few wealthy families, a high proportion of poor Caucasian families, and an increasing number of economically deprived ethnic minorities — Puerto Ricans, blacks, Mexican-Americans, or Chinese. In trying to determine what effect this population mixture may have on the social life of the city — its purchasing power, tax base, development of residential areas, welfare needs, and crime rate — the population specialist looks at past population composition and its apparent social repercussions. Then he compares present demographic and sociological data with former circumstances and hypothesizes the possible future of the city if the trend of middle-class out-migration should continue.

The interplay of the physical environment with population composition and social factors is also of interest to the sociologist. This is, indeed, where population study and ecology overlap. What, for instance, is the social and political picture in a nation such as India where the population is growing rapidly while the land area remains the same? In contrast, the United States expanded its territory for many years and thus had no problem of land scarcity until recent times, despite a growing population. Factors in a density analysis include the number of acres of productive farm land, the degree to which the nation is industrialized, and the possibilities for either out-migration or a reduction in the birth rate. Nations have gone to war, governments have toppled, famines have struck, and birth-control programs have been launched as a result of the pressures of population, so this is no idle matter.

Population analysts are also aware that cataclysmic events can have marked effects on the composition of a population, and concomitant pressures on society and social interaction. War, for instance, reduces the ratio of men of marriageable age and thus dooms many women to spinsterhood. After World War II the shortage of men in Europe was so acute that women advertised on bulletin boards to attract male survivors. War has other effects on the population that reverberate through the social structure. In Poland, for instance, war relaxed a rather rigid class system. Many young men who might otherwise never have received appointments and promotions to various high-ranking positions suddenly found themselves upwardly mobile, because of what Polish sociologists refer to as mass death of the controlling class in Poland.

Thus, while the analysis of birth rates, death rates, migration rates, and sex or race ratios may look dull at first glance, population is actually an exciting topic to study. The opposite of the case history, it is the study of society-wide — rather than individual or small group — phenomena. Instead of getting close to his subject, the population analyst is like a man high on a mountain, seeing and analyzing some of the massive pressures and variables that shape the social life stretched out before him.

How Population Analyses Are Made

The population expert obtains most of his data from official surveys, registration material, and special studies published in the form of census data and other vital statistics. His use of this demographic data is one form of what is called a *secondary analysis,* because the information was not gathered for the express purpose of one investigator's project, but is adapted by him to fit the goal of his study.

The type of data with which the population analyst works may be divided into four groups of variables. The first group contains basic demographic characteristics crucial to any population study.

Group I.   Basic Demographic Characteristics
   Births
   Deaths
   Migration
   Size of population
   Distribution of population

Data about these characteristics may be found in:

The United States Census Reports
Statistical Abstract of the United States
United Nations Demographic Yearbook *(for countries throughout the world)*

The remaining three groups of sociological variables can be viewed as related in a causal way to the items listed in Group I. Because changes in any item of any group will affect the other groups, they are all potentially important to a demographic analysis—depending, of course, on the subject under investigation.

Group II.   Basic Social Characteristics of a Population
   Age
   Sex
   Race or ethnicity
   It can be seen that the way in which proportions of the above occur in a population will affect—and be affected by—births, deaths, migration, and population composition. A predominantly old population or one with more men than women would experience a falling birth rate. If these factors were found to be concentrated in one racial or ethnic group, for instance, the racial composition of the population would eventually be affected. Data on age, sex, and race may be found in the same three sources cited for Group I.

Group III.   Social Acts and Statuses in a Population (Partial Listing)
   Marriage
   Divorce
   Annual income
   Educational level
   Occupation

Housing
Employment and unemployment
Voting behavior and party membership
Morbidity (illness rates)
Crimes or delinquent acts
Rural or urban residence
Ownership of such items as homes, automobiles, appliances
Caloric or protein intake

The interplay among Group III variables and the demographic factors of birth, death, migration, composition, and size is obvious. Marriage, divorce, income, and education all affect birth-rate levels. Income and availability of employment can affect housing and, in turn, rates of migration.

Data from Group III must be searched for by subject. This often includes locating the agency responsible for gathering such information. Consult a documents librarian for assistance. Sources for American data include:

Vital Statistics offices and U.S. Census—*marriage, divorce, birth, and death data.*

United States Department of Justice, FBI, Uniform Crime Reports, local police departments, and sheriffs' offices (especially in large cities)—*data on crime rates.*

National Prisoner Statistics *and* The Children's Bureau of the U.S. Social Security Administration—*data on delinquency cases that come to court.*

U.S. Department of Labor—*reports on labor statistics.*

U.S. Departments of Agriculture and Interior—*information on farm production, timber, fisheries, mining, gross national product, and other related items.*

Precinct reports and the World Almanac—*voting behavior.*

World Health Organization Reports—*detailed statistics on morbidity (illness).*

U.S. Department of Commerce—*information on cost of living, trade, banking, and other related items.*

The Statistical Abstract of the United States—*in one volume, annually selected data from many of the above sources. Although it is not complete in any one subject area, it is a fascinating compilation of information about those aspects of social life where official tabulation is available. Often state-by-state breakdowns are offered as well as national figures. Each volume carries data from selected past years, as well as the most current information within the limitations of the publication date, so that trends can be noted.*

And that's just the beginning! With the exception of the underdeveloped countries, foreign counterparts of these data can be found in most research libraries.

> ### Group IV.   Structural Components of Societies (Partial Listing)
> *Urbanization (degree of)*
> *Industrialization (degree of development)*
> *Social mobility*
> *Social class*
>
> *These are the most sophisticated variables, because they are* constructs *(complicated clusters of concepts) created by the population analyst to use in conjunction with Groups I, II, and III. For instance, increased urbanization of an area might affect both its crime rate and its male-female ratio. Industrialization affects morbidity (illness rates) and thus can affect age composition. These constructs are analytically very useful, but they are beyond the scope of this assignment. Sociologists who need ways of locating in the "real" world phenomena listed in Group IV often use the work of others as a guide; see, for example, Hollingshead's social class index (1961) or Lipset and Bendix's measure of social mobility (1959). Where no such material fits the needs of the study, the researcher creates his own analytic constructs. This is quite a complex operation and will be explained in part in Assignment Fifteen, "Scales and Indices."*

The major function of any population analysis is to *compare* data (drawn from the sources mentioned above). This means comparison between political units or through time or both. For instance, what good does it do to know that the death rate in an Asian country is 22 per 1000 if you don't know that the death rate is only 10 per 1000 or lower in most Western nations? It is only by such comparisons that rates, ratios, and indices come alive, and we can make statements about high or low rates or trends.

As with the explanatory survey, it is in comparing population data that the search for clues to causation takes on meaning. For instance, if we find that morbidity (illness) rates in several areas over time drop as urbanization increases, then we might infer that there is some causal connection there and could try to locate the urbanization components that might be responsible. Sanitation, hospitals, and medical technology are just a few factors that could be investigated. If, on the other hand, the illness rates were gathered for just a single point in time or for one geographic area instead of two or more, we would not be alerted to seek a possible causal link.

The Use of Percentages or the Creation of Rates

The crucial need for comparison in population analyses requires the conversion of raw figures into proportions, rates, or ratios; hence an important part of any population analysis is the method or methods by which demographers abstract data from societies of different size or composition and transform them into comparable units. Were the analyst to compare raw figures of, say, deaths in a nation with a large population to deaths in one with a small population, the small nation would appear much healthier than the large one. Some of the elementary (but important) ways of making data comparable are discussed below.

The most common means of converting absolute figures to relative ones in all the sciences is through the use of percentages — the rate per 100 — because percentaging removes the influence of population size. Demographers use the rate per 1000 or 100,000 more frequently than the percentage, but both of these are based on the same principle as a percentage. The birth rate of a given population, for example, is calculated by dividing the number of births in a year by the population of the society being studied and multiplying the result by 1000. This is called the *crude birth rate*. If one wanted to compare the crude birth rates in the United States in 1940 and 1960, the computation would be as follows:

$$1940 \text{ Crude Birth Rate} = \frac{2,588,647}{134,266,754} \times 1000 = 19.3$$

$$1960 \text{ Crude Birth Rate} = \frac{4,257,850}{183,285,009} \times 1000 = 23.2$$

The crude death rate is computed in the same way. The difference between the crude birth rate and the crude death rate is called the *crude rate of natural increase* (or decrease if there is a population loss).

Refinement of Rates

Rates such as this are called "crude" because that is what they are — unrefined. Often they are so gross as to result in lumping together data as unlike as apples and oranges, so to speak. For instance, suppose you are using crude birth rates to compare the fertility of American women with those of another country; and suppose further that there are twice as many women between the ages of 15 to 45 — the fertile years — in the second country as there are in the United States. To get some idea of the fertility of the women of each country would be next to impossible unless the rates were adjusted to reflect this difference in the proportions of women in the child-bearing years.

In response to this problem, sociologists and demographers have resorted to mathematical manipulation to obtain figures as free of contamination from unwanted phenomena as possible. In the problem cited above, they would calculate the births, not for the entire populations of the two countries, but only for the populations of women between the ages of 15 and 45. This calculation results in what is called an age- and sex-adjusted rate. By using it, the influence of the child-bearing components of population composition can be nullified. Death rates are also refined. Age-adjusted death rates compensate for inequalities resulting from comparisons of deaths in a country with a high proportion of older persons to those of countries with very low proportions of older persons. Obviously other rates such as marriages, divorces, crimes, and so on can also be adjusted when circumstances of the study require such data refinement. Computations involved in such conversions will not be a part of this assignment, but the student interested in pursuing the subject may consult the bibliography for materials containing more information.

The Creation of Tables

Like other researchers, the population analyst must forever keep his readers in mind. How is he going to present all the statistical data that are part of an average population study so that their import will be quickly grasped? The answer is that he becomes highly proficient in the production of tables, charts, and graphs.

As those of you who have done the survey research assignments know, one of the best ways to compare data is to set up tables containing those items that you want to compare. This is exactly what the demographer does. If he is interested in comparing the changing death rate of males in different states over a period of time (say 1920 to the present), he locates death statistics for these states (perhaps in ten- or twenty-year intervals), turns them into *rates* (by the method previously illustrated), and then presents the material in a table. For example, Table 14-1 (opposite page) was created with data drawn from various pages of the *Statistical Abstracts of the United States.* Such a table immediately suggests two things to the population analyst:

1. *The difference in death rates may have a social explanation.*
2. *Before looking for possible social causes, he may wish to refine the rates. For instance, there is a much higher percentage of blacks in Mississippi than there are in Nebraska, and the black*

death rate in the U.S. is higher than the white death rate. In this
comparison the investigator might want to restrict the figures to
whites, since there are so few blacks in Nebraska.

TABLE 14-1

COMPARISON OF CRUDE DEATH RATES OF MEN
IN NEBRASKA AND MISSISSIPPI SINCE 1920

Deaths/1000 population

Year	Nebraska	Mississippi
1920	10.0	12.2
1930	9.6	12.0
1940	9.6	10.7
1950	9.6	9.5
1960	9.5	10.0

Advantages and Disadvantages

The obvious advantage of population analysis is that it allows the sociologist to get the "big picture" of some important pressures in society.
Demographers are also proud of the fact that their findings are based on
what they often refer to as "hard data" — that is, officially recorded, indis-
putable statistical evidence drawn from the entire population (in the case
of births, deaths, and marriages) or from a very large sample like the
Census. This already gathered information is also advantageous to use
because it rarely requires supplementary field work.

One of the advantages of demography is also a disadvantage, however.
Since the data are already gathered, the sociologist has no control over
the quality, how the categories were set up, or what boundary lines of
time and space were adhered to. While he can refine the data as we have
discussed, he usually must make compromises when he uses it for his own
purposes.

Of course, population analysts are aware that they are attempting to
locate *clues* to social dynamics — not studying the dynamics *per se*. While
a sociologist might predict that the city's increasing ethnic minority populations may result in some specific social changes, he would have to do an
additional study — by means of observation, the depth interview, survey
research, etc. — of actual social dynamics to confirm his hypothesis.

Some Applications

Applications of population analysis have been varied. Sociologists have analyzed population data to understand the relationship between structural changes in the family and in society (Goode, 1963); why rates of illegitimacy are high in some countries (Hartley, 1966); and how family size is related to preferences in sex of children (Freeman et al., 1960).

Population analysts have also been concerned with the redistribution of population in cities (Redick, 1956) and have attempted to plan for the settlement of people at the edges of cities (Firey, 1946). The cost of welfare as it is related to birth control has been analyzed (Spengler, 1954), as has the positive effect of population growth on investments (Sweezy, 1940). The relationship between birth control and industrial development has been analyzed (Davis and Blake, 1956; Stycos, 1952), as have the demographic problems of American investments abroad (Whyte and Holmberg, 1956). Epidemiologists have attempted to discover whether the male-female differential in mortality is biologically or socially caused (Madigan, 1957). They have also explored whether social variables can explain heart disease (Reader, 1959).

II SOCIAL CHANGE AS A SUBJECT FOR POPULATION ANALYSIS

Because the composition of the population and its components both affect and reflect societal changes from the broadest to the most subtle, population analysis is an ideal approach to the topic of social change. Furthermore, of all the phenomena of human group life, population offers the researcher records that go back several centuries. Most civilized nations keep some type of population records that enable analysis of cross-cultural changes. Because such material is dated, the demographer is able to correlate various historically or sociologically significant events with it and make before-and-after studies. Trends over time can be traced in great detail because data was collected at regular intervals.

III PROJECT ASSIGNMENT

We have provided two assignments here — one for the beginning student, the other for the advanced — because the study of population, even when it is vastly reduced in magnitude (as it has been for these assignments) is still a very demanding method of sociological research.

FOR THE BEGINNING STUDENT

Go to the library and look at one of the U.S. Census books. In the front of the book is a discussion of how the census defines such things as a dwelling unit, a metropolitan area, and so on. These definitions actually tell you how the census-taker finds his data in the real world. Copy three such definitions from the book.

Take one of these definitions and use census material to make a table showing the change in this phenomenon through time in one state in the United States. For instance, take types of dwelling units in a metropolitan area and see if the proportion of people in each type has changed over a period of ten, twenty, and thirty years.

Suggest a hypothesis that might explain the change or lack of it, drawing on population analysis variables in Groups I, II, III, and IV.

The regular assignment for the more advanced student is a preliminary comparative study of two areas over time—A Southern U.S. state and a Northern U.S. state. You will attempt to account for trends in either the birth rate or the death rate of these states (Group I variables) by variables found in Groups II, III, or IV.

IV STEPS FOR THE POPULATION ANALYSIS PROJECT

A. In the Field

Go to the library and locate the *Statistical Abstracts of the United States.* Although these annual volumes do not carry complete information on any one subject, they are storehouses of data on all four levels of variables used in a population analysis and thus suitable for this type of assignment. For instance, the 1965 edition contains diverse data under the following section headings: (1) Population Composition; (2) Vital Statistics, Health, and Nutrition; (3) Immigration and Naturalization; (4) Education; (5) Law Enforcement, Federal Courts, and Prisons; (6) Area, Geography, and Climate; (7) Public Lands, Parks, Recreation, and Travel; (8) Labor Force, Employment, and Earnings; (9) National Defense and Veterans Affairs; (10) Social Insurance and Welfare Services—to list only about one-third of the sections!

1. For the two states you have selected, collect and *present in table form* either the birth rate or the death rate for three different years, *each* separated by at least ten years. (You may have to consult more than one book to get this spread, though all have some data from past years.)

2. Compare and discuss the change over time in this variable (the birth rate or the death rate) as it occurs in these two states. Form and discuss a simple hypothesis—based on sociological theory and your knowledge of differences between the Northern and Southern United States—to account for this change. For instance, birth rates might go up as morbidity goes down; birth rates might fall as population (per square mile) becomes dense, more urbanized, or more industrialized. Death rates might go down where morbidity goes down, more hospital services are available, employment and earnings are higher, or nutrition is better. Furthermore, changes in the age or sex proportions may affect all of the variables. Refer to Groups II, III, or IV for ideas.

3. Find some data in the *Abstracts* that represent such types of causative factors as number of hospitals, caloric intake, employment figures, and so on.

4. If the data are not in rate form, compute crude rate. Present a table showing the data you investigated that are possibly causal in terms of their incidence in the states and years (or as close to them as you can get).

B. Analysis of Your Data

Does your hypothesis seem feasible in light of the evidence? That is, does the explanatory variable you selected seem to be associated with the birth or death rates over time either positively (when one increases or decreases, so does the other) or negatively (when one increases or decreases, the other moves in the opposite direction)? If no special pattern is discernible, the possibility of a causal relationship is doubtful (although refining the rates might change the picture, were you able to do this.)

V PRESENTING YOUR RESULTS

Include the following in your report:

  1. *The states you are comparing and what you are comparing them on—birth rates or death rates.*

2. *A table showing either birth or death rates in your two states for three decades. Discuss the results, the hypothesis, and conclusions you draw from them.*

3. *A table showing rates of some variable from Groups II, III, and IV in relation to the change in birth or death rates. Do the implications of the table support your hypothesis; i.e., is the explanatory variable you selected either positively or negatively associated with the change in birth or death rates?*

4. *Suggestion of other factors from Groups II, III, and IV that might be investigated to give more understanding of the phenomenon being studied. Suggestions of rate refinements that might sharpen the comparisons.*

Keep your presentation to three typewritten pages excluding tables. Hand in the scratch paper from your library research with your report.

VI SELECTED BIBLIOGRAPHY

A. Methodology

Barclay, George W.
    1958   Techniques of Population Analysis. New York: Wiley.
Glick, Paul C.
    1962   "The 1960 census as a source for social research." American Sociological Review 27 (August):581–584.
Smith, T. Lynn
    1948   Population Analysis. New York: McGraw-Hill.

B. References and Studies

Davis, Kingsley
    1951   The Population of India and Pakistan. Princeton, N.J.: Princeton University Press.
    1956   "The amazing decline of mortality in underdeveloped areas." American Economic Review 46 (May):305–318.
    1965   "The sociology of demographic behavior." Pp. 309–333 in Robert K. Merton, Leonard Brown, Leonard S. Cottrell, Jr. (eds.), Sociology Today. New York: Basic Books.

——, and Judith Blake
   1956   "Social structure and fertility: an analytic framework."
           Economic Development and Cultural Change 4 (April):
           211–235.
Echler, Ross A., and Jack Zlotnick
   1949   "Immigration and the labor force." The Annals of the Amer-
           ican Academy of Political and Social Science 262 (March):
           92–101.
Firey, Walter
   1946   "Ecological considerations in planning for urban fringes."
           American Sociological Review 11 (August):411–423.
Freedman, Deborah, Ronald Freedman, and Pascal K. Whelpton
   1960   "Size of family and preference for children of each sex."
           American Journal of Sociology 66 (September):141–152.
Freedman, Ronald (ed.)
   1964   Population: The Vital Revolution. Garden City, N.Y.:
           Doubleday.
Goode, William J.
   1963   World Revolution and Family Patterns. New York: Free
           Press.
Hardin, Garrett
   1959   "Interstellar migration and the population problem." Jour-
           nal of Heredity 50 (March-April):68–70.
Hartley, Shirley M.
   1966   "The amazing rise of illegitimacy in Great Britain." Social
           Forces 44 (June):533–545.
Hauser, Philip M., and Otis Dudley Duncan
   1959   The Study of Population. Chicago: University of Chicago
           Press.
Hollingshead, A. B.
   1961   Elmtown's Youth. New York: Wiley. (First published 1949.)
Lipset, Seymour Martin, and Reinhard Bendix
   1959   Social Mobility in Industrial Society. Berkeley and Los
           Angeles: University of California Press.
Madigan, Francis C.
   1957   "Are sex mortality differentials biologically caused?" Mill-
           bank Memorial Fund Quarterly 35 (April):202–223.
Peterson, William
   1964   The Politics of Population. Garden City, N.Y.: Doubleday.
Reader, Leo G.
   1959   "Occupational and socioeconomic status as variables in
           heart disease research: a critique." The American Journal
           of the Medical Sciences 238 (September):298–300.

Redick, Richard W.
  1956   "Population growth and redistribution in central cities, 1940–1950." American Sociological Review 21 (February): 38–43.
Spengler, J. J.
  1954   "Welfare economics and the problem of overpopulation." Scienta 89:128–138, 166–175.
Stycos, J. Mayone
  1952   "Family and fertility in Puerto Rico." American Sociological Review 17 (October):572–580.
Sweezy, A. R.
  1940   "Population growth and investment opportunity." Quarterly Journal of Economics 55 (November):64–79.
Thomlinson, Ralph
  1965   Population Dynamics: Causes and Consequences of World Demographic Change. New York: Random House.
Thompson, Warren S.
  1953   Population Problems. New York: McGraw-Hill.
United Nations, Population Division
  1953   The Determinants and Consequences of Population Trends. New York: United Nations.
Whyte, William F., and Allan R. Holmberg
  1956   "Human problems of U.S. enterprise in Latin America." Human Organization 40 (Fall):1–40.
Wrong, Dennis
  1961   Population and Society. New York: Random House.

ASSIGNMENT FIFTEEN

METHOD:

Scales and Indices

RESEARCH TOPIC:

Health and Illness

I INTRODUCTION

Scales and Indices in Sociology

Man has always felt the need to measure his world. It is the quantity as well as the quality of things that is interesting and often exciting. Chemists identify elements by atomic weight, foodstuffs are sold by weight or volume, and clothes are sorted by size. In politics a candidate's popularity is measured by the votes he attracts, while in education academic excellence is indicated by grades. We continue to try to measure the world about us, either in concrete terms, as in "The length of the board is . . . ," or abstract ones, as "How angry she was!"

Man has had to create various devices that break phenomena into uniform pieces so that he can look at two similar items and have some quantitative means of stating their differences, as with the number of noise decibles that a jet transport makes during take-off versus the number a single-engine airplane makes. Sometimes men have used analogy with other, already measured, phenomena; a buffalo herd might be said to be "two days' ride from here," a person's age might be measured in terms of how many "moons" had been seen since his birth, and a rock would be so heavy that it would take "two men to carry it."

With the progress of the natural sciences — physics, chemistry, and biology — man has developed increasingly precise methods of dividing phenomena into standardized units and of counting them as well. He has gone from rather primitive measurements of length or distance (the ruler, yardstick, or mile), volume (the bushel, pint, or gallon), and weight (the pound or ton) to moderately elaborate instruments such as the clock, thermometer, pressure gauge, and the vernier caliper. These devices have helped to increase man's understanding of the physical world. Measurement of an object's various attributes is indispensable to the scientific enterprise because it is the basis of comparing how phenomena affect one another. With the aid of measuring instruments, scientists can determine that the volume of a certain liquid increases so many cubic centimeters when the temperature of the liquid reaches so many degrees, while the volume of another liquid reacts somewhat differently. From this clue, the scientist will begin to seek more data on the composition of each liquid.

Sociologists feel that if they can measure *social* attributes, it will help greatly to increase understanding of human group life. The effort to compare the intensities, qualities, or quantities of actions or emotions under various social conditions also requires some standardized, calibrated measuring equipment. To satisfy this requirement sociologists have developed special scales and indices to produce quantified definitions of social and social-psychological concepts. But the use of scales and indices alone is not in itself an approach to sociological research. Scales and indices are *tools* to be used in conjunction with other techniques such as the explanatory survey, population analysis, and sociometric techniques.

Sociologists distinguish three major types of scales to measure social attributes: nominal, ordinal, and interval. They employ these scales to measure fairly simple social phenomena like education or income levels as well as complex phenomena such as attitudes and the intensity with which they are held.

Nominal scales in one sense are not scales at all, but merely mutually exclusive subcategories of a given phenomenon. For instance, the general category "religious preference" can be divided into a nominal scale composed of Protestants, Catholics, and Jews, while the general category "political preference" can be divided into a nominal scale of Republicans, Democrats, and Independents. Observe that in the nominal scale there is no attempt to differentiate intensity of feeling for a particular subcategory. Only the proportion of the sample population belonging in each of the subcategories is available. This is analogous in the physical sciences to the recitation of elements and their proportion found in chemical compounds. Comparison of two populations on such a scale can still be quite helpful, however, when one is attempting to understand activities within each. For instance, one can look at two congressional districts with the following proportions of registered voters:

	District #1	District #2
Republicans	25%	42%
Democrats	55	41
Independent or undecided	20	17
	100%	100%

From this table one can select the area more likely to turn out for a parade of Democratic candidates, or the one in greater need of an intensive election campaign.

Ordinal scales are used to obtain some kind of qualitative ranking of phenomena, for instance, the relative intensity with which an attitude is held. The ordinal scale only establishes rank, however; it does not reveal the distance between ranks. When sociologists attempt to have subjects rate persons as playmates according to first, second, and third choices, as in the sociogram, they are creating an ordinal scale.

To take another example, if a student were to rate three psychology professors, the results might look something like this:

Professor Adams	*First Choice*
Professor Green	*Second Choice*
Professor Collins	*Third Choice*

Professor Adams was the student's first choice, but how much more appealing he is than the other two professors cannot be determined from this scale; we only know how he was ranked in comparison to the others. However, this can be a very useful kind of social information. The ordinal scale is one of the most popular in sociology because of the relative ease with which it can be adapted to many uses.

Other versions of this scale include those three-, five-, and seven-point scales in which an object or activity is ranked, such as:

		Excellent
Like very well		*Good*
Like fairly well	*or*	*Fair*
Like not at all		*Poor*
		Very poor

Here again there is no way of knowing how much intensity of feeling is attached to an object or activity given a "good" rating in comparison with one given a "fair" one. An ordinal scale in the physical sciences would be a rank-order list of the elements by weight without indicating the actual weight of each.

The student should be warned that ordinal scales such as those above are deceptively simple to construct but often difficult to analyze. Suppose three different groups of students were asked how they liked a certain instructor, and the results were as follows:

	Instructor Liked by Students			
	Very well	*Fairly well*	*Not at all*	
Class A	40%	20%	40%	= 100%
Class B	70	10	20	= 100
Class C	50	50	-	= 100

The questions that the analyst might well ask himself are: Is Class B more favorable to the instructor because 70 per cent said "very well," or is Class C really more favorable because there are no answers in its "not at all" category? There are two possible ways of handling this. One would be to combine the "very well" and "fairly well" categories and contrast them with the "not at all" category. The other would be to find the median of each distribution.

Interval scales go beyond ordinal scales in that units of measurement are constructed so there are equal intervals between measuring points. This offers an obvious advantage, since rigorous statements can be made about the nature of differences between rankings.

Interval scales are fairly easy to construct in the physical sciences (by the arbitrary division of lengths into smaller but equal units), but such calibration of social phenomena is not so simple. How can we divide equally the degrees of intensity of such attributes as prejudice toward minorities, anger at family members, or marital happiness? The measurement of inanimate objects has to reflect only the needs of the scientist, but the measurement of people's feelings or activities must reflect those feelings or activities accurately, or the measuring instrument is not doing what it purports to be doing. For this reason, in setting up an interval scale, the social scientist uses the combined judgment of other people in an attempt to calibrate the scale in a manner that reflects what people really think or experience about the social phenomenon being measured. The goal of such an approach is to arrive at a series of statements concerning attributes of the phenomenon being rated, each of which is equidistant and cumulative from the previous statement. This would be somewhat analogous to a ruler where the inches are equal in length and add up to a total of twelve. The way this is done in the social sciences is somewhat more difficult than in the physical sciences but still technically fairly simple. The mechanics will be discussed at greater length in the next section. It should be mentioned that, because interval scales often lack an absolute zero point, comparison across scales is hazardous—though results *within* a scale can be compared by degrees of intensity.

A good way to remember the usefulness and limitations of the nominal, ordinal, and interval scales is to keep the following progression in mind:

Nominal	*Ordinal*	*Interval*
Sally is tall	Sally is taller	Sally is three inches
Mary is short	than Mary	taller than Mary

How Scales and Indices Are Located, Constructed, and Used

There are a great many well-constructed scales already in existence, and you should investigate these before you attempt to devise a scale for your research purposes. Scales borrowed from others may be used just as they are or modified to fit the special needs of a specific study. Such scales have the advantage of previous testing through use. Further, comparable data is available if the investigator wishes to use it.

You can locate scales in the various sociology journals listed in Assignment Eighteen, "The Library Project." You can also find inventories of the scales that sociologists use, categorized by subject and source, in Bonjean, Hill, and McLemore, *Sociological Measurement: An Inventory of Scales and Indices, 1954–1965* (1967). Delbert C. Miller's *Handbook of Research Design and Social Measurement* (1964) discusses selected scales in some detail and provides a list of other sources for scales.

The investigator must be alert, however, to the problem of obsolescence in the measuring instrument he borrows from others. Where scales are composed of statements (such as the Thurstone Scale discussed later in this assignment), one must be careful to see that the statements fit current conditions. For instance, in an index of social class using the criterion of household furnishings, the presence of a "library table" would hardly rate a score today although it was once a part of such a rating created by F. Stuart Chapin (Miller, 1964, pp. 114–117). Likewise, scales utilizing annual income must be constantly revised to reflect the changing cost of living.

Where no scale will fit the specific measurement needs of the study, the sociologist must create his own. As we mentioned earlier, the ordinal scale is one of the most frequently used. The investigator writes a statement pertinent to his topic and then gives respondents an opportunity to answer positively, neutrally, or negatively on a three-, five-, or seven-point scale. Assignment of weights to the intervals is arbitrary and transforms the ordinal scale into a pseudo-interval scale. Some examples follow:

> *A. Most of the officials who run this city have its best interest at heart.*
>
> | *Agree very strongly* | *Agree* | *Not certain* | *Disagree* | *Disagree very strongly* |
> |---|---|---|---|---|
> | 5 | 4 | 3 | 2 | 1 |
>
> *B. Most of the officials who run this city know a lot about its problems.*
>
> | *Agree very strongly* | *Agree* | *Not certain* | *Disagree* | *Disagree very strongly* |
> |---|---|---|---|---|
> | 5 | 4 | 3 | 2 | 1 |
>
> *and so on.*

The investigator will use several related statements and average the scores he receives. This is, in fact, how many of the various indices * of social attributes are created using the ordinal scale principle; the investigator gains information about more than one type of phenomenon and then combines or averages his results. For instance, the investigator might decide that annual income, education, and occupation are good indicators of a person's social class. He will assign weights to their various values as follows, and add or average these to create an index:

Yearly Income		*Education*		*Occupation (from Census Categories)*	
Over $20,000	5	College graduate	5	Professional and managerial	5
$10,001- 20,000	4	Some college	4	Technical and sales	4
5,001- 10,000	3	High-school graduate	3	Service	3
3,001- 5,000	2	Some high school	2	Skilled labor	2
3,000 or under	1	Grade school or less	1	Unskilled labor	1

* The student will often hear reference made to both scales and indices. Strictly speaking, a scale is concerned with only one dimension of an attribute, while an index is thought to include a combination of many dimensions. For instance, a *scale* to measure level of education might be based on the number of years of schooling, whereas an educational index might include some combination of years of schooling, grade point average during this time, and score on a graduate record examination. In actual practice, however, the difference between scales and indices is often blurred so that they cannot be readily distinguished. This is because even if only one dimension of a phenomenon is used to construct a scale it is often a reflection of other dimensions as well. Thus years of schooling reflects in part the ability to get a passing grade and a willingness to stay in school up to a given time.

Suppose that a respondent made $40,000 a year, was a college graduate, and was in sales. His average score would be 14 divided by 3, or 4.66. Since 5 is the highest possible average, he would be relatively high in social class. Another respondent might be making $4000 per year, have only a grade school education, and be an unskilled laborer. His average score would be 4 divided by 3, or 1.33, relatively low in social class. Another way of combining these scores into an index would be to total them for each person and then to label those with scores of ten to fifteen upper class, from five to ten middle class, and from one to five lower class.

It is worth repeating that the researcher assigns these weights *arbitrarily,* without making any attempt to establish whether the social difference between, say, a high school diploma and some college is the same as the difference between some college and graduation from it. Furthermore, there is no way of saying that income, education, and occupation are all equally indicative of class position or that their parallel weight assignments are equivalent. The final result then, whether averaged or added, is merely a *rough estimate* of class gradations, notwithstanding the use of numbers.

Interval scales can be made by using demographic data — births, deaths, marriages, divorces, crime rates, monthly expenditures, and other statistics of interest. In such cases, the problem of intensity and equal distance between points is solved by the fact that the units are more easily discriminated than in other phenomena and thus can be *counted.* Obtaining the *range* of some data (usually by sampling) and then arbitrarily dividing it into equal subsections also is a way to construct an interval scale. Bogue (1963, pp. 92–93), for instance, used questionnaires to collect data concerning the amount of liquor consumed by men on Skid Row in an average day. After he felt he had the complete range of drinking patterns, which he presented in percentage form, he divided consumers of liquor into categories of light, medium, and heavy drinkers, thus creating an alcohol-consumption scale for future use.

Observations of social acts can be handled in the same way to create an interval scale, as, for example, in the use of observers stationed at several street intersections to do traffic counts. When all the data are put together, an investigator can create a scale of light, medium, and heavy traffic based on the actual numbers of cars passing various points in a city at any given time.

So far we have discussed making interval scales by starting with an ordinal scale and using the type of phenomenon that lends itself to counting — salaries in dollars, education in years, number of drinks, number of cars on the street. We have also shown how the sociologist uses three-, five-, and seven-point scales to show, say, degrees of agreement or disagreement in attitude. What does an investigator do if he wants an interval scale that measures more complicated nuances of attitude? Obviously this is a more demanding problem than is measurement wherein the units are pre-quantified in some way. Three behavioral scientists have attempted to work out techniques by which both the range and equal distance between subpoints can be built into an attitude rating scale. Their methods have been named after them: the Thurstone Scale, the Likert Scale, and the Guttman Scale. We shall confine our discussion to the Thurstone Scale, because it is the most basic of the three and the easiest to understand, and mention the other two only briefly.

The *Thurstone Scale,* an eleven-point interval scale, is developed in the following way:

1. *The investigator writes a number of positive and negative statements of varying intensity (sometimes as many as 50 to 100) pertaining to the phenomenon he wishes to measure.*

2. *He then asks people (often 50 to 100) to act as judges, and sort the statements into eleven piles — five degrees of favorable, one neutral, five degrees of unfavorable to the subject. (It is important to note that the investigator does not want the judges' personal opinions of the phenomenon, but rather their opinions concerning the* strength and direction *of the statements about the phenomenon — i.e., is the statement strongly or weakly positive or negative?) The major purpose is to find eleven statements that a majority of judges agree vary in graduated intensity from unfavorable to neutral to favorable. (Theoretically, if enough written statements were available, equivalent scales could be created with different sets of statements.)*

    Suppose the phenomenon to be tested concerns attitudes toward student demonstrators on college campuses. Some possible statements for the judges to rate as to positive or negative intensity might be:

    Student demonstrators should be suspended from college.

    Student demonstrators are trying to save this country from ruin.

    Student demonstrators are doing and saying what older people in this country would like to do and say but dare not.

    Student demonstrators ought to be sent to jail.

    Student demonstrators are for democracy.

    Student demonstrators are against democracy . . . and so on.

3. *The investigator records the results of each judge's assessment of the strength of each statement. That is, he keeps track of where each statement is sorted by each judge. He then finds the* median *score for each statement. (The median of any distribution of numbers is found by putting them in rank order and counting from the top or bottom to the* midpoint *of the numbers.) The median is used in this case to avoid any distortion caused by averaging. This would indicate the approximate point on an eleven-point scale that each statement represents, so far as the judges were concerned.*

Another criterion to use in selecting statements is the range *of judges' scores. Any statement with a large spread of scores would be viewed as unreliable because so much disagreement existed concerning its intensity. Those statements that were consistently sorted into scores very close to each other would be judged reliable indicators of that position on the eleven-point scale.*

In the brief illustration that follows, the median among five ratings for three statements is located by finding the halfway point scores placed in order on a continuum. We assume here that there are but five judges. (The more judges, the longer the distribution; but the median is still the midpoint.)

	Statement 1		Statement 2		Statement 3
	9		2		2
	10		3		3
median	10	median	3	median	9
	11		3		10
	11		4		11

The investigator would assign statement one to position 10 and statement two to position 3, but he would discard statement three as unreliable because of the wide spread in ratings it received from the judges. He will eventually need eleven statements in all.

4. *The eleven statements selected (each representative of one point in the scale) would then compose the eleven-point scale, presumably varying in intensity of feeling on a given topic in equal increments.*

5. *The scale is now ready to administer to a subject in the research project. Administration consists of asking the person to check*

the one statement he most agrees with. *(The items are not pre-sented to the subject in order, but randomly.) The assumption is that he also agrees with those of lesser intensity than his selected item, while disagreeing with any stronger statements.*

It should be mentioned that the scale-making technique presented here is, of necessity, limited to the simplest of operations, and that sometimes complicated statistical techniques are involved. There is also a variety of ways to administer scales. They can be handled by an interviewer or by the respondent.

The *Likert Scale* is an attempt to arrive at the average opinion of persons who have contradictory or ambivalent attitudes on a topic and who would not necessarily agree with all the statements below a certain point on a Thurstone scale or disagree with all the statements above it. Its complicated construction also depends on the use of judges. The *Guttman Scale* is a complicated combination of the Thurstone and Likert approaches to scaling. The student who wishes to study these techniques in greater depth is referred to the bibliography.

Advantages and Disadvantages

The most obvious advantage of scales and indices as a research tool is that by quantifying description they make sociological assessment of phenomena more exact. They also help to compare social phenomena under various conditions, and thus advance the determination of causality. Certainly, a "cohesiveness" scale that indicates that Community *A* rates 10.4 and Community *B* 13.9 is much more helpful than a statement like, "It appears that there is less cohesiveness in Community A than in B." A small change in some attribute of a phenomenon—its intensity, distribution, or appeal, for instance—is also more readily apparent if it can be perceived through some scaled measurement. Furthermore, the gains from such measurement attempts are *cumulative,* in that they enhance the possibility of testing research findings through the replication (repetition) of studies and thus aid in the refinement of both sociological theory and methods.

The construction of scales and indices also forces the researcher to think out the many ramifications of the phenomena he is studying. In some way he must create *order* out of what may first appear to be a multitude of social facts, and thus make the investigation of social behavior more systematic and the results more understandable.

Sociological scales and indices are, however, in their infancy and have a number of problems and disadvantages. A major problem for scale-makers is not how to construct a scale (which as you can see is a straightforward task technically), but rather how to be sure that the the scale is measuring what he says it is supposed to be measuring. This is known as the scale's "validity."

As with most abstract phenomena, tests to measure validity must be indirect. Usually the investigator relies on what is termed "face validity," i.e., the measuring scale approach seems to make sense on the face of it (as does the use of education, occupation, and income levels in combination for a social-class scale). Sometimes he will check to see if the subject's reaction to related phenomena is consistent with his scale rating; if the subject rates high on an achievement-motivation scale he should also be a hard worker, interested in school, and making good grades. Pragmatic or empirical validity is also used and refers to attempts to predict future behavior from measurement ratings.

These tests may all sound difficult and technical, but laymen concoct similar ones. In many social situations the need to be certain of the validity of one's measuring scale is often so urgent that laymen test it quite fearlessly. Note the girl who first asks her boyfriend, "How much do you love me?" and then proceeds to construct some test of his love in order to validate or disprove his claim in terms of the consistency of his responses. The slum gang's game of "playing the dozens"—a game based on trading personal insults—is an attempt to measure the point at which another person will "lose his cool." Loss of social poise is validated pragmatically: the subject stops talking and starts fighting.

Reliability refers to whether use of the scale in successive measurements of the same phenomenon will result in the same measure. In the Thurstone scale the reason for having many judges in the selection of scale items is to increase the universality, and thus the reliability, of the measuring instrument. But, how does the investigator know that the judges he has selected to "standardize" his scale actually have "standard" opinions? Might not a group of college student judges sorting statements about the police come up with a different measuring scale and intervals than would middle-aged, established citizens?

Regional differences might also result in differences in sorting statements. The same is true of scales constructed from demographic or observational data. Just how representative are they of the full range of behavior? A scale of crime incidence might be valid for Eastern seaboard cities of the United States, but not for cities in the South. Bogue's drinking scale, cited previously, was based on what Skid Row habitués consume—a quantity much larger than that in other areas of the city. This, of course, invalidates the scale for comparison from area to area—one of the reasons for using scales in the first place. It might be well to mention here that validity and reliability are so intertwined in practice that to increase one is to increase the other, and to question one is to question the other. If a scale is unreliable from group to group its validity as a measuring instrument is thereby reduced.

The problem of creating a uniform rating scale, presumably applicable to any respondent, is not solely a technical one; it touches on the very philosophy of social science. One of the major controversies concerning scales and indices is whether the investigator should rely entirely on the subjective judgment of respondents or whether he should arrive, either alone or with the aid of judges, at some all-purpose "objective" measurement — assuming this is possible.

This problem is most often discussed in connection with the creation of measuring instruments for social class (see Morris, Broom, and Selznick, 1963). Because subjective perspective on the class system varies according to the respondent's (or judge's) position in the social order, the investigator who attempts to reflect this has the problem of working with a different scale for each perspective. An alternative for the investigator is to create one "objective" scale based on his own knowledge of the society but with the realization that the scale does not fully match the subjective experiences of the respondents. The social class index described earlier in this assignment is of this latter variety.

Even more basic to the criticism of measurement as an endeavor in sociology is the doubt of some sociologists (primarily those who favor observation and depth interviewing as data-gathering techniques) that *any* scale could reflect social life as it is lived and experienced. They feel that people do not think in terms of three- or five-point scales when they make decisions (it *is* difficult to imagine a person asking himself if he feels "very well," "fairly well," or "not at all well" today). If one's choice of friends depends upon specific situations rather than upon any constants, is it realistic to devise a scale of personal preference for friends that is not tied to any situation at all? Can any science quantify and measure precisely what people themselves do not handle in this way? The controversy remains unsettled. (This may be in part because the average person puts up so little resistance to the social scientist's measuring efforts. Probably people like to *think* that they make decisions in an organized and quantifiable fashion.)

Finally, scale-makers have a tendency to forget that their findings, when valid, are more applicable to *groups* (where individual errors may tend to cancel each other out) than to individuals. (This is also true of measuring instruments in psychology.) The purpose of scales in sociology is primarily to measure group characteristics as accurately as possible; thus composite, not individual, scores are the goal of the scale-maker.

Some Applications

Despite the numerous problems, scales and indices continue to be used extensively in sociology, psychology, and demography. Psychologists, for instance, have constructed personality tests, IQ tests, occupational aptitude tests, authoritarianism tests, and self-concept scales. Social psychologists sometimes borrow these scales from psychologists. Demographers use cost-of-living indices, indices of urbanization and industrialization, and other composite measuring instruments to aid them in their analyses. *Sociological Measurement* (Bonjean, Hill, and McLemore) lists scales for such topics as achievement motivation, anomie and alienation, assimilation, class consciousness, social cohesion, conformity and deviance, crime and delinquency, interpersonal relations in the family, family cohesion, health and illness, discrimination and prejudice, job satisfaction, leadership qualities, marital satisfaction, political attitudes, religion, and the self-concept, to name but a few.

Such scales are used as part of an overall research design when the investigator wants to employ quantitative measurement to make the test of a hypothesis more stringent. For instance, he might first want to use a delinquency scale to locate "degrees of delinquency" in various areas of the metropolis in order to check the hypothesis that high delinquency areas are found near the centers of large cities. Marital happiness measurements are often compared with the bride and groom's personality attributes or social characteristics in an attempt to see whether they can expect connubial bliss.

II   HEALTH AND ILLNESS AS A SUBJECT FOR SCALES AND MEASUREMENT

Any area in which opposing concepts form a continuum of concern in everyday life and about which important decisions must be made is a good candidate for measurement; for instance, the sociology of health and illness (medical sociology). For instance, how can the general health level of one society be compared with another? (This task has been undertaken by the World Health Organization.) If public attitudes toward what constitutes health and illness, as well as what is a reportable symptom, were to be measured, the findings would probably reveal considerable class defferences in opinions on this matter (see for instance, Graham, 1958). Strength of attitudes for or against preventive medicine (vaccinations, inoculations, etc.), Medicare, and health insurance can also be scaled and quantified.

By what criteria are doctors considered good or bad? How do patients rank a doctor's skill and personality, and how do doctors rank a patient's cooperation? Hospitals and nursing personnel can be measured by patients. Nurses can also be measured about their attitudes toward their training, doctors, patients, and general hospital administration.

III PROJECT ASSIGNMENT

Consistent with other assignments that are fairly difficult for a beginner or even the novitiate upper-division student, a brief assignment will be offered as well as the regular assignment.

FOR THE BEGINNING STUDENT

Construct an *index* consisting of three different aspects of the same social phenomenon that can be used as indicators for it. (Use the social class example on p. 207 of this assignment as a guide.) For each indicator construct a three-, five-, or seven-point scale; use the totals or averages to construct your index.

Possible phenomena from which to construct your index might include measurements of health or illness, faith in one's doctor, willingness to spend money on preventive medicine, interest in medical achievements, ratings of treatment received at a hospital, and attitudes toward Medicare, to name a few.

What problems do you foresee in the use of this index?

Administer your index to five friends and report on the results. In what sort of an investigation might you use such a scale?

For a regular assignment, pretend you are an assistant project director assigned to develop some scales for a specific study in the sociology of health and illness. As your part of the project, you are first to locate a scale in the sociological literature that could be used in this study. Then you are to create a *Thurstone-type* scale of your own, on a different subject from that of the first scale but still related to the general topic of your research. In a memo to the project director you are to include a description of both of these scales (their advantages and possible drawbacks), a discussion on how they are to be used, and your recommendations.

IV   STEPS FOR THE SCALES AND INDICES ASSIGNMENT

A.   Before You Go into the Field

1.   Locate scales in the sociological literature on medical sociology. Use Bonjean, Hill, and McLemore's *Sociological Measurement* or the journals listed in Assignment Eighteen. (Stay out of the personality testing material – this is a sociology assignment.)

2.   Copy the scale from the journal or book you use, making notes on its administration and scoring (as well as a complete citation of your source).

3.   Decide on a topic related to the scale you selected from the literature for the scale you will construct.

4.   Write fifteen statements of varying "intensity," both positive and negative, concerning the subject of your investigation. Put each statement on a three-by-five card or slip of paper. (Number them 1 through 15 inconspicuously on the back of the cards to aid you in keeping track of them on a score sheet.) When you write the statements, keep the following suggestions in mind:

   A. *Limit each statement to* one idea *only. Avoid double-barreled sentences where the respondent might want to rank one part high, the other low.*

   B. *Avoid* extreme *statements that no one or everyone is likely to agree with.*

   C. *Keep the statements short and simple.*

   D. *Try to cover the full range of current feelings about the phenomenon in your statements. (Some researchers conduct preliminary depth interviews to get ideas for statements. You may not have time for this, however.)*

5.   Prepare some sort of tally sheet (see sample below) to keep track of results to aid you in item manipulation and scale development.

Figure 15-1

RANKING OF STATEMENTS

Judge	Statement Number														
	1	2	3	4	5	6	7	8	9	10	11	12	13	14	15
1	10	7	*dt.*	⌣											
2	11	3	*dt.*	—											
3	8	11	*dt.*	⌣											
4	10	5	*dt.*	⌣											
5	9	8	*dt.*	—											

B. In the Field

  1. Locate five persons to judge these items. (Because each person must do his judging individually, it is not necessary to get all five together.) Provide them with eleven spaces into which to sort the statements. Eleven cards numbered 1 to 11 and spread across a table will suffice.

  2. Record their judgments on a tally sheet (such as the sample above).

C. Construction of the Scale

  1. Rank-order the ratings of each statement, and find the median in each by counting down to the third score. For example, the ratings on the sample tally sheet would be ranked like this:

Item 1	*Item 2*	
8	3	
9	5	
Median 10	Median 7	. . . etc.
10	8	
11	11	
Spread: 3	Spread: 8	

  2. On the basis of the median scores, select one statement for each of the eleven points on the scale. In choosing between two statements with the same median, take the one with the smallest point spread (i.e., most agreement as to weight). In the sample above, Item 1 is better for a scale than Item 2. (With a total of fifteen statements you can eliminate the four with the greatest spread.)

  3. It will not be necessary for you to administer the scale to any respondents. This assignment is concerned only with the construction of scales.

V PRESENTING YOUR RESULTS

Remember that your results are to be organized as a memo to the project director. Include the following:

    1. A short introduction in which you discuss the specific sociological problem in the area of health and illness that you are going to investigate with the aid of scales.

    2. The already constructed scale that you located in a book or sociological journal, along with directions for administering and scoring it. Discuss what it will be measuring and how it will fit into the research planned.

3. *The eleven-item Thurstone-type scale that you have developed, showing the items in rank order from unfavorable to neutral to favorable. Discuss what facet of the phenomenon it will be measuring.*

4. *Any problems you foresee in the use of the scales, any doubts you have about the validity of each, and any suggestions you might have to increase validity.*

The presentations of the results of this scale and index assignment should not exceed four pages. This allows one-half page each for the presentation of the scales and three pages for discussion of administration, scoring, and general usefulness or drawbacks of the scales. Include your working papers with your final report.

VI SELECTED BIBLIOGRAPHY

A. Methodology

Cronbach, Lee J.
   1949   Essentials of Psychological Testing. New York: Harper & Row.
Edwards, Allan L.
   1957   Techniques of Attitude Scale Construction. New York: Appleton-Century-Crofts.
Selltiz, Claire, Marie Jahoda, Morton Deutsch, and Stuart W. Cook
   1964   Research Methods in the Social Sciences (especially Chaps. 5 and 10). New York: Holt, Rinehart & Winston.
Thorndike, R. L., and E. E. Hagen
   1961   Measurement and Evaluation in Psychology and Education. New York: Wiley.
Torgerson, Warren S.
   1962   Theory and Methods of Scaling. New York: Wiley.

B. Collections of Sociological Scales

Bonjean, Charles M., Richard J. Hill, and S. Dale McLemore
   1967   Sociological Measurement: An Inventory of Scales and Indices, 1954–1965. San Francisco: Chandler.

Miller, Delbert C.
  1964   Handbook of Research Design and Social Measurement.
          New York: McKay.

C. **Scales and Indices in Action**

Bell, Wendell, and Maryanne T. Force
  1956   "Urban neighborhood types and participation in formal as-
          sociations." American Sociological Review 21 (February):
          25–34.
Bogue, Donald J.
  1963   Skid Row in American Cities. Chicago: University of Chi-
          cago Press.
Clarke, Alfred C.
  1956   "The use of leisure and its relation to levels of occupational
          prestige." American Sociological Review 21 (June):301–
          307.
DeFleur, Melvin L., and Frank R. Westie
  1958   "Verbal attitudes and overt acts: an experiment in the sa-
          lience of attitudes." American Sociological Review 23 (De-
          cember):667–673.
Freeman, Howard, and Ozzie G. Simmons
  1959   "Social class and post-hospital performance levels." Ameri-
          can Sociological Review 24 (June):345–351.
Gibbs, Jack P., and Walter T. Martin
  1953   "A theory of status integration and relationship to suicide."
          American Sociological Review 18 (October):493–497.
Graham, Saxon
  1958   "Socio-economic status, illness, and the use of medical ser-
          vices." Pp. 129–154 in E. Gartley Jaco (ed.), Patients, Phy-
          sicians, and Illness. New York: Free Press.
Hollingshead, A. B., and F. C. Redlich
  1958   Social Class and Mental Illness. New York: Wiley.
Lipset, S. M., and R. Bendix
  1959   Social Mobility in Industrial Society. Berkeley and Los
          Angeles: University of California Press.
Lundberg, George A., and Lenore Dickson
  1952   "Interethnic relations in a high school population." Ameri-
          can Journal of Sociology 57 (July):1–10.
Meier, Dorothy, and Wendell Bell
  1959   "Anomie and differential access to the achievement of life
          goals." American Sociological Review 24 (April):189–202.

Morris, Richard T., Leonard Broom, and Phillip Selznick
    1963   "The study of social stratification." Pp. 182–201 in L.
            Broom and P. Selznick (eds.), Sociology. New York: Harper
            & Row.
Poole, W. C., Jr.
    1928   "Social distance and social pathology." Sociology and Social
            Research 12 (January-February):268–272.
Rettig, Salomon, and Benjamin Pasamanick
    1959   "Changes in moral values among college students: a fac-
            torial study." American Sociological Review 24 (December):
            856–863.
Runner, Jessie R.
    1937   "Social distance in adolescent relationships." American
            Journal of Sociology 43 (November):428–429.
Warner, W. Lloyd
    1949   Democracy in Jonesville. New York: Harper & Row.

METHOD:

Interaction Process Analysis

RESEARCH TOPIC:

Small Groups

I INTRODUCTION

Interaction Process Analysis, a Definition

In Assignment One we asked you to observe an instance of socialization and to set up a tally sheet to organize and enumerate the behaviors you were watching. At the time you may have wondered if there were some known or ready-made set of categories into which you could fit your observations. Indeed, there are many such ready-made sets, and they are extremely useful.

One of the most influential of these systems for coding (organizing by category) the behavior of individuals in social interaction is that conceived and devised by Robert F. Bales while studying small groups in the Harvard Social Relations Laboratory. Called Interaction Process Analysis (hereafter referred to as IPA), the Bales' system differs from that used in your first project in two major ways.

In Assignment One you were interested mainly in describing the actual content of behavior in the socialization process. For example, you wanted to describe how a group inculcates patterns of behavior into a new member. To do this you had to become aware of the rules for behavior in this group. Perhaps you observed how children learned the norms for crossing the street while a traffic-control officer was present. You tallied specific acts – the ritual, dance-like character of the boy whose job it was to direct the flow of traffic; the obedience of the other children to his commands, even when no traffic was in sight; the punishment of a child who tried to cross the street outside the marked walk by making him come back to the sidewalk and cross properly. And if you also observed on a nonschool day, you saw that the school-day rules or norms no longer applied to the situation. It was necessary for you to anticipate specific actions for your categories and perhaps to revise them after being in the field awhile to take account of unexpected behavior.

Bales' system of categories (see Fig. 16-1) is not concerned with the substantive content of the interaction, but rather with the types of inter-

Figure 16-1

IPA Code of Categories (Modified)*

Social-emotional Area: *Positive*		A	1. *Shows solidarity,* raises other's status, gives help, reward 2. *Shows tension release,* jokes, laughs, shows satisfaction 3. *Agrees,* shows passive acceptance, understands, concurs, complies
Task Area: *Neutral*	Answers	B	4. *Gives suggestion,* direction, implying autonomy for other 5. *Gives opinion,* evaluation, analysis, expresses feeling, wish 6. *Gives orientation,* information, repeats, clarifies, confirms
	Questions	C	7. *Asks for orientation,* information, repetition, confirmation 8. *Asks for opinion,* evaluation, analysis, expression of feeling 9. *Asks for suggestion,* direction, possible ways of action
Social-Emotional Area: *Negative*		D	10. *Disagrees,* shows passive rejection, formality 11. *Shows tension,* asks for help, withdraws out of field 12. *Shows antagonism,* deflates other's status, defends or asserts self

*Source: Bales, Robert F. *Interaction Process Analysis: A Method for the Study of Small Groups.* Reading, Mass.: Addison-Wesley, 1959, p. 9.

action that develop within all groups regardless of their function, history, or composition. To accomplish this, he developed a mutually exclusive, logically consistent system of categories that have been used to describe and analyze the sequence of interactional events in any group, the complex interrelationships among its members, and the different forms these patterns take when the structure and functioning of groups are altered by changes in sex composition, types of leadership, and so on.

If Bales' categories were used for observing the processes of interaction in an argument between a husband and wife, there would be no indication in the data whether the discussion was about the best way to discipline the children, what kind of a new car to buy, etc.* But you would have detailed information about whether it was the husband or the wife who made the most suggestions or gave the most opinions, and which spouse asked for suggestions and orientation. Furthermore, you would know if either spouse displayed intense or prolonged antagonism or disagreement, whether a feeling of acceptance and understanding prevailed, and the sequence in which these questions, answers, and positive and negative emotional reactions occurred.

Bales' system is intended to show that there are universal *processes* of interaction for groups involved in problem-solving activities. Like the sociologist Talcott Parsons, his colleague and collaborator, Bales sees the small group as a functioning social system with basic problems to resolve in order to maintain itself in a relatively stable state. (The assumption is that there is a tendency in *any* social system toward equilibrium or balance.) One set of *problems* for any group consists of trying to reach *goals,* solve issues, or accomplish tasks. Success at any of these creates momentary equilibrium. Possibly the group will also have to *adapt* to pressure from the outside. Solving internal problems and responding to outside pressures have been designated the "task-oriented areas" of the interaction process in Fig. 16-1, Sections B and C, because solutions to them largely depend upon the process of getting things done or problem-solving.

For example, a group of students may want to introduce some new, experimental courses into the college curricula (goal), but the faculty and administration are reluctant to allow the flexibility in course content that the students desire (problem). The students must make modifications in their suggested program (adaptation). If the problems are not resolved, or if the students violently disagree about how the problems should be solved, the student group may experience a disequilibrium that could destroy the group itself.

Groups also have to deal with emotional expressions of feelings that arise in interaction. If a problem is to be solved, there must be some attempt to maintain or regain integration within the group so that it does not fragment into conflicting sides. The students may have marked differences of opinion on the best way to go about obtaining the desired courses. Their arguments may cause tensions that must be resolved, through jokes, laughter, or expressions of trust and affection by the more affectively oriented members of the group. Handling emotional stresses and strains and maintaining integration are designated in Fig. 16-1, Sections A and D, "social-emotional areas, negative and positive." The instrumental and

---

* Bales does, however, use tape recorders (and sometimes film) in conjunction with observation to catch the topical content as a precaution against accidental loss of material and a check on reliability among observers.

affective aspects of interaction, then, are those processes the researcher is to observe and record. In doing so he must ignore any particular content that a given participant in the group might be expressing.

In observing a specific situation (Assignment One), the aim was insight into the meaning of an action for the individuals involved, but the aim of IPA is the discovery of general laws of interaction occurring in *all* groups. For example, is there a pattern of behavior that occurs in all groups? Bales and his associates report that indeed there does seem to be such a pattern that develops in the following *phases:** (1) *communication,* in which the group must come to some common definition of the problem they are trying to solve, (2) evaluation, in which the group must arrive at some *shared attitude* toward the situation, and (3) *control,* in which the group must make some kind of decision about what is going to be done about the problem.

Once such general laws for social groups are articulated there is the task of discovering what variables might alter the basic pattern. For instance, does the length of time spent in each of the phases listed above change when group members vary in age, sex, personality, social status, values, and so on? If so, how? What happens to a group with a permissive type of leadership, as opposed to one with an authoritarian type of leadership? It has been found that in the permissive group the leader gives relatively fewer opinions and suggestions, and that the group as a whole expresses more positive than negative feelings, as compared to the group with an authoritarian leadership pattern. Both groups, however, would show a "normal" pattern in that most of the interaction takes place in Sections B and C—Answers and Questions—of the IPA category code (see Figs. 16-2 and 16-3, for examples). This generalization certainly has implications for the training of group leaders.

Figure 16-2 †

The Profile for a Group with an Authoritarian Leader

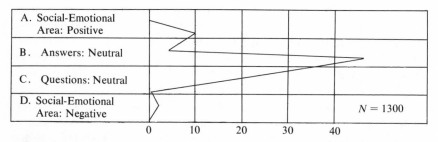

A. Social-Emotional Area: Positive					
B. Answers: Neutral					
C. Questions: Neutral					
D. Social-Emotional Area: Negative					$N = 1300$

0   10   20   30   40

† Source: Bales, Robert F. *Interaction Process Analysis: A Method for the Study of Small Groups*. Reading, Mass.: Addison-Wesley, 1959, p. 18 (adapted version of charts 4 and 5).

* With the use of Bales' system of categories, this pattern was discovered by observing the interaction of numerous groups. These observations were then analyzed by statistical techniques with which we do not attempt to deal in this manual.

Figure 16-3

The Profile for a Group with a Permissive Leader

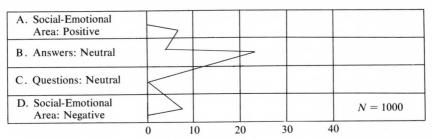

A. Social-Emotional Area: Positive					
B. Answers: Neutral					
C. Questions: Neutral					
D. Social-Emotional Area: Negative					$N = 1000$

0   10   20   30   40

Interest in types of interaction patterns is by no means without lay counterparts. People who ask "What was the general *tone* of the meeting?" are expressing this kind of interest in interaction processes, as are those who say, "Well, everyone was so uptight that nothing was accomplished except a lot of shouting." Is it any wonder that tension releasers—people who can joke or in some way make others feel more at ease and cooperative—are greatly in demand by both hostesses and boards of directors?

How to Do Interaction Process Analysis

All social groups, from dyads to total societies, find it necessary to deal with the task-oriented and emotional aspects of interaction, but Bales used small groups of from two to twenty members to obtain data on these processes. It is in these groups that detailed observations can be made on *all* expressions, verbal and nonverbal. For Bales, the small group consists of members who are interacting in face-to-face situations, and who *react* to one another. It does not include any group, however small, whose members are not *aware* of each other—although the group need not have any history of social bonds, as is the case for a primary group.

The basic unit of analysis in the IPA is "the act." An act includes any gesture, no matter how small or trivial, that can be observed. A smile, a frown, a sigh, shifting weight from one foot to another, tapping a pencil, stroking an ear, any vocal gesture from barely expressed grunts of disapproval to a single sentence of praise—all of these are individual acts. A more lengthy comment by a member would be coded into its smaller component units.

In a typical analysis, each act is coded into one of the twelve categories listed in Fig. 16-1 in two different ways:

1. Identification of the actor *by an arbitrarily assigned number.*
2. Identification of the recipient *of the action by a different number.*

For simplicity's sake each member of the group is identified by a number. The group as a whole is identified by 0, and anyone outside the group is X. So if number 1 asks number 2, "What is this meeting all about?" and number 2 answers that it is to find out why some members don't come to meetings, there would be *two* entries made on the coding sheet. The observer would code "1-2" in Category 7 ("asks for orientation"), and "2-1" in Category 6 ("gives orientation"). If number 4 looks annoyed at the question, this would be coded "4-1" in Category 12 ("shows antagonism"), and if number 5 asks "Where's Jim?" this would be coded 5-X in Category 7 ("asks for information").

An act is not coded in more than one category. This, of course, may cause some problems since almost any interaction at a verbal level contains emotional content. For example, a question like, "What the hell is going on here?" implies hostility. How would you code it? Bales developed two general rules to handle this type of ambiguity: (1) give preference to emotional content (Sections A and D) over Answers and Questions (Sections B and C), and (2) code the act into the category that indicates a response to the previous action or an anticipation of the next. The hostile question would thus be coded in Category 12 of Section D as a negative emotional response.

As you might expect, observers must be very alert to catch all the subtle nuances of group interaction. Bales has suggested that the novice should not record the total interaction between actor and recipient in each individual act, but only the act of the person designated the major actor. He should foreswear identification of the recipient until he becomes more skilled in the procedure. In the beginning it may be useful to have a partner in order to compare the results you obtain with those of another person. In this way you will become sensitive to other possible interpretations of who is acting, what constitutes an act, and in what category the act should be coded; you will also sharpen your own powers of concentration and observation.

There are many ways of analyzing data obtained by the use of IPA categories, including some complicated statistical techniques as mentioned earlier. The only way that will concern you in this assignment, however, is the relatively simple "group interaction profile." This is obtained by adding the total number of acts in all of the twelve categories, then calculating the percentage for each category of the total acts for all individuals in the group. These percentages are then plotted on graph paper, which allows the investigator to note very quickly whether there is more agreement than disagreement within the group, or whether there is more positive than negative emotional interaction. Figures 16-2 and 16-3 offer sample profiles using only the four major categories of (A) "Social-Emotional Area: Positive," (B) "Task Area: Answers," (C) "Task Area: Questions," and (D) "Social-Emotional Area: Negative." Observe that this is a condensation of the categories from Fig. 16-1 in that all types of answers in A ("shows solidarity," "shows tension release," "agrees") have been coded as "Social-Emotional: Positive." The same is true of B, C, and D. (See Fig. 16-1 for details on the content of categories.)

Advantages and Disadvantages

Interaction Process Analysis has several advantages over other observational techniques. First, IPA trains the investigator to think in abstract and general terms. Second, since the coding categories are uniform, the researcher can do *comparative* research on various types of small groups. For example, IPA allows the investigator to look at the effects of size, social status, age, personality, and cultural backgrounds of members, on the content of interaction process and thus on the structure of the group itself.

This system alerts the researcher to the dynamics of the situation by directing his attention to the type of act and to how each act elicits responses from other members of the group. This is certainly an efficient way to make the investigator aware of the "ongoingness" of social interaction, and of the need in coding to be more conscious of patterns and phases in social behavior. Since the categories are preset, there is no need for the researcher to try to construct them in the field at the same time as he is using them and thus risk failing to catch all relevant behavior. In other words, the researcher can concentrate all his attention on certain aspects of the situation, especially the problem-solving process, while ignoring others, such as the substantive or topical content. Finally, although it is not an integral part of the methodology, most observations of small group interaction based on IPA categories have been in laboratory situations, where the researcher has much more control of his group's size, social variables (sex, age, personality, status, etc.), and setting of goals than does the field worker.

Of course, some of the disadvantages are just the obverse of the advantages. The IPA system does not take account of the complexity and richness of social phenomena. It is a rigid system and thus does not allow for new insights or discoveries on the part of the investigator. For example, it does not make any difference what the group is engaged in, whether it is peace talks between two warring nations or a PTA meeting. What is coded is the same, and the profiles of both groups could be very similar.*

---

*As noted previously, it is the aim of Bales' system to discover *general laws* of group interaction. An empirical norm for group profiles has been established. Variations within this normative pattern are presumed to be due to differences in the social characteristics of the participants or in the social structure of the group.

Another disadvantage is that often the situations are not natural; rather they are contrived for observation in laboratory situations, with the participants instructed to pretend that they are interested in a given goal.

Another valid criticism is that Bales' categories do not really describe interaction process; instead they actually freeze interaction into frequencies of types of behavior.

Some Applications

IPA has been used to identify patterned ways in which groups handle internal and external problems. For example, Bales and Slater (1955) discovered there was a division of labor within the family that corresponds to the instrumental-affective dichotomy: the father handles those functions identified with adaptation and task orientation, and the mother copes with problems of group integration and management of feelings. The same differentiation of roles has been found to be characteristic of many other social groups as well. The IPA technique has also been used to identify the effect of social status (Strodtbeck, James, and Hawkins, 1957) and sex roles (Strodtbeck and Mann, 1956) in jury deliberations.

Perhaps one of the most important applications of this method, beyond the understanding of group processes and structure, is in training practitioners such as counselors, group leaders, teachers, and psychologists. The method allows them to evaluate their approaches to the guidance process. For example, a counselor who wishes to know whether he allowed enough leeway for the student to make his own decisions can look at his own profile to see how often and when he has interjected directive suggestions; then, if the data indicate it, he can try to modify his behavior in a less authoritarian direction (Bales, 1950).

II SMALL GROUPS AS A SUBJECT FOR INTERACTION PROCESS ANALYSIS

The IPA technique is devised for use on relatively small groups. Furthermore, since it requires an alert observer to catch all nuances of verbal and nonverbal expressions that are to be coded into the established categories, it is best suited for discussion rather than for action groups. As we mentioned earlier, one of the primary aims of this method is to discover social processes that enable a group to solve its problems and at the same time to maintain inner cohesion and equilibrium.

If the process patterns that lead to consensus or conflict can be located in small groups, it can be assumed that similar patterns operate in larger, more complex groupings, such as communities and societies. If this is so, problems of order, leadership, conflict, and consensus can thus be examined within small groups to reveal universal processes, and to answer such questions as: What are the patterns of interaction in a group with democratic leadership? What are the patterns of interaction in a group that maintains a high degree of solidarity? How about a group that dissolves or disintegrates under emotional strains and tensions? Is it possible to have two strong task-oriented leaders in the same group without a great deal of dissension? How is consensus among members maintained? How are issues resolved?

III PROJECT ASSIGNMENT

In this assignment you are to observe three or four of your friends in interaction as they discuss some topic of interest to them — violence on campus, poverty programs, United States involvement in war, conservation, pollution, population control, or whatever. This discussion can take place in either a contrived situation or a "natural" one. You could, for instance, ask your friends to get together to discuss an issue, or you could listen in on three or four strangers talking in the campus cafeteria, a coffee shop, or a bar. While the group is engaged in conversation, you will record their acts on the Modified Interactional Process Chart (Fig. 16-4). Later you will analyze these charts to prepare group profiles on graph paper, and finally discuss the results in the body of your report. We suggest that you select a partner for this assignment so that you will have the opportunity to compare your results with someone else who observed the same group (or groups) in interaction.

IV STEPS FOR THE INTERACTION PROCESS ANALYSIS ASSIGNMENT

A. Before You Go into the Field

1. Prepare several copies of the following modified IPA chart:

Figure 16-4

Modified IPA Chart

A. Social-Emotional Area: Positive	
B. Answers: Neutral	
C. Questions: Neutral	
D. Social-Emotional Area: Negative	

If you prepare these charts on standard-size typing paper, you will probably use only one sheet for each observation, or a total of three sheets.

2. You will use this "modified" category chart for your observations. But study Bales' original set of categories (Fig. 16-1) very thoroughly so that you will be able to code each act into the appropriate category without having to search for it at the time you are observing.

3. Plan to use three different groups, or the same group at three different times. If you have a partner, be prepared to compare your results with his.

B. In the Field

1. Select a place in which you can observe interaction between three or four people without being interrupted.

2. Plan to observe the interactions for three periods of approximately fifteen minutes each — no longer, since the degree of concentration required to code all acts is considerable.

3. Assign a number to each group member.

4. Code only the acts of the actor, not the recipient of the act. For example, if number 1 says "I think the President should go to Moscow for peace talks," code number 1 in "Answers" (which includes opinions, information, etc.). Remember to keep in mind the original set of categories listed in Fig. 16-1. Take it into the field with you to refresh your memory from time to time. The actual score-keeping for the first few moments of a three-man discussion might look like Fig. 16-5:

Figure 16-5

Modified IPA Chart

A. Social-Emotional Area: Positive	*112*
B. Answers: Neutral	*221/222*
C. Questions: Neutral	*33111*
D. Social-Emotional Area: Negative	*33*

C. Analysis of Your Data

1. For *each* group you observed, develop a group profile:

   A. *Count the total number of acts recorded.*
   B. *Count the total number of acts in each category for the entire group and compute the percentage in each category.*
   C. *Plot the percentage in each category for the group on graph paper.*

V PRESENTING YOUR RESULTS

Include in your report the following:

1. *The number of people in the group(s) you observed, and whether they were friends or strangers.*
2. *Whether you observed the same group or different groups in the three observation periods.*
3. *Whether you had a partner for this assignment.*
4. *Your group profiles (see IV, C above).*
5. *A discussion of your findings.*
   A. *If you observed the same group in interaction on three different occasions, compare the group profiles to see if there was any change in the pattern of interaction. How do you account for the change or stability?*

    *B. If you observed three different groups in interaction, compare
the profiles of these groups with each other. Note any differences you find. How do you account for these differences?*

    *C. If you had a partner, you should compare your results with
his, and discuss in a joint presentation of results why you
think you coded differently (if you did).*

    6. *The problems you encountered in the field. How do you think
they affected your data?*

    7. *Any hypotheses for further investigation that your findings sug-
gest. (You may assume the goals of the group to be mutual exchange of information and/or persuasion to a point of view.)*

Data gathering should be limited to approximately one hour and a half,
which will include the time you need (1) to prepare your coding charts,
(2) to set up your observation situation, and (3) to observe for three fif-
teen-minute periods. Limit your presentation of results to three typewritten pages if you did your IPA observations alone, or to five pages if you
had a partner (in the latter case you are to present your results as a joint
paper). The IPA tallies you made in the field should also be turned in
with your report.

VI SELECTED BIBLIOGRAPHY

A. Methodology

Bales, Robert F.
    1950   Interaction Process Analysis: A Method for the Study of
            Small Groups. Reading, Mass.: Addison-Wesley.
    1952   "Some uniformities of behavior in small social systems."
            Pp. 146–159 in Guy E. Swanson, Theodore M. Newcomb,
            and Eugene L. Hartley (eds.), Readings in Social Psychol-
            ogy. New York: Holt, Rinehart & Winston.
    1953   "The equilibrium problem in small groups." Pp. 111–161 in
            Talcott Parsons, Robert F. Bales, and Edward A. Shils
            (eds.), Working Papers in the Theory of Action. New York:
            Free Press.
Hare, A. Paul, Edgar F. Borgatta, and Robert F. Bales (eds.)
    1955   Small Groups. New York: Knopf.
Mills, Theodore M.
    1967   The Sociology of Small Groups. Englewood Cliffs, N.J.:
            Prentice-Hall.

Riley, Matilda W.
    1963   Sociological Research; A Case Approach. New York: Harcourt, Brace & World.

B. References and Studies

Bales, Robert F.
    1970   Personality and Interpersonal Behavior. New York: Holt, Rinehart, & Winston.
——, and Philip E. Slater
    1955   "Role differentiation in small decision-making groups." Pp. 259–306 in Talcott Parsons, Robert F. Bales et al. (eds.), The Family, Socialization and Interaction Process. New York: Free Press.
Psathas, George
    1960   "Phase movement and equilibrium tendencies in interaction process analysis in psychotherapy groups." Sociometry 23 (June):177–194.
Strodtbeck, Fred L., Rita M. James, and Charles Hawkins
    1957   "Social status in jury deliberations." American Sociological Review 22 (December):713–719.
Strodtbeck, Fred L., and R. D. Mann
    1956   "Sex role differentiation in jury deliberations." Sociometry 19 (March):3–11.
Talland, George A.
    1955   "Task and interaction process: some characteristics of therapeutic group discussion." Journal of Abnormal and Social Psychology 50 (January):105–109.

Part Five

The Summer Project
and Library Assignment

ASSIGNMENT SEVENTEEN

METHOD:

Ethnography

RESEARCH TOPIC:

Small Worlds

I INTRODUCTION

Ethnographic Research, a Definition

Have you ever listened to a speaker describe a situation and suddenly in your mind's eye you were there? You could almost see the people, smell the odors of the locality, and sense the shifting emotions of people as they interacted with each other. Such an experience of vicarious participation may come from reading an unusually vivid book or seeing a very good movie or well-acted play. It can also come from a good piece of ethnographic research. Ethnographic research is an investigator's application of his sociological methods and skills to a specific scene in order to learn enough about its people, situations, and human relationships to be able to present the reader with a slice of social life.

Ethnography is currently enjoying a resurgence among young sociologists. For years it has been a focal point of the continuing controversy between those who wish to fashion the discipline along the lines of the physical sciences, with emphasis on measurement, and those who believe the goal of sociology to be detailed description. The roots of ethnography are part anthropological, part "Chicago School" sociology.

Since the seminal days of their discipline, anthropologists have traveled to remote areas of the world in search of knowledge about human inter-action. They have lived and worked with the inhabitants of these remote places, studying and describing their everyday actions, cultures, and ways of life. An early (1896) definition of ethnography, attributed to A. H. Beattie, is that it is "purely descriptive, dealing with the characteristics, usages, social and political condition of peoples irrespective of their possible physical relations or affinities" (Beattie, 1964). The investigation of the day-to-day interactions of people in a society by one who is un-familiar with it at the outset is at the heart of the ethnographic method. It is his unfamiliarity that helps to explain the otherwise contradictory emphases of ethnographies on the mundane and the exotic, for to him everything is new and unusual. A few of the efforts of anthropologists were, in fact, popularized into movie travelogues complete with pictorial depictions of "strange" sex and marital customs, tribal dances, and other rituals. Older students may remember the narrator who traditionally closed such films with words such as, "And so, with the sun setting slowly in the West we say "Goodbye' to the quaint and romantic Isle of. . . ."

In the 1920's and 1930's the interests of anthropologists began to turn from describing exotic customs to analyzing, with the aid of various theoretical frameworks, just how the various approaches to life's mun-dane exigencies reflect, or are a result of, the basic needs of human groups, of man's personality, or of man as a social creature. Three different schools of inquiry have developed around each of these presumed causal factors: (1) the *functional,* in which various customs are analyzed to see how they maintain the society as a whole; (2) the *psychoanalytic,* in which personality development is viewed as a direct result of various culturally approved ways of weaning, toilet training, and other important childhood events; and (3) the *formal* or *phenomenological,* in which the investigator attempts to locate and describe *forms* of social interaction resulting from *individual* efforts to meet problematic situations. In the latter approach the central focus of the method is reconstruction of the *participants' perspective* on their situations rather than objective judg-ments of the investigator.

Because of the nature of their interests, most anthropologists have confined their studies to relatively small, isolated tribes of people in tech-nologically undeveloped areas. This concentration resulted in two methodological advantages: (1) The societies studied were not so large — either in population or area — as to be fragmented into subsocieties; and (2) the societies were sufficiently isolated from the effects of other groups to have developed unique, almost immutable cultures, presumably grow-ing out of their special situations.

Some sociologists picked up where earlier anthropologists left off. While many of their colleagues were studying rural and small-town, middle-class America, there was a group of "Chicago School" sociologists who focused their interests on the living patterns of large city subsocieties. The exotic people they studied were not primitive but rather deviant— slum dwellers, criminals, bohemians, and newly arrived immigrants from various parts of the world. Rather than studying "pure" societies, untouched by outside influences, these urban sociologists were interested, at least in part, in the impact of these subcultures on each other and on the city culture as a whole. As part of their theoretical framework, this school developed the ecological approach (discussed in detail in Assignment Five) with its concern for spatial and symbiotic patterns of group living. Students of the Chicago School have since expanded their interests beyond neighborhood groupings to life in such settings as mental institutions and prisons. Even more recently, ethnographer-sociologists have transferred their interests from blatantly deviant subsocieties to others that are usually regarded as conformist in the commonly accepted sense of the term, but with their own special cultures. Bars, dance halls, student and church groups are but a few examples of such subsocieties.

The sociological studies of subsocieties mentioned up to now have a geographic base—a location within the city—just as a tribe is located in a certain valley on a remote Pacific Island. But because sociologist-ethnographers often want to show the effects that one social world has on another, some of them became interested in studying ongoing subsocieties composed of individuals, without definable territories in the city, but with common norms, values, and interactional expectations. Such subsocieties are called *behavior systems.*

A behavior system is best described as composed of a group of people who share a unique subculture. This means that the members of the group have a similar outlook on life and can anticipate the general behavior patterns of the others without an intimate personal knowledge of each other. (This is, of course, one of the characteristics of socialized persons in any culture or subculture.) When such persons interact, they do so as an integrated unit, based on identification with each other. Because they compose a highly specialized subculture (often growing out of an occupation or avocation) members of behavior systems usually develop unique ways of communicating with one another, and not infrequently they employ a specialized language (see Sutherland and Cressy, 1960; Hollingshead, 1939). Criminals, artists, and people in various professions are but a few examples of behavior systems.

Sociologists who study behavior systems parallel anthropologists in their pursuit of the everyday lives of people whose small, special societies or subcultures are out of the ordinary by middle-class standards. Both disciplines are concerned with the universals of human interaction and human group life. However, like the urban sociologists (and unlike most anthropologists) those who study behavior systems are interested in inter-action between these small worlds and the larger culture.

At this point you might well ask what the difference is between a com-munity study and a "small world" ethnography. There are many similar-ities, since the focal point of both is a small society that has maintained regularized interactions over time. There are also some differences, not formalized by any means, between what is usually called a community study and what is usually called an ethnography. Community studies are first of all about communities—either small towns or neighborhoods within large towns—located within a specific geographic territory (see Assignment Nine). Communities usually are a larger unit (in terms of the number of people) than the behavior system and can, in fact, contain many such behavior systems. (One way of organizing data about a com-munity would be in terms of its behavior systems and their interrela-tionships.)

Community studies conducted by sociologists have, for the most part, focused on describing the community objectively rather than on appre-hending the perspectives of the inhabitants. Often the community under study is compared, either implicitly or explicitly, with the larger society or other communities. Rarely is its interaction with the society around it con-sidered; instead it is usually seen as a self-contained unit, with the emphasis on demographic variables, the role constellation of officials, power and its distribution, and the social class system and its conse-quences for life styles within the community. Ethnographic data—that is, in the modern sense—are rarely considered in a community study. There have been some outstanding exceptions to this, of course—*Street Corner Society* by William F. Whyte (1966) and *Tally's Corner* by Elliot Liebow (1967).

How an Ethnography Is Conducted

In contrast to such methods as survey research, Interaction Process Analysis, and other approaches that attempt to answer specific questions about social phenomena, an ethnography focuses on a *whole* social sub-unit as seen from the point of view of participants. This is the important distinguishing feature of this method, which by its very nature provides the investigator with a directive for the breadth of data to gather and the type of analysis to pursue. For instance, it means that in the study of an entire small society the data-gathering process is not completed until the investigator knows how the various participants interact with and view each other, how they learn things necessary for survival, how they were recruited to the system, and so on. Each part of an analysis must mesh with, and not contradict, the other parts, for the interest is in the whole picture and not isolated phenomena.

As to specific techniques of data gathering and analysis, there is no real agreement on the best way to apprehend and describe the perspectives of persons in a small world. This leaves the sociologist somewhat free to experiment and, occasionally, to flounder. Perhaps the best advice a beginner could get would be in the form of a discussion of ways of *locating* such necessary data as normative understandings, regularized relationships, and socialization techniques, followed by suggestions concerning methods of collecting and analyzing the data.

First of all, because he realizes that he is looking for the taken-for-granted activities of a small, specialized world, the ethnographer tries to view the culture and structure of that world as a stranger would, noticing the "strange customs" and trying to place them in the overall scheme of living there. Many investigators have found that one of their most fruitful approaches to data gathering is to find out how the society's participants get through an average day, week, month, or year—how they meet life's mundane needs, form everyday social understandings, etc. Both the definitions of needs and the strategies used to meet these problems must always be seen from the *perspective of the participant himself.*

Initiation rites and socialization activities in general are excellent ways of apprehending the perspective of a society's regular inhabitants. How are new members socialized to these small worlds? It is helpful to see if there are ways of socialization in this new world parallel to ways in worlds with which the investigator is familiar. Sororities and fraternities are not the only modern urban associations to have initiation rites. Policemen, prison inmates, soldiers, and some office gangs have individualized, customary induction procedures for novitiates. All social groups have ways of teaching a newcomer his place. Watch how people are sanctioned or expelled. Be alert for other situations that give clues to acceptable interactional boundaries in this world, because it is the ethnographer's task to recognize and describe these rites. Participants often go to great lengths to spell out their expectations at such times; in doing so they reveal their unique world view.

Almost all societies develop a division of labor. Ethnographers of small worlds are interested in the informal divisions of labor that spring up as solutions to the very special problems of existence in these worlds. Symbiotic relationships—in which two members use each other for some private reason—are also well worth investigating. Cliques within such societies are especially important, as they often point the way to various special value clusters.

Watch for leaders. Attempt to ascertain the qualities they have that endow them with authority in this small world. Leadership is a clue to desirable qualities of the culture. The interaction of persons in leadership roles with each other and with the rank and file can also be revealing. Attend all ceremonies and other important events — weddings, funerals, store openings, awards presentations. These special situations offer insights into both the culture and structure of the subsociety. Watch for emergencies. Reactions to emergencies tell an investigator many things about the structure and culture of the world, especially in terms of who or what is important or expendable, who has ultimate power and authority, and so on.

Be alert for "social types" — special kinds of persons found only in this special world. Find out what they are called by other participants. In Sykes' *The Society of Captives* (1965), such social types as the "merchant," the "ballbuster," and "the wolf" were explained from the viewpoint of inmate-participants in that society. The explication of these social types gave the investigator great insight into the informal social structure of the prison.

Ecological pressures are also important. The barriers to passage and the limitations on social intercourse or privacy that result from these physical structures are important influences on the perspectives of the people involved. For instance, in a study of bar behavior, the investigator found the placement of stools and booths affected social interaction (Cavan, 1966).

Another fruitful approach for an ethnographic investigator is to assemble career patterns of inhabitants or, in the case of behavior systems, participants. This is analogous to the life-cycle approach of anthropologists. For instance, what is the usual career of a felon? The Skid Row drunk? A girl singer with a dance band? Where do they start, where do they go, and how do their careers usually end? Julius A. Roth devoted his study of tuberculosis patients to this careers-through-time concept (Roth, 1963). Apprehending the general "atmosphere" — that is, the preponderance of collective symbolic meanings in the subworld — is also important. Is there an atmosphere of trust, distrust, fear, hostility, celebration, industriousness, accomplishment, or hopelessness? How are these meanings communicated? Such data would add a great deal to understanding a small world.

Now that we have discussed ways of ferreting out ethnographic data, let's move on to data collection and analysis. Observation and participant observation (Assignments One and Three) are the methods of data collection used most often by professional ethnographers. Certainly the goals of such a study — ascertaining the total behavior system — makes observing actual social interaction imperative. Some ethnographers feel that observation is the *only* worthwhile approach. Others feel, however, that any approach that aids in getting data needed to complete the picture is worth using. Such people often also use depth interviews (Assignment Two), case histories (Assignment Six), and role analyses (Assignment Seven) to construct the participants' perspective.

Well-informed persons (officials, gossips, and just plain know-it-alls) are often interviewed for the amazing amount of "inside dope" they can give a sociologist. Their statements must be checked for both exaggeration and, sometimes, pure fabrication, but these people can truly be gold mines of information and therefore worth interviewing at length. Some ethnographers also use content analysis (Assignment Nine) in an attempt to get at subjects' perspectives indirectly. The sermons delivered by prison chaplains to inmates or by mission personnel to alcoholics, for instance, reveal much about the type of men they consider their congregations to be (Wiseman, 1970). Letters, diaries, and other written documents, such as case histories by social control agents, can often reveal the shared perspective and symbolic meanings of inhabitants in the small world. The same is true, of course, of group conversations about key topics in the participants' world.

Ordinary people are involved in partial ethnographic investigations more often than in other kinds of sociological research. They must constantly try to understand the day-to-day activities of persons in the sub-societies of which they are a part (for example, occupational or training settings), and they must also try to apprehend the perspectives that *others* have about these interactions. They use both observations and informal questioning (not unlike depth interviewing) to increase their knowledge. People engage in these ethnographic investigations because they know they must learn the ropes and who's who well enough to get through the day without making a major blunder. A social fool is a poor amateur ethnographer.

The professional is more careful in his investigation than the layman. He is also more thorough, in that he goes beyond what the amateur needs to know in order to get by. Additionally, he is more systematic, in that he takes more time to verify his results and later to apply sociological concepts to his data to make them more understandable.

How does the investigator know when he has done a good job? He can ask himself, as he analyzes his data, if the pieces fit together into a coherent description of most of the action in the small world he is studying. Through his data and analysis, he can try to account for the existence, values, and meanings of minority as well as majority activities. A pragmatic test is also possible: Could a person who has read the analysis successfully enter and live as part of the world described in the analysis by following the "directions"—that is, the descriptions of norms, values, symbolic meanings, relationships, and interactions—contained in the analysis?

Advantages and Disadvantages

Like the cross-cultural studies of faraway tribes, local ethnographies of small, specialized worlds aid the sociologist (1) by expanding the applicability of his analytic concepts to various situations; and (2) by simultaneously revealing to him how various social forms are modified in different types of environments. Any study of the perspectives of others also helps the sociologist to see how truly relative the normative and non-normative are from culture to culture. This, too, aids him in seeing how important understanding a specific situation is to understanding motivation for action. The ethnography is an especially useful approach for locating social explanations of phenomena previously approached by psychologists primarily in terms of personality characteristics and pathologies that might better be viewed as deviations from middle-class behavior norms.

There are many disadvantages to ethnographies as well. One of the most serious is the difficulty of verifying findings or the replication (repetition) of the study. There is no systematic method by which to check the quality or adequacy of data from interviews or observations. Observers and participant observers often work themselves into a position in a small world so unique that they may develop a special view of it, making their findings somewhat difficult for a second investigator to replicate. One way to increase the validity of findings and conclusions is to show written analyses to the inhabitants themselves and get *their reaction* to these descriptions of the world they know so well.

Detractors of the ethnographic approach also complain about its lack of scientific rigor. Certainly, when worlds under study are often unfamiliar to the investigator, sociological insights gained through *verstehen* (insightful hunches) are questionable. The absence of careful sampling, statistical tests of significance, and other efforts to make data more "scientific" is deplored by many sociologists.

Some Applications

As we mentioned earlier, ethnographic studies have been made of prisons (Sykes, 1965, and Irwin, 1970); the mental hospital (Goffman, 1961); the emergency room of a hospital (Sudnow, 1967); hippies (Yablonsky, 1968), the police (Skolnick, 1966, and Sudnow, 1965); slums and ghettoes (Whyte, 1966, and Liebow, 1967); Skid Row alcoholics (Wallace, 1965, and Wiseman, 1970); and homosexual bars (Cavan, 1963). In all of these studies the investigators attempted to (1) describe the day-to-day social interactions and relationships — the cultures of these unique worlds — and (2) to communicate the perspective of the *actor — not* the investigator's idea of the actor's world to the reader.

Many of these studies have had a profound effect on the institutions studied, although that was not their purpose. Erving Goffman's *Asylums,* for example, has had a great impact on the administration of mental institutions and even on other total institutions such as prisons.

II SMALL WORLDS AS A SUBJECT FOR ETHNOGRAPHIC RESEARCH

Theoretically any setting or behavior system that offers a self-contained subsociety would be amenable to an ethnography, but in practice the most insightful research based on this approach has been of worlds that were foreign to the investigator. Thus the emphasis has been on deviant, unusual, or unique settings. In these worlds the investigator is usually a stranger and therefore more likely to be sensitized to all the interactions that seem mundane to participants. Successful ethnographies of the family, school, place of work, and other areas with which the sociologist is familiar are possible, of course, if the sociologist approaches with *the mental set of an outsider.* This means that phenomena must be "made strange" so as to constantly demand investigation and explanation.

For the beginner, the major research choice is between a geographic area such as a special type of work area and a behavior system without a physical locale. Examples of the former are the emergency ward of a hospital (or any other portion of hospital life), airports, post offices, a newsstand in the middle of a large city, a pornographic magazine stand, a neighborhood bar catering to the same clientele nightly, a florist shop, a beauty shop, a library, a high-powered advertising agency, a pick-up bar, an exclusive shop for ladies, and so on. Examples of behavior systems include beauty queens and their entourages, rodeo performers, homosexuals, airline hostesses, clubs of "singles," movie stars and their circle of directors, make-up men, the pimp-prostitute-taximan-customer-police behavior system, and many others.

III PROJECT ASSIGNMENT

You are to choose as a semester report some small world that appeals to you and to which you have reason to believe you can gain access for long periods of time. Do not select a world so familiar that its culture and structure are not somewhat "strange" to you. Your choice need not be a deviant world, but it should be unusual enough that it has not been the object of repeated studies. If you wish, you may join forces with another student. This is often helpful in terms of covering all the scenes of interaction, interviewing, and having someone to check the validity of insightful hunches.

A good ethnography takes a great deal of time and hard work. Data are not only accumulated slowly but are also constantly being revised in the light of new findings. A glance at the methodologies of some of the ethnographies in the bibliography will testify to this. Therefore do not select a small world that presents unusual problems regarding access, the availability of participants for observation or interviewing, complexity of some social structure, or other time-consuming difficulties.

IV STEPS FOR THE ETHNOGRAPHIC ASSIGNMENT

A. Before You Go into the Field

1. Decide on the small world you wish to study. Consider the amenability of its people and activities to observation, participant observation, and/or depth interviewing. (If you are planning to study an institution where official permission is needed, get your professor to write a letter on your behalf.)
2. Decide what you need to know, *at the very minimum,* to understand this world. Think about the various ways open to you to obtain data.
3. Keep in mind that ethnographic sociology is "played by ear," that is, as findings are made, new approaches to follow them up must be considered. Therefore too much advance planning tends to be a waste of time. Some ethnographers even suggest that the investigator assiduously avoid reading other related studies so as not to be influenced by them! Others feel that no usable field work can be done without a theoretical orientation of some sort to guide

collection of the data. (The symbolic interactionist framework (Blumer, 1962) is often recommended here.)

4. Plan on some way of keeping notes of field data. Participant observers must find a means of getting to a private place from time to time to write down observations. (The bathroom is one logical place. So is your car.)

B. In the Field

1. Just get started. Watch, participate, interview. Take voluminous notes. Do not try to focus your attention on any one thing too early in the investigation. Just try to understand the lives of people as they interact in this small world.

2. Remember that your physical appearance in the field should be such that you *blend* with the field. Dress and act in keeping with the expectations of your setting at all times.

3. Review your notes daily in private. Write down any conclusions you may have reached about interrelationships, socialization procedures, criteria for a well-socialized individual, norms, or anything else of sociological significance. *Initial all your conclusions* in your notes so you won't later mistake them for *findings or quotations from others!*

4. Take verbatim notes of conversations and depth interviews. (A tape recorder is an assistance if you can pay someone to transcribe the tapes; otherwise, this is too time consuming (about two and a half to three times recording time for the average student typist). It is better to learn to take fast but readable notes.

5. Watch for emerging patterns of interaction and their possible effects on participants' definitions of their situations.

6. Keep alert for important findings or concepts that seem to give you unusual insight into the subsociety you are investigating (see Becker and Geer, 1960, 267–289). These significant findings (significant because they have great effect on the entire small world) often give structure and guidance to both data collection and analysis of findings.

C. Analysis of Your Data

You will have a great deal of data before you have been in the field long. From the experiences of others come some ideas for handling it:

1. Start writing the report well before you have finished collecting data. Writing helps to organize the material and also points up the data that still needs to be collected in order for you to have a cogent analysis.
2. Put various interaction descriptions and quotations concerning the same subject on five-by-seven cards so that you can sort data into subject categories.
3. Formulate hunches about why people are acting as they do. Rethink these in terms of general sociological theories of society and accompanying concepts. Then note whether these general theories have been modified by actual activities in this world.
4. Other data organizing aids include:

   A. *Working your way (via descriptions) through the power structure of the world from top to bottom or vice versa.*
   B. *Depicting events in time sequence.*
   C. *Contrasting various scenes concerned with either the same phenomena or the same people.*
   D. *Reading other ethnographies and noting how they handled their analyses (see Bibliography).*

5. Present *evidence* for all major and most minor findings. In the survey research approach the evidence is the percentage of respondents who say or do one thing or another. In ethnographies the evidence is your recounting of incidents and quotations of conversations and interviews. Such latter evidence is usually presented indented and single-spaced in the report. (See "General Instructions for the Student," or look at some of the ethnographies listed in the bibliography for ideas on the form of presenting evidence.)

V PRESENTING YOUR RESULTS

Unlike previous studies, you are not limited in either time or space in the presentation of this report (although a thirty-page maximum might be suggested). Your report should contain the following:

   1. *The type of small world you studied.*
   2. *Why you selected it — that is, what you expected to find there of* sociological *importance.*

3. Your detailed descriptive analysis of this world. Interwoven in this description will be the presentation of the evidence *from your data for your conclusions.*

4. A discussion of sociologically relevant theoretical and conceptual developments emerging from this study. What theories or concepts seem to have been developed? How have existing theories or concepts been modified? (Such references should be footnoted in the proper form.) This is what differentiates ethnography from sheer journalism.

5. Summary and conclusions.

This undertaking will probably take an entire semester or summer of field research and writing. It should be, for the student interested in sociology, time most memorably spent. All reports should be typewritten.

VI   SELECTED BIBLIOGRAPHY

A.   General Discussion of Ethnographic Methods

Abel, Theodore
    1948   "The operation called *verstehen*." American Journal of Sociology 54 (November):211–217.
Adams, R. N., and J. T. Preiss (eds.)
    1960   Human Organization Research. Homewood, Ill.: Dorsey.
Back, Kurt
    1960   "The well-informed informant." Pp. 179–187 in R. N. Adams and J. T. Preiss (eds.), Human Organization Research. Homewood, Ill.: Dorsey.
Beattie, A. H.
    1964   "Ethnology." Gould and Kolb (eds.), A Dictionary of the Social Sciences. New York: Free Press.
Becker, Howard S., and Blanche Geer
    1964   "Participation observation: the analysis of qualitative field data." Pp. 267–289 in R. N. Adams and J. T. Preiss (eds.), Human Organization Research. Homewood, Ill.: Dorsey.
Blumer, Herbert
    1962   "Society as symbolic interaction." Pp. 179–192 in Arnold Rose (ed.), Human Behavior and the Social Processes. Boston: Houghton Mifflin.

Bruyn, Severyn T.
 1966 The Human Perspective in Sociology. Englewood Cliffs, N.J.: Prentice-Hall.
Cicourel, Aaron V.
 1964 Methods and Measurement in Social Sciences. New York: Free Press.
 1967 The Social Organization of Juvenile Justice. New York: Wiley.
Frake, Charles O.
 1964 "How to ask for a drink in Subanun." Pp. 127–132 in Gumpertz and D. Hymes (eds.), The American Anthropologist: The Ethnography of Communication 66 (December):127–132.
Garfinkel, Harold
 1967 Studies in Ethnomethodology. Englewood Cliffs, N.J.: Prentice-Hall.
Glaser, Barney G., and Anselm L. Strauss
 1965 "Discovery of substantive theory: a basic strategy underlying qualitative research." American Behavioral Scientist 8 (February):5–12.
 1967 The Discovery of Grounded Theory. Chicago: Aldine.
Hollingshead, A. B.
 1939 "Behavior systems as a field for research," American Sociological Review 4 (December):816–822.
McCall, George J., and J. L. Simmons
 1967 Issues in Participant Observation. Reading, Mass.: Addison-Wesley.
Merton, Robert K., and Patricia Kendall
 1946 "The focused interview." American Journal of Sociology 51: 541–557.
Schultz, Alfred
 1944 "The stranger." American Journal of Sociology 50 (May): 369–376.
Whyte, William F.
 1966 Street Corner Society. Chicago: University of Chicago Press.

B. Modern-Day Ethnographies

Cavan, Sherri
 1963 "Interaction in home territories." Berkeley Journal of Sociology 8:17–32.

1966   Liquor License: An Ethnography of Bar Behavior. Chicago: Aldine.

Coser, Rose L.
1962   Life on the Ward. East Lansing, Mich.: Michigan University Press.

Finestone, Harold
1964   "Kicks, cats, and color." Pp. 281–297 in Howard S. Becker (ed.), The Other Side. New York: Free Press.

Giallombardo, Rose
1966   Society of Women. New York: Wiley.

Goffman, Erving
1961   Asylums. Garden City, N. Y.: Doubleday.

Irwin, John
1970   The Felon. Englewood Cliffs, N.J.: Prentice-Hall.

Liebow, Elliot
1967   Tally's Corner. Boston: Little, Brown.

Love, Edmund G.
1956   Subways Are for Sleeping. New York: Harcourt, Brace & World.

Roth, Julius A.
1963   Timetables. Indianapolis, Ind.: Bobbs-Merrill.

Scheff, Thomas J.
1965   "Typification in diagnostic practices of rehabilitation agencies." Pp. 139–147 in Marvin B. Sussman (ed.), Sociology and Rehabilitation. Washington: American Sociological Association.

Scott, Marvin B.
1963   "A note on the place of truth." Berkeley Journal of Sociology 8:33–39.
1968   The Racing Game. Chicago: Aldine.

Skolnick, Jerome H.
1966   Justice Without Trial. New York: Wiley.

Sudnow, David
1965   "Normal crimes." Social Problems 12 (Winter):255–276.
1967   Passing On. Englewood Cliffs, N.J.: Prentice-Hall.

Sutherland, Edwin H., and Donald R. Cressey
1960   "Behavior systems in crime." Principles of Criminology. Philadelphia: Lippincott. (Chap. 13, pp. 237–250.)

Sykes, Graham M.
1965   The Society of Captives. New York: Atheneum.

Wallace, Samuel E.
1965   Skid Row as a Way of Life. Totawa, N.J.: Bedminster.

Werthman, Carl
    1963   "Delinquents in school: a test for the legitimacy of author-
            ity." Berkeley Journal of Sociology 8:39–60.
Wesley, William A.
    1964   "Violence and the police." Pp. 318–324 in R. W. O'Brien,
            C. C. Schrag, and W. T. Martin (eds.), Readings in General
            Sociology. Boston: Houghton Mifflin.
Wiseman, Jacqueline P.
    1970   Stations of the Lost. Englewood Cliffs, N.J.: Prentice-Hall.
Yablonsky, Lewis
    1968   The Hippie Trip: A Firsthand Account of the Beliefs and
            Behaviors of Hippies in America. New York: Pegasus.

ASSIGNMENT EIGHTEEN

METHOD:

Library Project

TOPIC:

Examination of Sociological Concepts and Hypotheses

I INTRODUCTION

The final assignment in this manual is the library project. Library research is not least in importance for the scientific investigator. The professional sociologist spends several weeks or months in the library researching his topic before he finally ventures into the field to collect his data. He tries to familiarize himself with the present state of knowledge in the subject of his interest. From the clues offered by past research, he develops testable hypotheses within a theoretical framework that is current in his field and acceptable to him. Often he refines his concepts and decides on operational definitions for them from the guidance provided by the work of others, and he becomes aware of methodological possibilities and problems by seeing how others have tackled similar research.

You will not be doing library research in a subject area for this assignment, however essential this phase of scientific investigation is for an adequate study in any field of knowledge. Instead, we want to introduce you more formally and explicitly to the sociological ideas that you have been using as project director of your miniprojects. We want you to become familiar with how practicing sociologists use theory to develop their hypotheses and concepts, and how they operationalize their concepts. First it is necessary to explain some of these terms.

Concepts

There is nothing strange, mysterious, or difficult about the term *concept*. Our language is composed of mutually understood concepts, and we use them every day in our ordinary speech. According to Webster's dictionary, a *concept* is *a generalized term for a class of objects,* an abstraction from "reality" that allows us to refer to reality. Concepts organize and categorize our world for us, and enable us to "see" and understand the empirical world around us. When we use the concept "tree," we are referring to "trees" in general. We all know and understand what is meant by this term even though each of us may have a picture in his head of a different kind of tree. A "pine tree" is a more specific concept, referring to all varieties of pine trees, and it narrows the focus so that each of us now thinks of a certain type of evergreen, though again each of us may "see" a different sort—Japanese pine, sugar pine, and so on. Furthermore for the professional forester or tree surgeon, there are a cluster of other concepts, more technical in nature, that go with the concept "tree" and expand its usefulness.

The sociologist uses concepts to aid him in referring to various aspects of human group life by categories; his concepts are more technical than those used by laymen and aid in the interrelationship of a wide range of social phenomena. To the average citizen, for example, *bureaucracy* refers to a government agency that is noted for bungling and red tape, but to the social scientist (and the sociology student) *bureaucracy* refers to a social structure with a division of labor established to accomplish special purposes. Universities, military organizations, factories, and the American League baseball teams are all bureaucracies, since they all have similar organizational characteristics. Sometimes the scientist's concepts eventually become a part of the layman's vocabulary. When this happens, the average citizen will also "see" details approximating the scientific, because his physical or social world has been reconceptualized for him.

In the foregoing exercises you worked with various sociological concepts such as socialization, primary groups, interaction, stereotypes, and so on. Each of these concepts was related to a family of other concepts that you found useful for your study. For instance, the concept *socialization* is related to positive and negative sanctions, peer group pressure, group acceptance or rejection, and so on.

The scientific concept is usually used more *precisely* than concepts that are used in the lay world. In chemistry, for instance, the elements composing a compound are specified by symbols—water is H_2O. This signifies a definition acceptable to all scientific workers in the field. The social scientist also tries to be extremely careful in specifying exactly what he means when he uses concepts such as role, status, culture, society, and deviant behavior. He too must specify what a concept includes and what it excludes. For instance, Max Weber, a famous German sociologist of the early twentieth century, outlined the major characteristics of an ideal or pure type of bureaucracy as including: (1) carefully defined positions or offices; (2) a hierarchical order with clear-cut lines of authority and responsibility; (3) selection of personnel on the basis of technical or professional qualifications; (4) rules and regulations governing official action; and (5) security of tenure and the possibility of a career by promotion in the hierarchy (Bendix, 1960). Sociology as a science has not yet reached the point where there is universal agreement about the components of certain basic concepts. Thus Weber's definition of the components of the concept of bureaucracy, unlike the acceptance of H_2O as water, has frequently been challenged.

An "Operational Definition" of a Concept

Even though the sociologist is careful to give definitions to concepts that will be useful to his investigation, he still has the problem of *locating* the phenomena he wants to study in the real world. How does the sociologist collect data on such concepts as social class, aggressive behavior, juvenile delinquency, sibling rivalry, or upward mobility? People do not go about with a label on them saying "upper class" or "lower class," nor are the boundaries of an area with urban blight so marked. Nevertheless, arbitrary decisions to demarcate these social phenomena must be made before they can be studied effectively. To investigate such complex concepts, the researcher must set forth the criteria by which he selects or rejects what might be instances of the phenomenon. The technical term for this process is to *operationalize the concepts:* making abstract ideas operable or usable, in this case for the specific purpose of researching them.

For instance, what would a sociologist consider an example, case, or instance of the concept *juvenile delinquent?* First, he has to be absolutely clear what he means by the term "juvenile." What age group is he talking about? From 12 to 18? Or 13 to 20? Or 16 to 21? He must specify the acceptable limits and then explain why he chose these limits for his particular study. The next problem is: What is he going to consider delinquent behavior? Should he count only those acts defined in the laws as felonies — major crimes such as murder, arson, robbery, rape, drug addiction, and so on? Or will he include misdemeanors as well — minor offenses such as truancy, intoxication, and malicious mischief? Finally, does a youngster have to have been arrested to be called a delinquent? Sent to Juvenile Hall? How many acts does he have to commit to become a hard case? Only after he has made these decisions can the sociologist go into the field and collect cases of the phenomenon he is studying.

Theories and Hypotheses

In a strict sense, a *theory* is the *formulation of apparent and at least partially verified relationships between certain observed phenomena.* Because verification is accomplished through empirical investigation a theory is not merely a "free flight of fancy." We rely on theory, either implicitly or explicitly, to understand the world. The nonprofessional in any subject area still has ideas about it. For example, a common-sense theory of human behavior is that it is "human nature" for man to be competitive and acquisitive. This common-sense theory, based on an accumulation of folk experience in the Western world, produces a way of understanding human actions from a particular point of view or perspective. Unlike scientific theories, however, rigorous, controlled observations have not been made to determine when, where, and under what circumstances the theory is true.

If concepts *categorize* the world, theory *orders* or *structures* these categories, expertly or crudely, to help *explain* relationships between them. In so doing, theory supplies guideposts for the scientist (or layman) about what he should look for in the physical, biological, and social worlds. Of course in pointing to what he should look for, theory tends to limit the investigator's vision as well, because by having a certain theoretical frame of reference, the scientist may overlook other explanations of relationships among phenomena. No scientific theory is static, however, because science is an ongoing enterprise in which others check and challenge both findings and the theory that inspired them.

Since theories are general statements about relationships in the world, they are too gross to be tested or confirmed all in one piece. *Hypotheses,* derived from theories, provide the more manageable links that connect the abstract theory with the empirical world. Through their use, bits and pieces of information that affirm, modify, or reject portions of that theory are discovered much as trial and error assures that the pieces of a jig-saw puzzle correctly put together results in a completed picture.

Hypotheses are hunches or educated guesses that make a statement about some kind of relationship between phenomena—an "if . . . then" statement. Not all investigations are *direct tests* of hypotheses, however; studies have other uses. As you noted when you were doing the foregoing assignments, some investigations have the more limited purpose of *de-*

scribing social phenomena. This does not mean that there is no under-lying hypothesis, however, for without one the investigator would lack guidance concerning what types of descriptive data would be useful for him to gather. In such cases the hypothesis is *implied* by the type of data gathered and the way it is handled.

In both the above ways of using a hypothesis, induction and deduction * are important. Sociologists and laymen alike use inductive and deductive logic. Often both are used in a single study, and the investigator works back and forth between the two.

For instance, the experienced sociologist, who has a theoretical frame-work to draw upon, may *deduce* a hypothesis from the theory and test it. If his hypothesis is proved or verified, then he can place greater credence on the explanatory power of the theory. Perhaps the sociologist will use the theoretical framework of *symbolic interaction,* with its emphasis upon the *symbol-making* capacity of man (Blumer, 1962). From this perspec-tive, what differentiates man from other animals, what makes him human, in his ability to create symbols and then respond to them. Using this theory the sociologist can hypothesize that *if* any human being were isolated so that he cannot learn to use a language, he would be lacking in human qualities. Not only would he be unable to speak intelligibly, he would also be unable to interact with others in any meaningful way. His behavior would be bizarre and irrational, or limited to those actions animals are able to perform. The sociologist could try to test or prove this hypothesis by locating individuals who have suffered such deprivation and noting their behavior patterns. He also would be careful to note those cases that did not confirm his hypothesis (Davis, 1947).

Whereas deduction consists of reasoning from the general to the spe-cific, induction goes in the opposite direction. The layman and the scien-tist have to make an imaginative leap from particular, specific observa-tions to a more general statement—to the beginnings or elaboration of a theory. For example, a young man may be successful in an attempt to se-duce a girl after several previous tries with other girls have failed. In try-ing to gain some generalized knowledge of the art of seduction (applicable to other similar cases), he will no doubt think over how he handled each attempt and what each girl was like, so far as he was concerned. He might hypothesize that *if* he does such-and-such, *then* she will succumb. If his hypothesis proves to be true, then he may fit it together with other pieces of data he has concerning his former actions and evolve a general theory

---

* Deduction is the application of some general premise or theory about social relations to various specific cases in order to understand them better. *Induction* is the pulling together of a number of isolated facts or individual cases that are probably all examples of the same phenomenon and arriving at some general conclusion about their meaning. For discussions of the interrelationship between inductive and deductive reasoning in research, see Glaser and Strauss (1965) and Nash (1966).

of seduction for use in future field operations. This will continue until he gets his face slapped; then he must fall back and refine his theory further.

The sociologist is more likely to be able to make a productive leap from the particular to the general than the layman, because the sociologist has a more precise theoretical framework in which to fit his data. For example, the sociologist who approaches his data from a functionalist perspective is apt to view persistent social phenomena as in some way useful to the ongoing social system. If he collects evidence that workers on a job do not always obtain their supervisor's permission to alter the sequence of the work, he will probably interpret these actions as functional to the social system of the occupational setting, because the work process is not slowed down by unnecessary interruptions.

The Relationship of Concepts to Theories and Hypotheses

It is probably obvious to you by now that theories and hypotheses are made up of clusters of related concepts. As we noted before, the investigator must define his concepts not only in *general* terms (the formal definition), but also in *operational* terms (what he is going to count as instances of the concept when he is investigating it in the field). The hypothesis, which in turn is deduced from theory or creates new concepts and theory, gives direction to the way the research is conducted — what relationships will be looked for, examined, and analyzed. The method or technique used to collect data will depend on the questions and the problem to be solved.

II JOURNAL ARTICLES AS SOURCES OF CONCEPTS AND HYPOTHESES

A very good way for the student to get a better understanding of how sociologists use and operationalize concepts and formulate hypotheses is not only to work in the field, as you have done for these project assignments, but also to look at the work of professionals. Like beginning singers who listen to the recordings of the old pros in order to get hints on phrasing, breathing, and tonal quality, neophyte sociologists can gain a great deal of insight into their chosen field by a critical reading of published research.

The research findings reported in professional sociological journals provide excellent examples of both concepts and hypotheses being used to test and develop theory or guide descriptive studies. The advantages of using journal articles for this purpose are many: the articles are fairly short and thus can be quickly perused for this information; journals from which to choose are numerous; and the student-sociologist has the opportunity to read professional versions of the type of research he has been doing rather than the predigested results offered in so many textbooks. Some of the journals in the field of sociology are:

> *American Behavioral Scientist*
> *American Catholic Sociological Review*
> *American Journal of Sociology*
> *American Sociological Review*
> *Annals of the American Academy of Political and Social Science*
> *British Journal of Sociology*
> *Human Organization*
> *Human Relations*
> *International Social Science Journal*
> *Journal of Marriage and Family Living*
> *Journal of Social Issues*
> *Journal of Social Psychology*
> *Merrill-Palmer Quarterly*
> *Pacific Sociological Review*
> *Population Review*
> *Social Forces*
> *Social Problems*
> *Sociology of Education*
> *Sociology and Social Research*
> *Sociological Inquiry*
> *Sociological Quarterly*
> *Sociometry*
> *Southwestern Social Science Quarterly*

As you peruse the journals you will also begin to develop a critical eye for well-explained hypotheses and well-operationalized concepts. You will discover too that, unfortunately, not all sociologists report their hypotheses and related concepts in a clear and understandable way. On the contrary, a disappointingly large proportion are careless about enlightening their readers about just what they are up to. These unfortunate lapses in scientific reporting can be educational in their own way, for they sharpen one's ability to tell good research procedures from sloppy ones. Soon you will be able to tell the difference between a well-thought-out study and one that is vaguely planned and carelessly executed.

III PROJECT ASSIGNMENT

In this assignment you are to examine current or back issues of *two* sociological journals for *two* examples of hypotheses used in connection with a field investigation. The hypotheses you select may be either of the type that is being tested or the type that is an implied guide to the collection of descriptive data. The field investigations in the articles may be any two of the many types described in this text. From each hypothesis you are to select one concept and discuss how the investigator defined it in both formal and operational terms. (Be aware that not all journal articles are concerned with field investigations. Some are discussions of theory or of the work of other sociologists. Where abstracts of articles are available, a glance at these often tells whether or not the article is a research report.) Additionally, using your own ideas about human group life, think of a problem that interests you and devise a hypothesis that presumably could be tested or used to investigate some phenomenon. Discuss how you would operationalize one of the concepts pertinent to your hypothesis. This makes three sets of hypotheses and concepts in all.

IV PRESENTING YOUR RESULTS

Restrict yourself to one typewritten page per hypothesis, related concept, and discussion. Do *not* attempt to summarize the article or report the findings as that is not part of the assignment. For each page include the following:

1. *The name of the author, year, article, journal, issue, page, in proper bibliographical style. (Put your own contribution on p. 3 and label it as such.) Fictitious example:*
   Jones, John J.
        1970   "Reference group identification." American Sociological Review 50 (January):159–169.
2. *A brief summary of the research problem and the hypothesis discussed in the article. One or two sentences will do. Examples:*
      Jones is attempting to test the hypothesis *that the identification of delinquent boys with their gang is much stronger than the identification of nondelinquent boys with their friendship groups.*
   Or:

Jones is attempting to describe *the characteristics of the delinquent boy's reference group as compared to that of the nondelinquent boy. Implied by the data gathered is the hypothesis that age, sex, social class, grades received in school, car ownership, and participation in school activities are important to such a description.*

3. *A key concept used in the hypothesis. Give the following information about this concept:*

    A. *Its definition. Example:*

        Identification *is defined by Jones as* the feeling that one's identity is connected with another person or object.

    B. *How the concept was operationalized so that the researcher could find actual cases of the concept to study. Example:* Jones operationalized identification *as the reported feelings of having one's own destiny or reputation bound up with the destiny or reputation of another. He used a questionnaire to get this information.*

4. *A brief assessment of the operationalized concept in terms of the ease with which an investigator could find instances, cases, or examples of it. How vague is the researcher? Imagine yourself using his directions to locate ten cases — would it be easy or difficult in terms of knowing which cases do or do not represent the concept and so should be accepted or rejected?*

V BIBLIOGRAPHY

Ackoff, Russell L.
    1965   The Design of Social Research. Chicago: University of Chicago Press.

Bendix, Reinhard
    1960   Max Weber: An Intellectual Portrait. Garden City, N.Y.: Doubleday (especially pp. 418–425).

Blumer, Herbert
    1962   "Society as symbolic interaction." Pp. 179–192 in Arnold Rose (ed.), Human Behavior and the Social Processes. Boston: Houghton Mifflin.

Conant, James B.
    1953   Modern Science and Modern Man. Garden City, N.Y.: Doubleday.

Davis, Kingsley
    1947   "Final note on a case of extreme isolation." American Journal of Sociology 52 (March):432–437.
Dewey, John
    1966   Logic, The Theory of Inquiry. New York: Holt, Rinehart & Winston. (First published 1939.)
Durkheim, Emile
    1962   The Rules of Sociological Method. Glencoe, Ill.: Free Press. (Translated by Sarah A. Solovay and John H. Mueller and edited by George E. G. Catlin. First published in translation 1938).
Gibson, Quentin B.
    1960   The Logic of Social Enquiry. London: Routledge.
Glaser, Barney G., and Anselm L. Strauss
    1965   "The discovery of substantive theory: a basic strategy underlying qualitative research." American Behavioral Scientist 8 (February):5–12.
Greer, Scott A.
    1969   The Logic of Social Inquiry. Chicago: Aldine.
Gross, Llewellyn (ed.)
    1959   Symposium on Sociological Theory. Evanston, Ill.: Harper & Row.
Kaplan, Abraham
    1964   The Conduct of Inquiry; Methodology for Behavioral Science. San Francisco: Chandler.
Knop, Edward
    1967   "Suggestions to aid the student in systematic interpretation and analysis of empirical sociological journal presentation." The American Sociologist 2 (May):90–92.
Kyburg, Henry E., and Ernest Nagel (eds.)
    1963   Induction: Some Current Issues. Middletown, Conn.: Wesleyan Press.
Merton, Robert K., and Paul F. Lazarsfeld (eds.)
    1950   Continuities in Social Research. New York: Free Press.
Nagel, Ernest
    1961   The Structure of Science. New York: Harcourt, Brace & World.
Nash, Manning
    1966   Primitive and Peasant Economic Systems. San Francisco: Chandler (p. 10).
Popper, Karl R.
    1959   The Logic of Scientific Discovery. New York: Basic Books.

Rose, Arnold M.
   1954   Theory and Method in the Social Sciences. Minneapolis, Minn.: University of Minnesota Press.
Weber, Max
   1949   The Methodology of the Social Sciences. Glencoe, Ill.: Free Press. (Translated and edited by Edward A. Shils and Henry A. Finch. Originally published 1903 and 1917.)
Whitehead, Alfred North
   1946   Science and the Modern World. New York: Macmillan.

See also the bibliography in "Introduction: General Instructions for the Student."

Epilogue

In the foregoing assignments the emphasis was on techniques for collecting data in the social sciences. We arbitrarily assigned these methods to subject areas for pedagogical reasons. We want to emphasize, however, that you should keep in mind the point made in the "Introduction: General Instructions for the Student." The methodology to be used in a research study is selected *after* the investigator has chosen his problem. The research question suggests the method or methods to be used. Different subject areas can be substituted for the ones we selected, and we hope your instructor will feel free to make such substitutions.

We developed these assignments for the novice in sociology. As beginning students, you went into the field with little or no idea of what sociology was all about. With limited or no theoretical background, you were required to decide on a problem to study and then collect data pertinent to it with the help of the assignments, your own common sense, and what you were learning in your classes and other reading in sociology. For many of you, guesses or hunches about what was happening were largely derived from what you already knew of the social world from a variety of sources—personal experiences with others, television, drama, education, and so on. The concepts you used were taken, more than likely, from an introductory sociology text. (Upper division students, of course, have a greater wealth of knowledge on which to draw.) Even with these limitations, it is likely that in the course of your investigations, both beginning and upper division students made some genuine discoveries about the dynamics of human group life, the methods by which to capture them, and how these methods shape the ultimate research results. At least, that is what we *hope* happened! We hope, too, that you enjoyed your brief tour through sociological investigation and will now read the work of others with keener interest, a critical eye, and a greater understanding of sociology and sociologists.

70 71 72 73   7 6 5 4 3 2 1